ANCIENT DNA AND THE EUROPEAN NEOLITHIC

Ancient DNA and the European Neolithic: Relations and Descent

Neolithic Studies Group Seminar Papers 19

Edited by

Alasdair Whittle, Joshua Pollard and
Susan Greaney

Oxford & Philadelphia

Published in the United Kingdom in 2023 by
OXBOW BOOKS
The Old Music Hall, 106-108 Cowley Road, Oxford, OX4 1JE

and in the United States by
OXBOW BOOKS
1950 Lawrence Road, Havertown, PA 19083

Paperback Edition: ISBN 978-1-78925-910-0
Digital Edition: ISBN 978-1-78925-911-7 (epub)

A CIP record for this book is available from the British Library

Library of Congress Control Number: 2022949327

Printed in the United Kingdom by CMP Digital Print Solutions

Typeset in India by Lapiz Digital Services, Chennai.

For a complete list of Oxbow titles, please contact:

UNITED KINGDOM
Oxbow Books
Telephone (01865) 241249
Email: oxbow@oxbowbooks.com
www.oxbowbooks.com

UNITED STATES OF AMERICA
Oxbow Books
Telephone (610) 853-9131, Fax (610) 853-9146
Email: queries@casemateacademic.com
www.casemateacademic.com/oxbow

Oxbow Books is part of the Casemate Group

Front cover: Image designed by Joshua Pollard.
Back cover: Image based on four of five generations and their relationships in the Hazleton North long cairn identified by aDNA analysis. Source: Vicki Cummings and Chris Fowler.

Foreword

This book presents the proceedings of an online seminar held in November 2021, organised by the Neolithic Studies Group (NSG), that forms part of an ongoing series of NSG Seminar Papers.

The NSG is an informal organisation comprising archaeologists with an interest in Neolithic archaeology. It was established in 1984 and has a large membership based mainly in the UK and Ireland, but also including workers from the nations of the Atlantic seaboard. The annual programme includes two or three meetings spread throughout the year and includes seminars held in London and field meetings at various locations in north-west Europe.

Membership is open to anyone with an active interest in the Neolithic of Europe. The present membership includes academic staff and students, museums staff, archaeologists from government institutions, units, trusts, and amateur organisations. There is no membership procedure or application forms and members are those on the current mailing list. Anyone can be added to the mailing list at any time, the only membership rule being that the names of those who do not attend any of four consecutive meetings are removed from the list (in the absence of apologies for absence or requests to remain on the list).

The Group relies on the enthusiasm of its members to organise its annual meetings and the two co-ordinators to maintain mailing lists and finances. Financial support for the group is drawn from a small fee payable for attendance of each meeting.

Anyone wishing to contact the Group and obtain information about forthcoming meetings should contact the co-ordinators at the following addresses:

TIMOTHY DARVILL
Department of Archaeology and Anthropology
Bournemouth University
Poole
Dorset BH12 5BB

KENNETH BROPHY
Department of Archaeology
University of Glasgow
Glasgow
G12 8QQ

Alternatively, visit the NSG website: http://www.neolithic.org.uk/

Neolithic Studies Group Seminar Papers

Contents

List of contributors

BRUNO ARIANO
Smurfit Institute of Genetics
Trinity College Dublin
Dublin
D02 PN40
Ireland

ESZTER BÁNFFY
German Archaeological Institute
Romano-Germanic Commission
Palmengartenstr. 10–12
Frankfurt am Main 60325
Germany

TOM BOOTH
Francis Crick Institute
1 Midland Road
London
NW1 1AT
UK

SELINA BRACE
Natural History Museum
Cromwell Road
London
SW7 5BD
UK

DANIEL G. BRADLEY
Smurfit Institute of Genetics
Trinity College Dublin
Dublin
D02 PN40
Ireland

MAXIME N. BRAMI
Palaeogenetics Group
Institute of Organismic and Molecular
Evolution (iomE)
Johannes Gutenberg University Mainz
55099 Mainz
Germany

LARA M. CASSIDY
Department of Genetics
Trinity College Dublin
Dublin
D02 PN40
Ireland

YOAN DIEKMANN
Palaeogenetics Group
Institute of Organismic and Molecular
Evolution (iomE)
Johannes Gutenberg University Mainz
55099 Mainz
Germany
and
Research Department of Genetics, Evolution
and Environment
University College London
Gower Street
London
WC1E 6BT
UK

EVA FERNÁNDEZ-DOMÍNGUEZ
Archaeo-DNA lab
Department of Archaeology
Durham University
Durham
DH1 3LE
UK

SUSAN GREANEY
Department of Archaeology and History
University of Exeter
Laver Building
North Park Road
Exeter
EX4 4QE
UK

KRISTIAN KRISTIANSEN
Department of Historical Studies
University of Gothenburg
Box 200
40530 Gothenburg
Sweden
and
Lundbeck Foundation GeoGenetics Centre
Øster Voldgade 5-7
1350 Copenhagen
Denmark

JOSHUA POLLARD
Department of Archaeology
University of Southampton
Avenue Campus
Highfield
Southampton
SO17 1BF
UK

BIANCA PREDA-BĂLĂNICĂ
Department of Cultures
University of Helsinki
P.O. Box 4 (Fabianinkatu 24, 121C)
00014 Helsinki
Finland

MARTIN B. RICHARDS
Department of Biological and Geographical
Sciences
School of Applied Sciences
University of Huddersfield
Queensgate
Huddersfield
HD1 3DH
UK

ALISON SHERIDAN
c/o Department of Scottish History and
Archaeology
National Museums Scotland
Chambers Street
Edinburgh
EH1 1JF
UK

LEO SPEIDEL
Genetics Institute
University College London
99–105 Gower Street
London
WC1E 6AA
UK
and
Francis Crick Institute
1 Midland Road
London
NW1 1AT
UK

ALASDAIR WHITTLE
Department of Archaeology and Conservation
Cardiff University
John Percival Building
Colum Drive
Cardiff
CF10 3EU
UK

Chapter 1

Introduction: questions of descent, relationships and identity

Alasdair Whittle and Joshua Pollard

THE AIM OF THIS VOLUME

This volume, coming out of the annual Neolithic Studies Group day conference (held online in November 2021), explores the impact of recent archaeogenetic work focused on the Neolithic and Copper Age in Europe. Its temporal and geographic scope runs broadly from the 7th to the 3rd millennia cal BC, with a particular but by no means exclusive interest in Britain and Ireland, and with one paper that examines evidence from the Near East, going back to the 10th millennium cal BC (and even earlier). Our aim is to bring a range of colleagues from the disciplines of archaeogenetics and archaeology under the same cover, and to foster extended dialogue, critique and discussion in a way that is routinely not possible in the normal medium of short papers in scientific journals.

THE aDNA REVOLUTION

There has been a fundamentally important aDNA revolution in recent years. This development offers a series of key insights not available by other means into central questions within archaeology relating to population histories, descent and relationships, and by implication also identity, at many scales and of many different kinds. These are all complex matters, which raise a host of challenges for both geneticists and archaeologists.

The idea of revolution can often be exaggerated, but the term certainly seems to fit in the case of archaeogenetics, especially over the last decade (Rutherford 2016; Reich 2018; Jones and Bösl 2021). As a viable science its beginnings were precarious (see Richards, this volume), but enhanced method and widespread application now offer remarkable insight into key population dynamics in human history. One recent characterisation by an archaeologist refers to 'Next Generation Sequencing (NGS), the recovery of dense concentrations of endogenous DNA from the petrous bone of the human skull, and the sequencing of entire human genomes (the complete set of genetic information for a given organism)' (Thomas 2022, 1); it is increasingly worthwhile to keep an eye out for the distinction between genome-wide and genuinely whole genome analyses. These innovations and improvements have come to expand radically the amounts of information available, compared to the situation just a decade and more ago when the main emphasis was on mitochondrial and Y-chromosome data (*e.g.* Sykes 1999; Bramanti *et al.* 2009; Brandt *et al.* 2013; 2015; but see also Richards, this volume, for the continuing value of those datasets). Adam Rutherford (2016, 4) has referred to 'an epic poem in your cells…an incomparable, sprawling, unique, meandering saga'. The ability now of archaeogeneticists to trace the descent of populations and detailed relationships among groups and individuals is astonishing, especially if one is old enough to remember the research days of, say, the 1970s and 1980s (*e.g.* Whittle 1977), when big questions like the nature of the Mesolithic–Neolithic transition in Britain had to be addressed with archaeological evidence and assumptions alone, and when the closest DNA came to making a contribution was the suggestion of the relevance of modern blood-group patterning across Europe to earlier population histories (Ammerman and Cavalli-Sforza 1984; Reich 2018, xv–xvii).

Since about 2015, there has been a veritable flood of publications rolling out this aDNA revolution (Reich 2018, xviii), with a global reach and stretching far back in time into the Palaeolithic (Rutherford 2016, 26–7). It is hard to think now of an archaeological question not affected by the aDNA revolution.

One of the greatest impacts of recent archaeogenetic work has been felt in the study of the European Neolithic and Copper Age. That area and that timespan have been centrally involved in the great flow of recent papers. There are several important headlines. Three major ones involve arrivals of new population, at the start and end of the European Neolithic/Copper Age, underlining older archaeological opinion about colonisation and population movement (*e.g.* Ammerman and Cavalli-Sforza 1984; Gimbutas 1989; Sheridan 2010; Rowley-Conwy 2011). First, at the start of the Neolithic, paper after paper seems to demonstrate the reality of the arrival of new people of Aegean and ultimately Near Eastern genetic ancestry, in dominant numbers, now across nearly every region of Europe, though not always in exactly the same proportions and of course appearing across a shifting timescale from the 7th to the early part of the 4th millennium cal BC (*e.g.*, selectively, Skoglund *et al.* 2014; Mathieson *et al.* 2015; 2018; Szécsényi-Nagy *et al.* 2015; 2017; Cassidy *et al.* 2016; 2020; Hofmanová *et al.* 2016; González-Fortes *et al.* 2017; Lipson *et al.* 2017; Olalde *et al.* 2018; Brace *et al.* 2019; Rivollat *et al.* 2020; Allentoft *et al.* 2022; Ariano *et al.* 2022; Marchi *et al.* 2022).

The next startling headline, without doubt also the most controversial, figures the appearance in central and parts of western Europe of people of steppe-related genetic ancestry, manifested archaeologically in the Corded Ware-Single Grave phenomenon of the early 3rd millennium cal BC, and very probably linked to the slightly earlier Globular Amphorae culture and beyond that to the Yamnaya culture and related groups far to the east (Anthony 2007; Allentoft *et al.* 2015; 2022; Haak *et al.* 2015; Scorrano *et al.* 2021). This shift in genetic signatures has been seen as the consequence of a 'massive' or 'mass' migration (Haak *et al.* 2015, 207; Reich 2018, 110), spurred on in one account especially by horse-riding male warrior bands, the forerunners of a new and much more mobile, pastoral population (Kristiansen *et al.* 2017).

The third arrival has been seen as on a more restricted scale. Bell Beaker people across central Europe from broadly the middle of the 3rd millennium cal BC onwards also had steppe-related ancestry, but counter to the suggestions of the long-established archaeological literature, there is no clear support for significant Beaker-using population movements within continental western and central Europe as a whole, because sampled Beaker people in Iberia showed significant continuity with preceding populations and Beaker people in central Europe had significant steppe-related ancestry (Olalde *et al.* 2018; Reich 2018, 115). However, seemingly resolving another long-standing debate, it seems clear that Beaker-using people did come into Britain and Ireland in significant numbers, in Britain from around 2400 cal BC and perhaps predominantly from the area of the Lower Rhine and the Low Countries (Olalde *et al.* 2018; Parker Pearson *et al.* 2019; see also Armit and Reich 2021; Brace and Booth, this volume), echoing the models of much earlier studies based on material culture and funerary rite (Clarke 1970).

There have been other stories of great significance. Following early Neolithic arrivals in central Europe, there is genetic evidence for the surprisingly long survival in certain contexts of people of Mesolithic or hunter-gatherer descent (Bollongino *et al.* 2013) and in the Carpathian basin for the gradually increasing representation of characteristically hunter-gatherer haplotypes (Szécsényi-Nagy *et al.* 2015; 2017). We are also probably witnessing a shift to more detailed studies of particular contexts, whose results offer important insights into the relatedness of smaller social groups (Sánchez-Quinto *et al.* 2019). There have been stunning recent results at this more intimate scale, from the brothers at Trumpington Meadows, Cambridgeshire (Scheib *et al.* 2019; *cf.* Fowler 2022), or the very close, incestuous interbreeding at Newgrange, Co. Meath (Cassidy *et al.* 2020; see also Cassidy, this volume), to the five-generation patriline within the long cairn at Hazleton, Gloucestershire (Fowler *et al.* 2022). Add to these investigations a welter of other information – from details of personal appearance including skin, eye and hair colour (Rutherford 2016, 64) and even stature, to aspects of diet, including lactose tolerance (Anguita-Ruiz *et al.* 2020; Evershed *et al.* 2022), disease, including evidence now for plague as far back as the 3rd millennium cal BC (Rasmussen *et al.* 2015), and the histories of a spectrum of species of domesticated crops and animals (*e.g.*, selectively, Brown *et al.* 2015; Scheu 2018; Librado *et al.* 2021) – and it is plain, despite the risk of hype (Jones and Bösl 2021) on the one hand and of undue pessimism (Furholt 2019a) on the other, that the idea of a revolution in understanding having taken place is well justified.

QUESTIONS TO BE ASKING

All these developments raise a series of important questions, which it is the aim of this volume to debate. When as archaeologists without scientific training or technical expertise in either genetic procedures or increasingly sophisticated statistical analyses we read paper after archaeogenetic paper, we come across recurrent questions and matters that involve interpretation. We want to be assured that the most precise chronologies possible are being applied (Whittle 2018); at times in the short space routinely available in leading scientific journals rather compressed or fuzzy chronologies are often deployed. For example, the development of both the LBK in central and western Europe, and the appearance and spread of the Neolithic in Britain and Ireland, may have played out over several centuries, but some of the accounts of the genetics involved seem to rely on a kind of frozen, generalised snapshot. We would like to know more about scales, from varying kinds of population movement to the effects of indigenous involvement (*e.g.* Mithen 2022), from respectively hunter-gatherers at the start of the Neolithic to the already established communities living across central and western Europe by the early 3rd millennium cal BC. There can be all manner of conditions of and reasons for colonisation, migration and movement (Anthony 1990); these can be part of varying social strategies as much as a response to external push or pull factors (*e.g.* Hofmann 2015; 2016; 2020), and so scale can vary enormously. Likewise, we are interested in the effect of local, existing knowledge. If, as is repeatedly suggested in the literature, the contribution of hunter-gatherers to initial early Neolithic genetic signatures was real but small (*e.g.* Brandt *et al.* 2014; Nikitin *et al.* 2019), how did that translate in terms of the transmission of knowledge, for example of the lie of the land and of lithic resources (Mateiciucová 2008)? The question is pertinent, too, when considering later migration events, such as that of Beaker groups into Britain and Ireland, where early co-presence in areas around major Late Neolithic monument complexes suggests landscape knowledge transmitted through close contact with local communities. We are interested, for the same sorts of reasons, in whether processes of population arrival and replacement, and of small-group composition, were uniform or diverse; we want to resist the universal application of single models. Two brief examples would be the uneven and varying archaeological evidence for the Corded Ware presence in central and western Europe, with novel pottery alone perhaps the sole indicator of change in the Alpine foreland (Ebersbach *et al.* 2017), and the nature of family and lineage groups in cemeteries and collective burial deposits. We will have to see whether these all represent closed and tightly defined social groupings (*e.g.* Haak *et al.* 2008), or whether more open access and more fluid arrangements can also be found in future investigations (*cf.* Fowler *et al.* 2022, 1); we will briefly discuss the case of Hazleton further below.

Related to questions of uniformity and diversity, we are interested in sampling density. We acknowledge that whole genome analysis and statistical tools (Speidel, this volume) now open up for analysis a multiplicity of relationships and genetic histories even from small numbers of analysed individuals (Booth 2019, 3), but acceptance of that important point does not remove the general desirability of increasing the density of sampling across Europe, not least if possible for Mesolithic populations. Like many others, we are concerned that interpretation of aDNA results should not be confined within restrictive and rigid definitions of culture and identity (a worry voiced by many commentators, including Frieman and Hofmann 2019; Crellin and Harris 2020). The obvious main target here has been the notion of a bounded, self-defining and uniform Corded Ware culture, which may be quite inadequate to catch the varying range of innovations across central and western Europe in the late 4th and early part of the 3rd millennium cal BC (Furholt 2014; 2017; 2019a; 2019b; see also Kristiansen, this volume). Finally, we are interested in how aDNA results can help us to do better archaeology. Take the Beaker phenomenon, for which neither conventional culture-historical accounts of repeated movements and migrations nor the processual emphasis on a package of cultural ideas and practices have turned out adequately to capture the complexities of the situation across continental Europe and Britain. What are the subtler clues that archaeologists could revisit, in the light of aDNA results?

There is space here, by way of introduction to the kinds of interpretive challenges that recurrently face us, only to take three of these examples a little further. Above, we have raised questions mainly for the archaeogeneticists, but there are questions too for archaeologists.

First, we reflect briefly on the debate about the end of the Neolithic (in the broad sense, without going into details here of regional Copper Age schemes). We have outlined above the principal genetic findings of recent years, and noted interpretations of massive or mass migration, with the further refinement in one model of male warrior bands with horses and wheeled vehicles leading this major incursion from the east. The most persistent and fierce critic of this view has been Martin Furholt (2014; 2017; 2019a; 2019b). He has underlined the case for Corded Ware and indeed Yamnaya variability (Furholt 2014; 2019b, 119, 121; *cf.* Heyd 2017; 2021; Preda-Bălănică *et al.* 2020; and see Preda-Bălănică and Diekmann, this volume), supporting the empirical cases with a repeated emphasis on the generally if not universally polythetic nature of culture. In explicit response to Kristiansen *et al.* (2017), he proposes instead the spread of a network of related but regionally and chronologically varying mortuary practices, which he dubs the Single Grave Burial Ritual Complex (SGBR: Furholt 2019b). So far, however, despite fierce criticism of what he sees as conventional and out-dated aDNA-based narratives (Furholt 2019a), he has not sought to explain how such a network of practice might be conceptualised in detailed social terms, other than by reference to rather general notions of social integration on the one hand and of local histories on the other (Furholt 2019b, 123, 125) nor how its operation might have affected the very considerable increase in steppe-related ancestry revealed by the geneticists (even accepting the valid point that indigenous population might well be under-represented in such a mortuary shift; *cf.* Booth *et al.* 2021). We reflect that it is hardly necessary to accept either of the two visions of culture proposed, since culture can be seen as performance and varies accordingly (Carrithers 1992), and that archaeologists have become unaccustomed to specific and particularising historical narratives, often seeming to prefer generalised models, routinely imported from other disciplines (Whittle 2018). There is plenty at stake here beyond the specifics of Yamnaya and Corded Ware aDNA.

In contrast, there seems to be much greater consensus about the general impact of aDNA studies on our view of the processes of change at the start of the Neolithic across Europe; colonisation by new people seems the undisputed major driving force. Lest we become in turn complacent about this horizon, we see all this as shifting and resetting the terms of debate rather than ending it. There are still many questions to be addressed anew, in terms of timing, variability, directionality and sources (see Bánffy, this volume). There are, as raised above, important matters of how to quantify the contribution of indigenous people to early Neolithic genetic signatures and how to evaluate this in wider social and cultural perspectives. It is worth noting that a recent paper has attempted to make the case for a larger Mesolithic input in the case of Britain (Thomas 2022), even though it seems to us to require too much special pleading (*cf.* Thomas 2013). And if the latest picture from aDNA for Denmark is of an almost complete replacement of hunter-gatherers (Allentoft *et al.* 2022), what happens to older archaeological arguments for continuity there in terms of lithic traditions and knowledge of the landscape?

Finally, the need for continuing interrogation and interpretation seems to us equally vital as attention shifts to the close encounters of mortuary and other deposits. The analysis of the Hazleton collective deposit offers an interesting case in point (Fowler *et al.* 2022). A prominent feature of the remarkable array of relationships within the two chambers of the monument was the finding that one man had reproduced with four women, though the investigations could not demonstrate whether that represented 'serial monogamy or polygyny' (Fowler *et al.*

2022, 3). The study goes on to suggest the enduring importance of maternal sub-lineages and the inclusion of biologically unrelated people, within a dominant patriline. One commentator, in contrast, has expressed 'deep suspicion that an alpha male was able to impregnate several women and that he was considered to be more important to the community than the women', referring further to 'the "hippy" trap' of assuming that the community had any say in the selection (Catling 2022, 62). This is perhaps unhelpful, and not for the first time (_cf._ Frieman and Hofmann 2019) modern assumptions collide with complex evidence from the past. One way to take things further may be more Bayesian chronological modelling, using genetic relationships as informative priors, and a recurrent awareness of, and willingness to explore, the potentially varied constitution of kinship and other forms of social relatedness in settings remote from our own (_cf._ Brück 2021; see also Kristiansen, this volume)

HISTORIES OF DESCENT, RELATIONSHIPS AND IDENTITY: THIS VOLUME

There is therefore no shortage of things to think about in relation to descent and relationships, and to the implications of the new and still accumulating aDNA results for how we should consider individual and group identities.

In the papers presented here, Martin Richards offers a timely, critical overview of the development of aDNA studies and emphasises the continuing contribution of the analysis of uniparental markers. Kristian Kristiansen defines a series of challenges in aDNA research, ranging from matters of sampling, research ethics, terminology, open access to data, and a shift from interdisciplinarity to transdisciplinarity ('a unity of intellectual frameworks'). He outlines, too, interpretive challenges that include the investigation of how genetic admixture processes relate to cultural admixture processes, and the translation of biological mating processes into rules of kinship and marriage. Bruno Ariano and Daniel Bradley address the question of whether Neolithic seascapes were accelerants or retardants of genomic exchange. Given that agriculture was spread via migration rather than acculturation, for the examination of subsequent networks among genomically similar Neolithic populations a more in-depth interrogation of genomic diversity is needed. This is provided by a next generation of analyses that consider similarity within and between genomes based on shared chunks of chromosomes. The detailed data required for these methods can be obtained by genome-wide imputation in a cost-effective leveraging of partially sequenced genomes. These genealogical approaches parse fine structure among European Neolithic genomes and unveil the retarding effects of seascapes for genetic relations, rather than their connectivities. Such analyses highlight how limited reproductive networks were on some island communities, such as those on Malta, Orkney and Gotland, an observation that might be balanced against material evidence for varying maritime connection. Leo Speidel considers new statistical tools that we can use to infer the joint history of hunter-gatherers and farmers in Europe, extrapolating their genealogical relationships to times where data are comparatively sparse.

The bulk of the other papers give case studies relating in the first place to particular times and places, but engaging consistently with the sorts of broader issues already discussed. Eva Fernández-Domínguez uses genome-wide ancient human DNA data to show that a strong genetic substructure existed among the first farming populations of the Fertile Crescent (*c.* 8000 cal BC). This suggests multiple origins of farming and a local evolution of farmer groups from preceding hunter-gatherer populations with limited gene flow at the onset of the Neolithic. To date, the available Neolithic palaeogenomic data indicate a mainly Anatolian origin for the continental route of the Neolithic expansion, punctuated by local episodes of admixture with local hunter-gatherer groups. According to other lines of evidence, however, an earlier parallel, sea-mediated expansion from the Levantine and Anatolian coasts cannot be discarded. She strongly advocates the integration of multi-disciplinary approaches, including aDNA, in the search for a more nuanced understanding of the population changes associated with the emergence of farming in the Near East. Maxime Brami and Yoan Diekmann consider whether foragers became farmers in south-east Europe, hinging on the interpretation of the famous site of Lepenski Vir; armed with aDNA results, they challenge many previously accepted readings of the evidence, arguing for a much more active and dominant role for incoming farmers of Aegean ancestry. Eszter Bánffy ranges across south-east and central Europe, with special reference to the Carpathian basin, in a further effort to reconcile aDNA data with the archaeological record, as well as some contradictions, and to underline the diversity of the Neolithic transition. By bringing together information about the genetic ancestry of individuals and the mortuary archaeology of burial practices, Bianca Preda-Bălănică and Yoan Diekmann investigate the relationship between descent and identity in the kurgans and flat cemeteries of the region, from the 5th to the 3rd millennium cal BC. While many individuals with no steppe-related ancestry are buried according to Balkan-Carpathian basin burial practices, they find that a significant number of them were also buried according to Pontic-Caspian steppe practices. Their results suggest that operating with the prevalent dichotomy only obscures the complexity of processes taking place in the region, indicating that ancestry is at most one factor amongst others contributing to social identity.

Three papers then consider aspects of the Neolithic in Britain and Ireland. Selina Brace and Tom Booth combine to provide an updated and authoritative review of ancestry change in Neolithic Britain, incorporating new results, adding greater detail than presented by Brace *et al.* (2019) and giving some contrast with the later ancestry shift that occurs in Britain from *c.* 2500 cal BC. They note that initial EEF (Early European Farmer) migrations into Britain probably took place over several hundred years, followed by little further intermarriage with groups from continental Europe. A complex picture is presented of matters of origins, admixture with local Mesolithic groups and genetic relatedness in varied 4th millennium cal BC contexts. There is evidence of substantial population continuity into the first half of the 3rd millennium cal BC, but of surprisingly low population sizes during this period; while the persistence of Neolithic-descended populations through the second half of the 3rd millennium cal BC alongside new continental migrants carrying steppe-related ancestries is emphasised.

In her genomic survey of the Mesolithic–Neolithic transition in Ireland, Lara Cassidy reviews analyses so far of both Mesolithic and Neolithic people. She suggests that relative population sizes were key factors in the process; the Mesolithic population was probably both small and isolated by the 5th millennium cal BC, and probably vastly out-numbered by Neolithic newcomers, who may well have arrived from points of origin shared with migrants into Britain. Alison Sheridan and Alasdair Whittle then reflect on how aDNA results have impacted on their differing models of the processes involved in the Neolithisation of Britain and Ireland, and seek to identify remaining and future challenges for both geneticists and archaeologists.

To round things off and to look to the future, Susan Greaney argues for a 'slow science' approach to collaborative aDNA research that makes room for nuanced and reflexive interpretation drawing on the humanities, particularly anthropological and archaeological theory. Genetic change and relatedness need to be considered in the light of the partial nature of the archaeological record and the samples available to researchers, couched using careful terminologies, interpreted alongside other strands of archaeological evidence and grounded in critical approaches to social identity and kinship beyond the biological and indeed, beyond the human.

As in the wake of most revolutions, there is still much to do.

ACKNOWLEDGEMENTS

We are very grateful to both Tim Darvill and Kenny Brophy of the Neolithic Studies Group and our co-editor Susan Greaney for their help and advice throughout the processes of organising and running the online meeting, and then achieving this volume; Alison Sheridan also gave invaluable editorial help. We thank Eske Willerslev, Volker Heyd, Chris Fowler and Neil Carlin, who gave excellent talks on the day but were unable to contribute here because of other commitments; Volker gave us up-to-date references for recent Yamnaya research. Martin Richards, Maxime Brami, Bianca Preda-Bălănică and Yoan Diekmann have bravely stepped in to provide papers and maintain the breadth of our coverage. Finally, we thank Julie Gardiner and Jessica Hawxwell of Oxbow Books for their patient guidance.

REFERENCES

Allentoft, M.E., Sikora, M., Refoyo-Martínez, A., Irving-Pease, E.K., Fischer, A., Barrie, W. *et al.* 2022. Population genomics of Stone Age Eurasia. *bioRxiv* preprint May 5, 2022, doi. org/10.1101/2022.05.04.490594.

Allentoft, M.E., Sikora, M., Sjögren, K.-G., Rasmussen, S., Rasmussen, M., Stenderup, J. *et al.* 2015. Population genomics of Bronze Age Eurasia. *Nature* 522, 167–72.

Ammerman, A.J. and Cavalli-Sforza, L.L. 1984. *The Neolithic transition and the genetics of populations in Europe*. Princeton: Princeton University Press.

Anguita-Ruiz, A., Aguilera, M. and Gil, Á. 2020. Genetics of lactose intolerance: an updated review and online interactive world maps of phenotype and genotype frequencies. *Nutrients* 12(9), doi.10.3390/nu12092689.

Anthony, D.W. 1990. Migration in archaeology: the baby and the bathwater. *American Anthropologist* 92, 895–914.

Anthony, D. 2007. *The horse, the wheel and language: how Bronze Age riders from the Eurasian steppes shaped the modern world*. Princeton: Princeton University Press.

Ariano, B., Mattiangeli, V., Breslin, E.M., Parkinson, E.W., McLaughlin, T.R., Thompson, J.E. *et al.* 2022. Ancient Maltese genomes and the genetic geography of Neolithic Europe. *Current Biology* 32, doi.org/10.1016/j.cub.2022.04.069.

Armit, I. and Reich, D. 2021. The return of the Beaker folk? Rethinking migration and population change in British prehistory. *Antiquity* 95, 1464–77.

Bollongino, R., Nehlich, O., Richards, M.P., Orschiedt, J., Thomas, M.G., Sell, C., Fajkosova, Z., Powell, A. and Burger, J. 2013. 2000 years of parallel societies in Stone Age central Europe. *Science* 342, 479–81.

Booth, T. 2019. A stranger in a strange land: a perspective on archaeological responses to the palaeogenetic revolution from an archaeologist working amongst palaeogeneticists. *World Archaeology* 51, 586–601.

Booth, T., Brück, J., Brace, S, and Barnes, I. 2021. Tales from the Supplementary Information: ancestry change in Chalcolithic–Early Bronze Age Britain was gradual with varied kinship organization. *Cambridge Archaeological Journal* 31(3), 379–400.

Brace, S., Diekmann, Y., Booth, T.J., van Dorp, L., Faltyskova, Z., Rohland, N. *et al.* 2019. Ancient genomes indicate population replacement in Early Neolithic Britain. *Nature Ecology and Evolution* 3, 765–71.

Bramanti, B., Thomas, M.G., Haak, W., Unterlaender, M., Jores, P., Tambets, K. *et al.* 2009. Genetic discontinuity between local hunter-gatherers and Central Europe's first farmers. *Science* 326, 137–40.

Brandt, G., Haak, W., Adler, C.J., Roth, C., Szécsényi-Nagy, A., Karimia, S. *et al.* 2013. Ancient DNA reveals key stages in the formation of central European mitochondrial genetic diversity. *Science* 342, 257–61.

Brandt, G., Knipper, C., Nicklisch, N., Ganslmeier, R., Klamm, M. and Alt, K.W. 2014. Settlement burials at the Karsdorf LBK site, Saxony-Anhalt, Germany. In A. Whittle and P. Bickle (eds), *Early farmers: the view from archaeology and science*, 95–114. Oxford: British Academy.

Brandt, G., Szécsényi-Nágy, A., Roth, C., Alt, K.W. and Haak, W. 2015. Human paleogenetics of Europe – the known knowns and the known unknowns. *Journal of Human Evolution* 79, 73–92.

Brown, T.A., Cappellini, E., Kistler, L., Lister, D.L., Oliveira, H.R., Wales, N. and Schlumbaum, A. 2015. Recent advances in ancient DNA research and their implications for archaeobotany. *Vegetation History and Archaeobotany* 24, 207–14.

Brück, J. 2021. Ancient DNA, kinship and relational identities in Bronze Age Britain. *Antiquity* 95, 228–37.

Carrithers, M. 1992. *Why humans have cultures: explaining anthropology and social diversity*. Oxford: Oxford University Press.

Cassidy, L.M., Martiniano, R., Murphy, E.M., Teasdale, M.D., Mallory, J., Hartwell, B. and Bradley, D.G. 2016. Neolithic and Bronze Age migration to Ireland and establishment of the insular Atlantic genome. *Proceedings of the National Academy of Sciences of the United States of America* 113, 368–73.

Cassidy, L.M., Ó Maoldúin, R., Kador, T., Lynch, A., Jones, C., Woodman, P.C. *et al.* 2020. A dynastic elite in monumental Neolithic society. *Nature* 582, 384–8.

Catling, C. 2022. Neolithic blended families. *Current Archaeology* 385, 62.

Clarke, D.L. 1970. *Beaker pottery of Great Britain and Ireland*. Cambridge: Cambridge University Press.

Crellin, R. and Harris, O.J.T. 2020. Beyond binaries: interrogating ancient DNA. *Archaeological Dialogues* 27, 37–56.

Ebersbach, R., Doppler, T., Hofmann, D. and Whittle, A. 2017. No time out: scaling material diversity and change in the Alpine foreland Neolithic. *Journal of Anthropological Archaeology* 45, 1–14.

Evershed, R.P., Smith, G.D., Roffet-Salque, M., Timpson, A., Diekmann, Y., Lyon, M.S. *et al.* 2022. Dairying, diseases and the evolution of lactase persistence in Europe. *Nature* 608, 336–45.

Fowler, C. 2022. Social arrangements. Kinship, descent and affinity in the mortuary architecture of Early Neolithic Britain and Ireland. *Archaeological Dialogues* 29, 67–88.

Fowler, C., Olalde, I., Cummings, V., Armit, I., Büster, L., Cuthbert, G.S., Rohland, H., Cheronet, O., Pinhasi, R. and Reich, D. 2022. A high-resolution picture of kinship practices in an Early Neolithic tomb. *Nature*, doi.org/10.1038/s41586-021-04241-4.

Frieman, C. and Hofmann, D. 2019. Present pasts in the archaeology of genetics, identity, and migration in Europe: a critical essay. *World Archaeology* 51, 528–45.

Furholt, M. 2014. Upending a 'totality': re-evaluating Corded Ware variability in Late Neolithic Europe. *Proceedings of the Prehistoric Society* 80, 67–86.

Furholt, M. 2017. Massive migrations? The impact of recent aDNA studies on our view of third millennium Europe. *European Journal of Archaeology* 21, 159–91.

Furholt, M. 2019a. De-contaminating the aDNA-archaeology dialogue on mobility and migration: discussing the culture-historical legacy. *Current Swedish Archaeology* 27, 53–68.

Furholt, M. 2019b. Re-integrating archaeology: a contribution to aDNA studies and the migration discourse on the 3rd millennium BC in Europe. *Proceedings of the Prehistoric Society* 85, 115–29.

Gamba, C., Jones, E., Teasdale, M., McLaughlin, R., Gonzalez-Fortes, G., Mattiangeli, V. *et al.* 2014. Genome flux and stasis in a five millennium transect of European prehistory. *Nature Communications* 5, 21 October 2014, doi: 10.1038/ncomms6257.

Gimbutas, M. 1989. *The language of the goddess*. San Francisco: Harper and Row.

González-Fortes, G., Jones, E.R., Lightfoot, E., Bonsall, C., Lazar, C., Grandal-d'Anglade, A. *et al.* 2017. Paleogenomic evidence for multi-generational mixing between Neolithic farmers and Mesolithic hunter-gatherers in the Lower Danube basin. *Current Biology* 27, 1–10.

Haak, W., Brandt, G., de Jong, H.N., Meyer, C., Ganslmeier, R., Heyd, V. *et al.* 2008. Ancient DNA, strontium isotopes, and osteological analyses shed light on social and kinship organization of the Later Stone Age. *Proceedings of the National Academy of Sciences of the United States of America* 105, 18226–31.

Haak, W., Lazaridis, I., Patterson, N., Rohland, N., Mallick, S., Llamas, B. *et al.* 2015. Massive migration from the steppe was a source for Indo-European languages in Europe. *Nature* 522, 207–11.

Heyd, V. 2017. Kossina's smile. *Antiquity* 91, 348–59.

Heyd, V. 2021. Yamnaya, Corded Wares and Bell Beakers on the move. In V. Heyd, G. Kulcsár and B. Preda-Bălănică (eds), *Yamnaya interactions. Proceedings of the International Workshop held in Helsinki, 25–26 April 2019*, 383–414. Budapest: Archaeolingua.

Hofmann, D. 2015. What have genetics ever done for us? The implications of aDNA data for interpreting identity in Early Neolithic central Europe. *European Journal of Archaeology* 18, 454–76.

Hofmann, D. 2016. Keep on walking the role of migration in Linearbandkeramik life. *Documenta Praehistorica* 43, 235–51.

Hofmann, D. 2020. Not going anywhere? Migration as a social practice in the early Neolithic Linearbandkeramik. *Quaternary International* 560–561, 228–39.

Hofmanová, Z., Kreutzer, S., Hellenthal, G., Sell, C., Diekmann, Y., Díez-del-Molino, D. *et al.* 2016. Early farmers from across Europe directly descended from Neolithic Aegeans. *Proceedings of the National Academy of Sciences of the United States of America* 113, 6886–91.

Jones, E.D. and Bösl, E. 2021. Ancient human DNA: a history of hype (then and now). *Journal of Social Archaeology* 21, 236–55.

Kristiansen, K., Allentoft, M.E., Frei, K.M., Iversen, R., Johannsen, N.N., Kroonen, G., Pospieszny, Ł., Price, T.D., Rasmussen, S., Sjögren, K.-G., Sikora, M. and Willerslev, E. 2017. Re-theorising mobility and the formation of culture and language among the Corded Ware culture in Europe. *Antiquity* 91, 334–47.

Librado, P., Khan, N., Fages, A., Kusliy, M.A., Suchan, T., Tonasso-Calvière, L. *et al.* 2021. The origins and spread of domestic horses from the western Eurasian steppes. *Nature* 598, 634–40.

Lipson, M., Szécsényi-Nagy, A., Mallick, S., Pósa, A.M., Stégmár, B., Keerl, V. *et al.* 2017. Parallel ancient genomic transects reveal complex population history of early European farmers. *Nature* 551, 368–72.

Marchi, N., Winkelbach, L., Schulz, I., Brami, M., Hofmanová, S., Blöcher, J. *et al.* 2022. The mixed genetic origin of the first farmers of Europe. *Cell*, doi.org/10.1016/j.cell.2022.04.008.

Mathieson, I., Lazaridis, I., Rohland, N., Mallick, S., Patterson, N., Alpaslan Roodenberg, S. *et al.* 2015. Genome-wide patterns of selection in 230 ancient Eurasians. *Nature* 528, 499–503.

Mathieson, I., Alpaslan Roodenberg, S., Posth, C., Szécsényi-Nagy, A., Rohland, N., Mallick, S. *et al.* 2018. The genomic history of southeastern Europe. *Nature* 555, 197–203.

Mateiciucová, I. 2008. *Talking stones: the chipped stone industry in Lower Austria and Moravia and the beginnings of the Neolithic in central Europe (LBK), 5700–4900 BC*. Brno: Masarykova univerzita.

Mithen, S. 2022. How long was the Mesolithic–Neolithic overlap in Western Scotland? Evidence from the 4th Millennium BC on the Isle of Islay and the evaluation of three scenarios for Mesolithic–Neolithic interaction. *Proceedings of the Prehistoric Society* 88, 1–25.

Nikitin, A.G., Stadler, P., Kotova, N., Teschler-Nicola, M., Price, T.D., Hoover, J., Kennett, D.J., Lazaridis, I., Rohland, N., Lipson, M. and Reich, D. 2019. Interactions between earliest *Linearbandkeramik* farmers and central European hunter gatherers at the dawn of European Neolithization. *Scientific Reports* 9, 19544, doi.org/10.1038/s41598-019-56029-2.

Olalde, I., Brace, S., Allentoft, M.E., Armit, I., Kristiansen, K., Rohland, N. *et al.* 2018. The Beaker phenomenon and the genomic transformation of northwest Europe. *Nature* 555, 190–6.

Parker Pearson, M., Sheridan, A., Jay, M., Chamberlain, A., Richards, M.P. and Evans, J. (eds) 2019. *The Beaker people: isotopes, mobility and diet in prehistoric Britain*. Oxford: Oxbow Books.

Preda-Bălănică, B., Frînculeasa A. and Heyd, V. 2020. The Yamnaya impact north of the Lower Danube: a tale of newcomers and locals. *Bullétin de la Société Préhistorique française* 117, 85–101.

Rasmussen, S., Allentoft, M.K., Nielsen, K., Orlando, L., Sikora, M., Sjogren, K.-G. *et al.* 2015. Early divergent strains of *Yersinia pestis* in Eurasia 5,000 years ago. *Cell* 163, 571–82.

Reich, D. 2018. *Who we are and how we got here: ancient DNA and the new science of the human past*. Oxford: Oxford University Press.

Rivollat, M., Jeong, C., Schiffels, S., Küçükkalıpçı, İ, Pemonge, M.-H., Rohrlach, A.B. *et al.* 2020. Ancient genome-wide DNA from France highlights the complexity of interactions between Mesolithic hunter-gatherers and Neolithic farmers. *Science Advances* 6, eaaz5344, 29 May 2020.

Rowley-Conwy, P. 2011. Westward Ho! The spread of agriculture from central Europe to the Atlantic. *Current Anthropology* 52, S431–51.

Rutherford, A. 2016. *A brief history of everyone who ever lived: the stories in our genes*. London: Weidenfeld and Nicholson.

Sánchez-Quinto, F., Malmström, H., Fraser, M., Girdland-Flink, L., Svensson, E.M., Simões, L.G. *et al.* 2019. Megalithic tombs in western and northern Neolithic Europe were linked to a kindred society. *Proceedings of the National Academy of the United States* 116, 9469–74.

Scheib, C.L., Hui, R., D'Atanasio, E., Wilder, A.W., Inskip, R.A., Rose, A. *et al.* 2019. East Anglian early Neolithic monument burial linked to contemporary megaliths. *Annals of Human Biology* 46(2), 145–9.

Scheu, A. 2018. Neolithic animal domestication as seen from ancient DNA. *Quaternary International* 496, 102–7.

Scorrano, G., Yediay, F.E., Pinotti, T., Feizabadifarahani, M. and Kristiansen, K. 2021. The genetic and cultural impact of the steppe migration into Europe. *Annals of Human Biology* 48, 223–33.

Sheridan, J.A. 2010. The Neolithisation of Britain and Ireland: the 'big picture'. In B. Finlayson and G.M. Warren (eds), *Landscapes in transition*, 89–105. Oxford and London: Oxbow Books and Council for British Research in the Levant.

Skoglund, P., Malmström, H., Omrak, A., Raghavan, M., Valdiosera, C., Günther, T. *et al.* 2014. Genomic diversity and admixture differs for Stone-Age Scandinavian foragers and farmers. *Science* 344, 747–50.

Sykes, B. 1999. *The human inheritance: genes, language, and evolution*. Oxford: Oxford University Press.

Szécsényi-Nagy, A., Brandt, G., Haak, W., Keerl, V., Jakucs, J., Moeller-Rieker, S. *et al.* 2015. Tracing the genetic origin of Europe's first farmers reveals insights into their social organization. *Proceedings of The Royal Society B* 282/1085, 2015, 20150339; DOI: 10.1098/rspb.2015.0339.

Szécsényi-Nagy, A., Roth, C., Brandt, G., Rihuete-Herrada, C., Tejedor-Rodriguez, C., Held, P. *et al.* 2017. The maternal genetic make-up of the Iberian peninsula between the Neolithic and the Early Bronze Age. *Scientific Reports* 2017-12, doi: 10.1038/s41598-017-15480-9.

Thomas, J. 2013. *The birth of Neolithic Britain.* Oxford: Oxford University Press.

Thomas, J. 2022. Neolithization and population replacement in Britain: an alternative view. *Cambridge Archaeological Journal*, doi:10.1017/S0959774321000639.

Whittle, A. 1977. *The earlier Neolithic of southern England and its continental background.* Oxford: British Archaeological Reports.

Whittle, A. 2018. *The times of their lives: hunting history in the archaeology of Neolithic Europe.* Oxford: Oxbow Books.

Chapter 2

Living with archaeogenetics: three decades on

Martin B. Richards

The aftermath of the Neolithic transition has the longest pedigree of any topic in archaeogenetics and is an ideal lens through which to track the growth of the discipline. Here, I retrace from a personal perspective the history of archaeogenetic accounts of the European Neolithic, including some of the missteps and stumbles along the way. In particular, I emphasise the neglect of the uniparental markers, especially mitochondrial DNA, in much recent work. I argue that incorporating such analyses can move on the narratives written using aDNA from sweeping, broad-brush narratives to more nuanced discussion of the detailed processes involved in colonisation and integration. As a case study, I take a closer look at the mitochondrial and Y-chromosome evidence from Neolithic Britain and Ireland, illustrating the complexity of the picture emerging for both the Neolithic transition and the arrival of Beaker-using people, at the beginning and end of the period.

In the spring of 1990, I replied to an advert in the *New Scientist* for a postdoctoral position working with archaeological DNA (or 'ancient DNA', aDNA). I knew little about archaeology but had become jaded by microbial genetics during my doctoral work in Manchester and was very keen to move closer to the humanities. I began work at the University of Oxford's Institute of Molecular Medicine in August, tasked with solving the mystery of the Anglo-Saxon settlement of Britain by Robert Hedges and Bryan Sykes, with whom Erika Hagelberg had just published the first DNA supposedly amplified from archaeological bone samples in *Nature* (Hagelberg *et al.* 1989). Whether it really had been was a moot point. It was the early days of the polymerase chain rection (PCR, amplifying short fragments of DNA for sequencing) and Bryan had built – and, characteristically, then marketed – his own water-bath-based PCR machines. But within a few months, I was bogged down with the seemingly intractable problems of PCR contamination – of extraneous DNA being preferentially amplified over any traces surviving in the sample. It began to seem that aDNA research might have been born prematurely.

EARLY DAYS

At the time, the most influential archaeogeneticists, although we tended to call ourselves molecular anthropologists in those days, were Allan Wilson in Berkeley and Luca Cavalli-Sforza, the godfather of human population genetics, in Stanford. They were both working with contemporary data, with research focused on modern human origins and the Neolithic transition in Europe, respectively. I found the 'classical-marker' approach of Cavalli (Ammerman and Cavalli-Sforza 1984) uninspiring, but the phylogeographic analyses of mitochondrial DNA (mtDNA) by Wilson and his colleagues fresh and exciting. It was only three years since the commotion generated by the Berkeley group's big *Nature* paper, published on New Year's Day, 1987, and backing the out-of-Africa model (Cann *et al.* 1987).

As well as phylogeography and mtDNA analysis, Wilson's lab had also pioneered both PCR itself and the recovery of DNA from what always seemed to be called 'ancient remains'. (Despite, or perhaps because of, the release of *Jurassic Park* in 1993, there was a widespread avoidance of over-hyped talk of 'fossil DNA'.) Although Svante Pääbo's 1985 *Nature* cover article on Egyptian mummies (Pääbo 1985) failed to stand the test of time, like most early work with humans as well as claims about dinosaurs, Russ Higuchi's work with the extinct 19th-century quagga, published the year before, also in *Nature* (Higuchi *et al.* 1984), showed the potential, since it was unlikely that there was any quagga (or closely-related zebra) DNA lurking in the Berkeley lab waiting to contaminate the PCRs there.

So, I was extremely enthusiastic about Bryan Sykes' proposal that we take our lead from Berkeley and work simultaneously on *both* archaeological samples and modern mtDNA sequences. At the same time, it was Cavalli's research area that we were especially interested in. Since I was soon reading Colin Renfrew's books on the European Neolithic and Indo-European languages, I was very keen to apply Wilson's approach to Europe.

Robert had been asked to carbon-date the Tyrolean Iceman, and showed that he was older than had been expected by the archaeologists. He was dated to the Late Neolithic, around 5200 years ago. But Robert had been given more bone than the accelerator needed, and of course Bryan pushed for us to have a go at his DNA too. By now we had quite a lot of experience and had been fortunate to be able to prepare samples in a different part of Oxford (the Research Lab in Keble Road) and set up PCRs in a different building again, at the John Radcliffe Hospital, next to the Institute of Molecular Medicine.

The project's technician, Kate Smalley, and I carried out independent extractions and PCR sequencing of his mtDNA control-region with (for once) a clear result, which we contributed to a 1994 publication in *Science*, led by Oliva Handt and Svante Pääbo in Munich – the official group assigned to the DNA analysis (Handt *et al.* 1994). Despite months of patient PCR cloning work, they had been struggling with the sample they had received, which seems to have been less generous than the one given to Robert, and, in the end, we sent them some of ours to confirm the result. We promoted it as the first case of an aDNA sequence authenticated by replication in two different laboratories.

We also managed convincingly to sequence some 4000-year-old Archaic Indian samples from Newfoundland. But after four years' hard slog, that was pretty much our only success in terms of aDNA at the time. Despite our seemingly modest targeting of only 300 or so base pairs of mtDNA, the Anglo-Saxons had pointedly refused to provide us with any useful data (Richards *et al.* 1993; 1995). The problems with contamination seemed overwhelming and we started to think that they might be insurmountable. It seemed that the bubble might have burst. In 1995, I moved to working full time on contemporary human mitochondrial variation. We heard that Svante had decided to abandon working with human aDNA at around the same time (Pääbo 2014).

Our single major success of the 1990s, the Iceman sequence, was only 350 base-pairs (bp) long. This was a dozen or so years before 'next-generation DNA sequencing' (NGS) took off. NGS revolutionised not only genomics in general, but aDNA work in particular, because it meant we could work with extremely short fragments, and that we could recognise damage signatures, making the confident authentication of archaeological sequences finally a reality. By then I was at the University of Leeds where I experienced the revolution first-hand. Luca Ermini, a visiting student from the lab of Franco Rollo, one of the pioneers of extracting aDNA from plant remains at the University of Camerino (Rollo *et al.* 1988), used the earliest form of NGS, 454 sequencing, to generate the 16,568 bp of the whole mitochondrial genome of the Iceman (Ermini *et al.* 2008). The 3.2 billion bp of his whole genome came only four years later (Keller *et al.* 2012). While his mtDNA lineage was virtually extinct in the present day, the rest of his genome turned out to look like that of a Sardinian. There was a perfectly simple explanation, but it was years before we realised what it was.

FINDING FARMER FOUNDERS

We did not completely abandon aDNA in the 1990s. But we did focus most of our attention on modern mtDNA patterns. I had been lucky enough to be contacted early on by an enthusiastic young German chemist (and Anglophile), Peter Forster, and, through him, to have met the unorthodox graph theorist Hans-Jürgen Bandelt in Hamburg who, in a way, became my scientific 'guru'. With the help of their insights and expertise, we learnt to analyse the lineages graphically with networks, rather than with the parsimony-tree approach for which Allan Wilson's group had been severely lambasted. And they also developed a very simple molecular-clock dating approach, termed 'ϱ dating', that could be used hand in hand with the networks, a method that, despite mathematically rather illiterate comments in some quarters, stands up perfectly well today (Macaulay *et al.* 2019). Peter also laid the groundwork for what we came to call founder analysis – a heuristic approach to dating migrations. In essence, this is simply subtracting the source variation – that is, the mutational variation that arose before arriving in a particular sink population – from the molecular age estimates in a particular sink population. In this way, we can convert an overall coalescence age – based on the total variation in a sink population – to a migration time, by dating the founder lineages that arrived when the population formed (Forster *et al.* 1996; Saillard *et al.* 2000; Macaulay and Richards 2013).

In a way, this was also what the Berkeley group had been doing when they estimated the age of the non-African lineages to date the out-of-Africa migration. It was also the approach of someone with an equal claim to Wilson to have pioneered human mitochondrial analysis, working initially on Native Americans and later also on Europeans: Antonio Torroni, in Rome (Torroni *et al.* 1993; 1996), who became another close colleague. Although sometimes misunderstood by more conservative population geneticists, this approach has been a keystone of our phylogeographic analyses of contemporary uniparental marker variation ever since.

It was more complicated for Europe, where the lineages were more entangled with those of the assumed Near Eastern source, than for America. Even so, our innovations were essentially small tweaks to the phylogeographic approach of the earlier work – in particular, to help head off some of the storm of criticism that had assailed the Berkeley group from all sides in the early 1990s. Founder analysis wasn't quite the chronological dimension we'd like to have got from aDNA, but it gave us a handle on approaching archaeological questions with modern variation.

Using this approach, we tried to evaluate the scale of the Neolithic dispersal into Europe and the extent to which the local Mesolithic populations had contributed to the ancestry of Europeans. We did this rather heuristically in 1996, and more formally and with a much larger dataset in 2000, by which time Hans had thrown himself into the task of tightening up the analysis, and we were now working closely with Vincent Macaulay, a Bayesian refugee from physics (Richards *et al.* 1996; 2000).

Unfortunately, what I thought we had achieved seemed to get obscured by the smoke created by our intruding into what turned out to be an area of major contention. When Peter and I identified a particular set of lineages (within what later became known as haplogroup J) with a distinct pattern in Europe and clear Near Eastern ancestry, my immediate response was: *We've found the farmers!* But the implication was that a good three-quarters of modern European maternal ancestry was pre-Neolithic. Bryan's response, therefore, which was undoubtedly what generated the headlines (and a *New Scientist* cover, seven years after that advert for my job), was: *Cavalli got it wrong*. Thus, we ended up in a miniature version of the kind of storm suffered by the Berkeley group over human origins.

Frustratingly, we were frequently regarded as supporting the cultural diffusion of farming across Europe, when in fact we were proposing a pioneer-dispersal model, involving leapfrog colonisation of Near Eastern migrants, with later assimilation of Mesolithic hunter-gatherer groups into the farmer-islands. It was certainly a view that emphasised the contribution of the indigenous inhabitants of Europe, along the lines of Marek Zvelebil's view from archaeology (Zvelebil 1986; 1995; 2000; 2001a; 2001b) but also of dispersal and colonisation (Rowley-Conwy 2011), and not just from the Balkans or south-east Europe (Zvelebil 2001a) but also from the Near East. Most of us thought of ourselves as refining Cavalli's 'demic diffusion' view, rather than overturning it, although it is fair to say that, like Marek, who referred to the image of 'Panzer divisions' (Lewin 1997), we were not too enthusiastic about the idea of a 'wave of advance'.

ANCIENT DNA STRIKES BACK

I am not sure this was very wrong, as far as it went, but by comparing Europe *en bloc* with the Near East *en bloc*, we underestimated the demographic impact of those pioneers in central and western Europe. When the first ancient mtDNA from Mesolithic central Europeans began to appear in 2009, most carried haplogroups U4 and U5, with earlier Palaeolithic Europeans also including other branches of haplogroup U – mainly U8b and U2e (Bramanti *et al.* 2009). Haplogroup U branched off from other lineages around 50,000 years ago, and we had proposed it being carried by the earliest Upper Palaeolithic populations. But we also saw haplogroups H and V, T2 and K (which is actually a part of U8; by no means all of haplogroup U was indigenous to Palaeolithic Europeans) and later on even parts of J, as arriving – or, at any rate, spreading across most of Europe – with the Late Glacial (Soares *et al.* 2010).

Now, we not only have data from pre-Neolithic and Neolithic human remains, but much of the data are not from short mtDNA sequences but whole mitochondrial genomes (or 'mitogenomes') (Brandt *et al.* 2014; Posth *et al.* 2016). And as a result, we now know that whilst many of these lineages are indeed seen in eastern and southern Europe before the Neolithic, they are in quite a small minority there – the U4 and U5 lineages mostly predominate – and, crucially, they were already present in Anatolia in the Early Neolithic.

Moreover, aDNA from hundreds of Early Neolithic Europeans, coming especially from Wolfgang Haak at the Max Planck Institute in Jena, David Reich in Harvard, and their colleagues, showed that the 'Neolithic mitochondrial package' included more than just haplogroups J, T1, U3 and a few sub-clusters of H and W that we had proposed in 2000 (Brandt *et al.* 2013; Haak *et al.* 2005; 2010). The main Early Neolithic lineages in central Europe were J1c, T2b, T2c, T2e, K1a, some V and H, a few assimilated U5 lineages (but less than 5%) and, most surprisingly, N1a1a. In the south, the situation was even more varied. We had J2b, K1b and X2b lineages as well, some T1a, more (and more diverse) haplogroup H (although still nothing like the high frequencies at which we see it today), and a larger and more diverse selection of assimilated Mesolithic haplogroup U lineages. There were fewer N1a1a lineages, but they were still there, and we could trace their ancestry right back into the western Anatolian Neolithic.

N1a1a is vanishingly infrequent in modern Europeans, and in fact the frequency of the other lineages in the LBK (*Linearbandkeramik*) was also drastically different from in present-day central Europeans. The conclusion had to be that the pattern for Europe had not been fixed in the early Neolithic but had been overwritten later on. This invalidated a crucial assumption of Cavalli's, that the first, and therefore most important, principal component of European genome-wide variation was due to the Neolithic expansion from the south-east into the Mesolithic population of Europe. It was an assumption that we had made ourselves when archaeologists often pointed out to us that subsequent population movements might have smothered the Neolithic pattern.

It was this assumption that led us to overlook statements about the Late Neolithic Corded Ware like this one from Andrew Sherratt: 'one of the largest and most revolutionary transformation(s) of European prehistory' (Sherratt 1994, 193). Or rather, we imagined it was largely a social and cultural revolution, based on the formation of new contact networks, rather than a demographic one as well (Soares *et al.* 2010). This was why the conclusions from the genome-wide work from the Jena/Harvard and Copenhagen labs respectively, published back-to-back in *Nature* in 2015 (Allentoft *et al.* 2015; Haak *et al.* 2015), seemed so ground-breaking from our point of view.

They showed that genetic patterns changed enormously in Europe in the 3rd millennium cal BC, due to dispersals from the Pontic-Caspian steppe. They did this mainly using genome-wide and Y-chromosome data, although prefigured by an earlier study of Corded Ware and Bronze Age mtDNA that pointed to the introduction of new maternal lineages too (Brandt *et al.* 2013). One with an extraordinarily wide distribution and shallow time depth, for example, is T1a, a rare lineage that we had attributed to dispersal earlier in the Neolithic (Pala *et al.* 2012). T1a did indeed spread to a limited extent along the Mediterranean with the early Neolithic, but it was distributed much more widely across Europe and Asia, from eastern Europe via the Caucasus, in the late Neolithic/Early Bronze Age. Its distribution matches that of a new genome-wide component, with its source ultimately in Iran, that spread across the Caucasus on to the steppe and then both west and east. It reached almost every part of Europe, bar Sardinia. This was why the Iceman, who lived before this development, resembled present-day Sardinians, who somehow isolated themselves from this continent-wide transformation.

We know now that there was assimilation of hunter-gatherers in Europe after around 6000 years ago, throughout the middle Neolithic and into the late Neolithic, especially on the fringes, such as the western Mediterranean, the regions adjacent to the North Sea, and east-central Europe, but also in the interstices in central Europe (Bollongino *et al.* 2013). This had been expected on archaeological grounds (Zvelebil and Dolukhanov 1991; Sherratt 2004), although the case had been overstated for western Europe (Zvelebil 2001a). But there are two ironies when trying to look back on this from present-day variation.

First, some of the groups with the most assimilation succumbed to the newcomers from the east and much of that variation was lost forever, although it survives in north-east Europe more than elsewhere (Saag *et al.* 2017; 2021; Mathieson *et al.* 2018). But the second concerns the newcomers themselves. Pastoralism on the western steppes emerged from intermarriage between local steppe hunter-gatherer elites and Neolithic groups (primarily women) dispersing from Mesopotamia and Iran via the Caucasus (Wang *et al.* 2019). This meant that not only was a fresh set of Near Eastern Neolithic lineages introduced into Europe (on the female side), but a fresh set of Mesolithic European hunter-gatherer lineages were introduced (on the male side), alongside, of course, the mixed heritage in the rest of the genome.

Complicating things even further, when the Corded Ware-using groups formed in eastern Europe, they did so by incorporating yet *another* substantial ancestry component – that of the local Neolithic of eastern Europe (again, evidently mainly women) – who were, in turn, themselves largely descendants of the early pioneer farmers of east-central Europe (Papac *et al.* 2021; Saag *et al.* 2021). But overall, the upshot was that, when we look back from the present at lineages across Europe from the end of the Neolithic, the hunter-gatherer ancestry we see is not primarily due to assimilation of western and central European Mesolithic groups. Much of it derives from the Eastern European Mesolithic.

Having said this, in a final twist, it looks as if the Eastern European Late Mesolithic *itself* was the result of a merging of local hunter-gatherers with others who had expanded from western and central Europe in the postglacial. This can be seen in the appearance of U5b2 lineages in the east, alongside the more local U5a and U4. Moreover, there seem to have been local turnovers and replacements of populations throughout the Mesolithic and Neolithic in northern and eastern Europe. In retrospect, the assumption we shared with Cavalli that we might be able to recover the main episodes solely from today's genetic patterns seems overly ambitious. At the same time, in the light of these nuances, the new popular narratives framed around 'mass migrations' seem crude and simplistic.

COMPLICATIONS IN SOUTH-EAST EUROPE

Even given these subtleties, we were left with some nagging doubts. Some researchers have been quite dismissive of both mtDNA and phylogeographic analyses over the years, but from our perspective there had not been any knock-out criticisms. The founder analyses that we have performed over the years continued to suggest that around three-quarters of the present-day mitochondrial lineages arrived before the Neolithic in Europe. How then could we explain these results? Were they really wrong?

Although our early analyses, based only on short mtDNA sequences, lacked the clear resolution that we can see with complete mitogenomes, this does not seem to have skewed the results very much – we see the same pattern with the latter. Again, we have worked very hard on the mitochondrial molecular clock in the intervening years, and we feel quite confident about the mutation rate we are using, which is also quite well supported by completely independent studies, some based on aDNA calibration points (Soares *et al.* 2009; Fu *et al.* 2013; Pala *et al.* 2014).

Moreover, the results should not be skewed by subsequent movements within Europe. Nor should they be adversely affected by subsequent movements into Europe from the Near East – in fact, such movements are what it is expressly designed to detect. And if there had been heavy back-migration from Europe to the Near East – from sink to source – since the Neolithic, that should reduce the estimates, not increase them (Richards *et al.* 2000).

One very real possibility is that the modern Near East just does not represent the source adequately, but the aDNA data that we have do not really support that view. There has been a huge amount of mixing between the two distinct source pools of the Near East – the western and eastern limbs of the Fertile Crescent – and some Iron Age and medieval arrivals from Central and East Asia, but not much more migration from Europe than we had already allowed for in the 1990s. For example, we still see N1a1a in Anatolia today, despite its dwindling presence in Europe since the early Neolithic. So why do we continue to obtain this result, if it has been discredited by aDNA studies? There is a nagging feeling that the results might still be telling us something meaningful after all.

Pedro Soares tested this using data from haplogroups J and T, generated during a PhD project co-supervised by Luisa Pereira (Pereira *et al.* 2017). Previous work by Maria Pala had suggested that these haplogroups might not have dispersed entirely from the Near East in the Neolithic, but that some lineages may already have reached south-east Europe from the Levantine glacial refuge after the Last Glacial Maximum (Pala *et al.* 2012). This was backed by aDNA evidence for haplogroup J2b1 dating to around 10,000 years ago, in Mesolithic Sardinia (Modi *et al.* 2017).

So, we separated the mitogenome lineages from central and eastern Mediterranean Europe from those in Iberia and central/northern Europe when we carried out the founder analysis. When we did this, we found that two-thirds of those in Mediterranean Europe dated to the Late Glacial, and only one-third to the Neolithic. But when we dated those in Iberia and central/northern Europe, including Mediterranean Europe with the Near East as the source, the situation was reversed – most of the lineages dated to the Neolithic. Pedro's group have since found a similar pattern for other lineages – most notably, including some from haplogroup H.

The simplest explanation for this pattern seems to be that the Neolithic Near East was not the sole source for Neolithic Europe but that some lineages had already expanded into the eastern Mediterranean in the Late Glacial and were assimilated by the later Neolithic pioneers moving across the Aegean from Anatolia, 9000 years ago. Perhaps this is also hinted at by the presence of lineages belonging to the supposed 'Neolithic mitochondrial package' in the Iron Gates Mesolithic, including various haplogroup K and H lineages, and indeed J2b1, as also seen in the Sardinian Mesolithic (Modi *et al.* 2017; Mathieson *et al.* 2018).

There are further complexities when we look at the patterns of uniparental markers across Europe. Although the genome-wide picture has suggested to many something like Jared Diamond's portrayal of early farmers steamrolling across the continent (Diamond 1997), the Y-chromosome data are much more equivocal. The male lineages most clearly associated with Neolithic dispersal from the Near East are G2a2-L1259, along with the much less frequent H2d-ABR039, H2m-SK1192, E1b1-P2, T1a1-L162, and perhaps J2a-M410. Yet these lineages form less than three-quarters of continental early Neolithic male lineages, in the most recent Harvard database, although they do comprise all of those amongst the LBK heartland in Germany and Austria. What is more, in south-east Europe, and the Mediterranean as far as Iberia, they are down to less than half. Numerous male lineages from the Mesolithic persisted into the Neolithic in Europe: C1a2-V20 and R1a1-M459 in south-east Europe, R1b-M343 in Mediterranean Europe and, most strikingly, I2a1-L460 across the continent. The British Neolithic carries only I2a1-L460 male lineages, with no G2a2-L1259 whatsoever.

This is not the heavy assimilation we see later during the middle Neolithic in the genome-wide patterns. These male lineages look to have been assimilated very early, some in south-east Europe, some in the south-west, and possibly some in the north-west. There is little evidence of early assimilation in central Europe, fitting nicely with the archaeological picture of a major, rapid demic expansion there (Price *et al.* 2001). But either we are seeing a significant sex bias, or the male lineages are corroborating our suspicions regarding the female lineages, with a high level of early assimilation in south-east and Mediterranean Europe.

THE NEOLITHIC OF BRITAIN AND IRELAND: THE VIEW FROM THE UNIPARENTAL MARKERS

This brings us finally to the situation in Britain and Ireland, which is different again. For such a tiny corner of the world, trying to tease out the pattern of settlement using contemporary variation is a fairly hopeless task, although numerous efforts were made, and a few broad conclusions, such as the influence of Norwegian Vikings on the Northern Isles, were possible (Wilson *et al.* 2001; Leslie *et al.* 2015). The impact of aDNA work on our understanding has therefore been profound.

The genome-wide aDNA data of the past few years have confirmed that Britain and Ireland were resettled both in the early Neolithic and the Chalcolithic (Cassidy *et al.* 2016; Olalde *et al.* 2018; Brace *et al.* 2019), thus supporting a form of pioneer colonisation, appearing first in south-east England from northern France and dispersing throughout Britain and Ireland (Whittle *et al.* 2011; compare Sheridan 2010; Rowley-Conwy 2011). And we have finally been able to revisit the issue of the Anglo-Saxon settlement, which, again, we see had a major, lasting impact on the British gene pool (Gretzinger *et al.* 2022).

But, of course, there is much more to it than that, just as Booth *et al.* (2021) have argued in elegant detail for the Beaker period. Archaeogeneticists have a distressing tendency to write each paper as though they have solved one of the perennial questions of archaeology, or to posit new, and often spurious, questions that they know they can answer (or have already answered but not yet published), whilst ignoring gaps that seem obvious to everyone else. In practice, notwithstanding the enormous and genuine progress of the last few years, no archaeological 'problem' of any interest is ever quite resolved by the appliance of science, as, for example, Hofmann (2015) has spelled out in the case of the LBK. The problem is not helped when some geneticists do not engage sufficiently with archaeological (or linguistic and other) expertise, and work with simplistic, discredited or outdated models (Pluciennik 1998; Bandelt *et al.* 2002; Vander Linden 2016; Fernández-Domínguez 2018; Furholt 2018; 2019) – although, to be fair, efforts are being made to address this (Eisenmann *et al.* 2018) – or ignore the political implications of their work (Hofmann *et al.* 2021).

In the case of Neolithic Britain and Ireland, there has been little attention yet devoted by archaeogeneticists to the scale of colonisation, the number of colonisation episodes, or the routes taken, in contrast to the intensive work by archaeologists (*e.g.* Sheridan 2007; 2010; Whittle *et al.* 2011; Cummings 2017; Shennan 2018). And, having worked with uniparental markers for 30 years, my close colleagues and I are frequently surprised at the extent to which they (especially the mtDNA) have been neglected since the dawning of the NGS age, just at the time when there is a torrent of new and highly informative data from the avalanche of ancient whole-genome studies (Bandelt 2018). In fact, of course, the phylogeographic approach becomes far more powerful when aDNA is available in large volumes. The uniparental markers can help us to pinpoint the fine details (let alone difference in behaviour between the sexes) that may otherwise be overlooked with the all-encompassing but blunt approach of the whole genome (Richards and Macaulay 2013). It is worth briefly taking a closer look at the British-Irish case to see what we might learn if we paid more attention to the uniparental systems.

MALE 'FORAGER' LINEAGES

There are a quite lot of data now for the British and Irish Mesolithic and Neolithic (there are no pre-Mesolithic data as yet): 92 males with whole-genome profiles on the Harvard database (Cassidy *et al.* 2016; 2020; Olalde *et al.* 2018; Brace *et al.* 2019; Sanchez-Quinto *et al.* 2019; Dulias *et al.* 2022). Of course, most of these are Neolithic; only five are Mesolithic (there are a further three Mesolithic females), of which one is typed to only poor resolution, as is also true for three of the Neolithic samples. We should also bear in mind that Y-chromosome haplotypes and their place in the phylogeny for aDNA are estimates; they are always based on scoring fragmentary data, with many gaps, and may (for example) be positioned deeper in the tree than they should be, due to missing data towards the tips. Finally, Y-chromosome nomenclature is a huge challenge for almost all of us, because of the tradition that the subclades in the tree be renamed wholesale almost every year by ISOGG, the organisation recognised as setting the standard. Since the names of lineages routinely switch in confusing ways, to accommodate the sprouting of new branches caused by the addition of new data, it is important to clarify the terminal single nucleotide polymorphism (SNP) defining whatever haplogroup we are talking about, cumbersome as it may seem.

The Neolithic male lineages in Britain and Ireland include a diverse array of mainly I2a1b-M436 and I2a1a-P37 lineages (in a similar 2:1 ratio in both regions), exclusively I2a1-L460 in Britain, but with two Irish individuals belonging to haplogroup H2-P96. These are lineages with a source in the Near East, possibly the distinctive eastern Fertile Crescent Neolithic population, and thought to have dispersed into north-west Europe via the Mediterranean route (Rohrlach *et al.* 2021). All the British and remaining Irish Neolithic male lineages belong to haplogroup I2a1-L460, with large numbers of closely related haplotypes within the two subclades, I2a1a-P37 and I2a1b-M436. Overall, the more common lineages are shared between Britain and Ireland, suggesting that there was likely a common pool, and that the unshared lineages are just due to sampling.

The five male Mesolithic individuals from England, Wales, and Ireland all belong to haplogroup I2-M438. Of the four that are well typed, all belong to one of the two subclades of I2a1-L460: three I2a1b-M436 and one I2a1a-P37. There is a single individual carrying I2a1a2-M423 in Ireland, one with I2a1b1-M223 in Wales, and two with I2a1b2a-L38: one in Ireland and the other in England, at the famous Cheddar Gorge in Somerset. These are clearly very closely related to those seen in the Neolithic, and several of them are shared with Neolithic individuals. As a result, Brace *et al.* (2019) suggested 'stability' on the male lineage from Mesolithic into Neolithic, in contrast to their argument for almost complete Neolithic replacement of the mtDNA and autosomes.

However, these lineages are also shared with both other Mesolithic and other Neolithic groups in western and northern Europe, so we cannot assume that the sharing of a local lineage implies local ancestry and assimilation. In fact, many Mesolithic Y-chromosome lineages are both ancient and extremely widely dispersed, so these could have arrived from almost anywhere in continental Europe. For example, the major western Neolithic lineage, I2a1a2-M423, dates to 14,200 years (YFull: https://www.yfull.com/tree/; Adamov *et al.* 2015) and is seen in the Mesolithic of Ireland, Luxembourg, and Sweden. It is very frequent in an arc across the Neolithic of Atlantic Europe, in Iberia, France, Ireland, Britain (in fact, predominating in the Neolithic of Orkney, where it persists into the Bronze Age), and Scandinavia, and virtually absent elsewhere (Dulias *et al.* 2022).

So, although the most parsimonious explanation might at first sight seem to be local assimilation in Ireland or Sweden, given the high frequency and diversity of these lineages in Iberia and France the explanation is probably more complex. They comprise more than a third of I2a1 lineages in Neolithic France and Iberia and more than half of those in France alone (Brunel *et al.* 2020; Rivollat *et al.* 2020; Seguin-Orlando *et al.* 2021). I2a1 itself comprises almost two-thirds of lineages in France and Iberia but only around 15% in central Europe, where I2a1a2 is almost absent.

I2a1a was involved in the Late Glacial Magdalenian expansions across Europe, dispersing as far as the Serbian Iron Gates and Mesolithic Ukraine, but with I2a1a2 present in both France and Spain in the early Neolithic. I2a1b is seen earliest in the Mesolithic of Italy, although it appears rapidly across Europe, again from Britain and France to the Iron Gates and Ukraine, so it perhaps may also have been caught up in the Late Glacial dispersals, although it is curiously absent from (well-sampled) Iberia before 4000 cal BC. Thus, even though both are present in Mesolithic Britain, I2a1a and I2a1b might well have been assimilated from Mesolithic enclaves on the Mediterranean, such as that suggested in northern Italy by Broodbank (2013, 150) and then dispersed both into north-west Europe along the Rhône and Loire rivers (the Chasséen) and around the Mediterranean coast to Iberia (Shennan 2018), perhaps with further episodes of assimilation of related lineages *en route*.

FEMALE 'FARMER' LINEAGES

This is not to say that there was no assimilation within Britain and Ireland, so that the Mesolithic hunter-gatherers were completely lost. Brace *et al.* (2019) themselves pointed to minor levels of continuity into the Neolithic in Scotland, and we have identified at least one potentially local Mesolithic mitochondrial lineage that has survived into the present day (Dulias *et al.* 2022). Interestingly, if we examine the British and Irish Mesolithic mitochondrial lineages, we see a rather different pattern.

There are six distinct lineages amongst the seven well-typed Mesolithic individuals, of which, curiously, three belong to the Eastern European U5a2, with the remainder belonging to the West European U5b1 and U5b2. (A caveat to what follows is that we are looking at the level of subclade resolution here; these 'lineages' are far from being identical at the individual sequence haplotype level.)

What is especially intriguing is that, because the U5a2 lineages are on the edge of their range, they do not match with other western, central or Mediterranean European individuals either in the Mesolithic or Neolithic, but two of the three do match with Neolithic individuals from Britain (and one subclade seen in Mesolithic Ireland, U5a2d, persists into present-day England). Indeed, the same seems to be true for one of the U5b1 lineages (at least, it is seen in the English Chalcolithic), and the U5b2a lineage also lacks matches in western European lineages that postdate the Upper Palaeolithic. With the caveat noted above, that these observations should be confirmed by a more detailed phylogenetic analysis of the lineages (which, as for the Y chromosome, is challenging with aDNA because of the poor quality of the data), this makes assimilation the most likely explanation for all of these lineages: that is, more than half of the known local Mesolithic maternal lineages.

The basal U5a2 lineage, on the other hand, lacks matching lineages anywhere, and the other U5b1 lineage is seen in Mesolithic individuals in northern Italy, as well as numerous Iberian and French Neolithic individuals, supporting the suggestion above that there was assimilation of Mesolithic people by Neolithic immigrants along the Mediterranean before they dispersed north-west.

Still, these likely assimilated hunter-gatherer lineages only amount to around 2% of maternal lineages in the Neolithic of Britain and Ireland overall. Even if we sum all of the U5 lineages in Neolithic Britain and Ireland, they only amount to 13% of the lineages, and the majority of these were most likely assimilated on the continent. So, overall, it does seem that the uniparental markers support the conclusions from the genome-wide evidence that rather few traces of the local Mesolithic people survived into the Neolithic. This is concordant with the view of some (by no means all) archaeologists that the insular Mesolithic population was thin on the ground and perhaps dwindling already well before the arrival of the newcomers (Tolan-Smith 2008; Mallory 2017), in contrast to the intensification that was taking place around the coasts of Atlantic Europe and at the Iron Gates, but similarly to inland continental Europe (Rowley-Conwy 2011).

On the other hand, the detailed analysis of mtDNAs raises the possibility that perhaps most of the local population were indeed assimilated by the newcomers (Whittle *et al.* 2011), but that there were relatively very few of them to assimilate, or that the new arrivals spread more rapidly. The precision with which this implies we can tease out both the survival of those lineages, and the sources of those that arrived subsequently, suggests a fruitful avenue for future research that investigates the fine processes involved, evaluating the extent and nature of colonisation and integration or assimilation in different times and places, rather than sweeping summaries concerning replacement of one population by another.

We can take a similar approach to the next major 'replacement' in Britain: the arrival of Beaker-using people just after 4500 years ago. Again, genome-wide and Y-chromosome studies have pointed to a replacement of 90–95% (Olalde *et al.* 2018) but once more – and to a greater extent than with the Mesolithic–Neolithic transition – a detailed look at the mitochondrial lineages suggests a greater degree of continuity, and a sex bias undetected by genome-wide approaches. Whilst less than 6% of the male Neolithic lineages survived into Beaker, Chalcolithic and Bronze Age Britain, around 20% of the mitochondrial lineages persisted, suggesting greater assimilation of female than male lineages (Dulias *et al.* 2022), consistent with the much more complex and nuanced process inferred by Booth *et al.* (2021). Moreover, the process was, not surprisingly, far from monolithic, depending on social configurations at the local level. For example, in Orkney, we found that the situation was reversed, with the autosomal and female lineages being largely replaced, whilst the Neolithic male lineages persisted until at least the Middle Bronze Age (Dulias *et al.* 2022).

CONCLUSION: THE END OF THE BEGINNING?

All of this is a far cry from Cavalli-Sforza's early work on the wave of advance in Neolithic Europe. Even so, is it fair to describe his work as being 'wrong', as does David Reich in his popular account of the NGS revolution (Reich 2018)? Was Cavalli really mistaken and has aDNA now finally got it right? Has there really been a huge paradigm shift in archaeogenetics?

Thanks to NGS, aDNA has undeniably come of age. At Huddersfield, we now have a thriving aDNA Facility, led by Ceiridwen Edwards, and have run a successful Leverhulme Trust doctoral programme that generated hundreds of ancient genomes. I have been astonished at what she and they have been able to achieve in the last few years.

Still, without wishing to minimise the technological advances, which are genuinely awe-inspiring to someone who was attempting to study aDNA in the 'dark ages' of the 1990s, it is hard to say that we are really now working with a completely new set of ideas. Instead, the turn from contemporary variation towards aDNA that the technology has made feasible has meant a more serious engagement with archaeology for many genetic researchers, which, rather than some great transformation, has led to more subtle approaches to the interpretation of historical genetic data. It seems more reasonable to say that Cavalli was partly right and that hopefully we are a bit more right today, but despite all the insights of the past few years, we still have a long way to go.

ACKNOWLEDGEMENTS

I gratefully acknowledge the critical comments and suggestions of Maria Pala and Pedro Soares, as well as their collaboration, support and friendship over many years. My work in this area was supported by a Leverhulme Trust Doctoral Scholarship program from 2015–2021. I would also like to thank Daniela Hofmann, Martin Furholt and Eva Fernández-Domínguez for the opportunity to discuss and think about some of these issues, and to the Centre for Advanced Study (CAS) at the Norwegian Academy of Science and Letters in Oslo for providing a forum in which to do so, as part of the project *Exploring the Archaeological Migration Narrative: The Introduction of Farming and Animal Husbandry in Southern Norway*. I am also grateful for access to the Allen Ancient DNA Resource for mitogenome and Y-chromosome haplogroups: https://reich.hms.harvard.edu/allen-ancient-dna-resource-aadr-downloadable-genotypes-present-day-and-ancient-dna-data, version 50.

REFERENCES

Adamov, D., Guryanov, V., Karzhavin, S., Tagankin, V. and Urasin, V. 2015. Defining a new rate constant for Y-chromosome SNPs based on full sequencing data. *Russian Journal of Genetic Genealogy (Русская версия)* 7, 68–89.

Allentoft, M.E., Sikora, M., Sjogren, K.G., Rasmussen, S., Rasmussen, M., Stenderup, J. *et al.* 2015. Population genomics of Bronze Age Eurasia. *Nature* 522(7555), 167–72.

Ammerman, A.J. and Cavalli-Sforza, L.L. 1984. *The Neolithic transition and the genetics of populations in Europe*. Princeton University Press.

Bandelt, H.-J. 2018. David Reich's *Who we are and how we got here: ancient DNA and the new science of the human past*. *Current Anthropology* 59, 659.

Bandelt, H.-J., Macaulay, V.A. and Richards, M.B. 2002. What molecules can't tell us about the spread of languages and the Neolithic. In C. Renfrew and P. Bellwood (eds), *Examining the language-farming dispersal hypothesis*, 99–107. Cambridge: McDonald Institute for Archaeological Research.

Bollongino, R., Nehlich, O., Richards, M., Orschiedt, J., Thomas, M., Sell, C., Fajkosová, Z., Powell, A. and Burger, J. 2013. 2000 years of parallel societies in Stone Age Central Europe. *Science* 342(6157), 479–81.

Booth, T.J., Bruck, J., Brace, S. and Barnes, I. 2021. Tales from the Supplementary Information: ancestry change in Chalcolithic-Early Bronze Age Britain was gradual with varied kinship organization. *Cambridge Archaeological Journal* 31, 379–400.

Brace, S., Diekmann, Y., Booth, T. J., van Dorp, L., Faltyskova, Z., Rohland, N. *et al.* 2019. Ancient genomes indicate population replacement in Early Neolithic Britain. *Nature Ecology and Evolution* 3, 765–71.

Bramanti, B., Thomas, M. G., Haak, W., Unterlaender, M., Jores, P., Tambets, K. *et al.* 2009. Genetic discontinuity between local hunter-gatherers and Central Europe's first farmers. *Science* 326, 137–40.

Brandt, G., Haak, W., Adler, C.J., Roth, C., Szécsényi-Nagy, A., Karimnia, S. *et al.* 2013. Ancient DNA reveals key stages in the formation of central European mitochondrial genetic diversity. *Science* 342, 257–61.

Brandt, G., Szecsenyi-Nagy, A., Roth, C., Alt, K.W. and Haak, W. 2014. Human paleogenetics of Europe – the known knowns and the known unknowns. *Journal of Human Evolution* 79, 73–92.

Broodbank, C. 2013. *The making of the Middle Sea: a history of the Mediterranean from the beginning to the emergence of the Classical World*. London: Thames & Hudson.

Brunel, S., Bennett, E.A., Cardin, L., Garraud, D., Barrand Emam, H., Beylier, A. *et al.* 2020. Ancient genomes from present-day France unveil 7,000 years of its demographic history. *Proceedings of the National Academy of Sciences of the United States of America* 117(23), 12791–8.

Cann, R.L., Stoneking, M. and Wilson, A.C. 1987. Mitochondrial DNA and human evolution. *Nature* 325(6099), 31–6.

Cassidy, L.M., Maolduin, R.O., Kador, T., Lynch, A., Jones, C., Woodman, P.C. *et al.* 2020. A dynastic elite in monumental Neolithic society. *Nature* 582(7812), 384–8.

Cassidy, L. M., Martiniano, R., Murphy, E. M., Teasdale, M. D., Mallory, J., Hartwell, B. and Bradley, D.G. 2016. Neolithic and Bronze Age migration to Ireland and establishment of the insular Atlantic genome. *Proceedings of the National Academy of Sciences of the United States of America* 113, 368–73.

Cummings, V. 2017. *The Neolithic of Britain and Ireland.* Abingdon: Routledge.

Diamond, J.M. 1997. Language steamrollers. *Nature* 389, 544–6.

Dulias, K., Foody, M.G.B., Justeau, P., Silva, M., Martiniano, R., Oteo-Garcia, G. *et al.* 2022. Ancient DNA at the edge of the world: Continental immigration and the persistence of Neolithic male lineages in Bronze Age Orkney. *Proceedings of the National Academy of Sciences of the United States of America* 119(8), e2108001119. https://doi.org/10.1073/pnas.2108001119.

Eisenmann, S., Bánffy, E., van Dommelen, P., Hofmann, K.P., Maran, J., Lazaridis, I. *et al.* 2018. Reconciling material cultures in archaeology with genetic data: the nomenclature of clusters emerging from archaeogenomic analysis. *Scientific Reports* 8, 13003. https://doi.org/10.1038/s41598-018-31123-z.

Ermini, L., Olivieri, C., Rizzi, E., Corti, G., Bonnal, R., Soares, P. *et al.* 2008. Complete mitochondrial genome sequence of the Tyrolean Iceman. *Current Biology* 18, 1687–93.

Fernández-Domínguez, E. 2018. Comment on: Massive migrations? The impact of recent aDNA studies on our view of third millennium Europe. *European Journal of Archaeology* 21, 184–6.

Forster, P., Harding, R., Torroni, A. and Bandelt, H.-J. 1996. Origin and evolution of Native American mtDNA variation: a reappraisal. *The American Journal of Human Genetics* 59, 935–45.

Fu, Q., Mittnik, A., Johnson, P.L.F., Bos, K., Lari, M., Bollongino, R. *et al.* 2013. A revised timescale for human evolution based on ancient mitochondrial genomes. *Current Biology* 23, 553–59.

Furholt, M. 2018. Massive migrations? The impact of recent aDNA studies on our view of third millennium Europe. *European Journal of Archaeology* 21, 159–78.

Furholt, M. 2019. Re-integrating archaeology: a contribution to aDNA studies and the migration discourse on the 3rd millennium BC in Europe. *Proceedings of The Prehistoric Society* 85, 115–29.

Gretzinger, J., Sayer, D., Justeau, P., Altena, E., Pala, M., Dulias, K. *et al.* 2022. The Anglo-Saxon migration and the formation of the Early English gene pool. *Nature* 610(7930), 112–19.

Haak, W., Balanovsky, O., Sanchez, J.J., Koshel, S., Zaporozhchenko, V., Adler, C.J. *et al.* 2010. Ancient DNA from European early Neolithic farmers reveals their Near Eastern affinities. *PLoS Biology,* 8, e1000536.

Haak, W., Forster, P., Bramanti, B., Matsumura, S., Brandt, G., Tanzer, M. *et al.* 2005. Ancient DNA from the first European farmers in 7500-year-old Neolithic sites. *Science* 310, 1016–18.

Haak, W., Lazaridis, I., Patterson, N., Rohland, N., Mallick, S., Llamas, B. *et al.* 2015. Massive migration from the steppe was a source for Indo-European languages in Europe. *Nature* 522(7555), 207–11.

Hagelberg, E., Sykes, B. and Hedges, R. 1989. Ancient bone DNA amplified. *Nature* 342(6249), 485.

Handt, O., Richards, M., Tromsdorf, M., Kilger, C., Simanainen, J., Gueorguiev, O. *et al.* 1994. Molecular genetic analyses of the Tyrolean Ice Man. *Science* 264, 1775–78.

Higuchi, R., Bowman, B., Freiberger, M., Ryder, O.A. and Wilson, A.C. 1984. DNA sequences from the quagga, an extinct member of the horse family. *Nature* 312(5991), 282–4.

Hofmann, D. 2015. What have genetics ever done for us? The implications of aDNA data for interpreting identity in Early Neolithic central Europe. *European Journal of Archaeology* 18, 454–76.

Hofmann, D., Hanscam, E., Furholt, M., Baca, M., Reiter, S.S., Vanzetti, A. *et al.* 2021. Forum: populism, identity politics, and the archaeology of Europe. *European Journal of Archaeology* 24, 519–55.

Keller, A., Graefen, A., Ball, M., Matzas, M., Boisguerin, V., Maixner, F. *et al.* 2012. New insights into the Tyrolean Iceman's origin and phenotype as inferred by whole-genome sequencing. *Nature Communications* 3, 698.

Leslie, S., Winney, B., Hellenthal, G., Davison, D., Boumertit, A., Day, T. *et al.* 2015. The fine-scale genetic structure of the British population. *Nature* 519(7543), 309–14.

Lewin, R. 1997. Ancestral echoes. *New Scientist* 155(2089), 32–7.

Macaulay, V. and Richards, M.B. 2013. Mitochondrial genome sequences and their phylogeographic interpretation. In *Encyclopedia of Life Sciences (eLS)*. Chichester: John Wiley & Sons, Ltd. https://doi.org:10.1002/9780470015902.20843.pub2

Macaulay, V., Soares, P. and Richards, M.B. 2019. Rectifying long-standing misconceptions about the rho statistic for molecular dating. *PLoS One* 14(2), e0212311. https://doi.org/10.1371/journal.pone.0212311.

Mallory, J.P. 2017. *The origins of the Irish*. London: Thames and Hudson.

Mathieson, I., Alpaslan-Roodenberg, S., Posth, C., Szecsenyi-Nagy, A., Rohland, N., Mallick, S. *et al.* 2018. The genomic history of southeastern Europe. *Nature* 555(7695), 197–203.

Modi, A., Tassi, F., Susca, R.R., Vai, S., Rizzi, E., Bellis, G. *et al.* 2017. Complete mitochondrial sequences from Mesolithic Sardinia. *Science Reports* 7, 42869. https://doi.org/10.1038/srep42869.

Olalde, I., Brace, S., Allentoft, M.E., Armit, I., Kristiansen, K., Booth, T. *et al.* 2018. The Beaker phenomenon and the genomic transformation of northwest Europe. *Nature* 555(7697). https://doi.org/10.1038/nature26164.

Paabo, S. 1985. Molecular-cloning of ancient Egyptian mummy DNA. *Nature* 314(6012), 644–5.

Pääbo, S. 2014. *Neanderthal man: in search of lost genomes*. New York: Basic Books.

Pala, M., Chaubey, G., Soares, P. and Richards, M.B. 2014. The archaeogenetics of European ancestry. In *Encyclopedia of Life Sciences (eLS)*. Chichester: John Wiley and Sons. https://doi.org/10.1002/9780470015902.a0024624.

Pala, M., Olivieri, A., Achilli, A., Accetturo, M., Metspalu, E., Reidla, M. *et al.* 2012. Mitochondrial DNA signals of Late Glacial re-colonization of Europe from Near Eastern refugia. *American Journal of Human Genetics* 90, 915–24.

Papac, L., Ernee, M., Dobes, M., Langova, M., Rohrlach, A. B., Aron, F. *et al.* 2021. Dynamic changes in genomic and social structures in third millennium BCE central Europe. *Science Advances* 7(35). https://doi.org/10.1126/sciadv.abi6941.

Pereira, J.B., Costa, M.D., Vieira, D., Pala, M., Bamford, L., Harrich, N. *et al.* 2017. Reconciling evidence from ancient and contemporary genomes: a major source for the European Neolithic within Mediterranean Europe. *Proceedings of the Royal Society Series B*, 284(1851):20161976.

Pluciennik, M. 1998. Deconstructing 'the Neolithic' in the Mesolithic-Neolithic transition. In M. Edmonds and C. Richards (eds), *Understanding the Neolithic of north-western Europe*, 61–83. Glasgow: Cruithne Press.

Posth, C., Renaud, G., Mittnik, A., Drucker, D.G., Rougier, H., Cupillard, C. *et al.* 2016. Pleistocene mitochondrial genomes suggest a single major dispersal of non-Africans and a Late Glacial population turnover in Europe. *Current Biology* 26(6), 827–33.

Price, T.D., Bentley, R.A., Luning, J., Gronenborn, D. and Wahl, J. 2001. Prehistoric human migration in the Linearbandkeramik of central Europe. *Antiquity* 75, 593–603.

Reich, D. 2018. *Who we are and how we got here: ancient DNA and the new science of the human past*. Oxford: Oxford University Press.

Richards, M., Côrte-Real, H., Forster, P., Macaulay, V., Wilkinson-Herbots, H., Demaine, A. *et al.* 1996. Paleolithic and Neolithic lineages in the European mitochondrial gene pool. *American Journal of Human Genetics* 59, 185–203.

Richards, M., Macaulay, V., Hickey, E., Vega, E., Sykes, B., Guida, V. *et al.* 2000. Tracing European founder lineages in the Near Eastern mtDNA pool. *American Journal of Human Genetics* 67, 1251–76.

Richards, M., Smalley, K., Sykes, B. and Hedges, R. 1993. Archaeology and genetics: analysing DNA from skeletal remains. *World Archaeology* 25, 18–28.

Richards, M.B., Hedges, R.E.M. and Sykes, B.C. 1995. Authenticating DNA extracted from ancient skeletal remains. *Journal of Archaeological Science* 22, 291–9.

Richards, M.B. and Macaulay, V.A. 2013. It is unfair to compare genetic ancestry testing to astrology. *The Guardian, 08/04/2013.* https://www.theguardian.com/science/blog/2013/apr/08/unfair-genetic-ancestry-testing-astrology.

Rivollat, M., Jeong, C., Schiffels, S., Kucukkalipci, I., Pemonge, M.H., Rohrlach, A.B. *et al.* 2020. Ancient genome-wide DNA from France highlights the complexity of interactions between Mesolithic hunter-gatherers and Neolithic farmers. *Science Advances* 6(22), eaaz5344. https://doi.org/10.1126/sciadv.aaz5344.

Rohrlach, A.B., Papac, L., Childebayeva, A., Rivollat, M., Villalba-Mouco, V., Neumann, G.U. *et al.* 2021. Using Y-chromosome capture enrichment to resolve haplogroup H2 shows new evidence for a two-path Neolithic expansion to Western Europe. *Scientific Reports* 11(1). https://doi.org/10.1038/s41598-021-94491-z.

Rollo, F., Amici, A., Salvi, R. and Garbuglia, A. 1988. Short but faithful pieces of ancient DNA. *Nature* 335(6193), 774.

Rowley-Conwy, P. 2011. Westward ho! The spread of agriculture from central Europe to the Atlantic. *Current Anthropology* 52, S431–51.

Saag, L., Varul, L., Scheib, C.L., Stenderup, J., Allentoft, M.E., Saag, L. *et al.* 2017. Extensive farming in Estonia started through a sex-biased migration from the steppe. *Current Biology* 27(14), 2185–93.

Saag, L., Vasilyev, S.V., Varul, L., Kosorukova, N.V., Gerasimov, D.V., Oshibkina, S.V. *et al.* 2021. Genetic ancestry changes in Stone to Bronze Age transition in the East European plain. *Science Advances* 7(4). https://doi.org/10.1126/sciadv.abd6535.

Saillard, J., Forster, P., Lynnerup, N., Bandelt, H.-J. and Nørby, S.S. 2000. mtDNA variation among Greenland Eskimos: the edge of the Beringian expansion. *The American Journal of Human Genetics* 67, 718–26.

Sánchez-Quinto, F., Malmström, H., Fraser, M., Girdland-Flink, L., Svensson, E.M., Simoes, L.G. *et al.* 2019. Megalithic tombs in western and northern Neolithic Europe were linked to a kindred society. *Proceedings of the National Academy of Sciences of the United States of America* 116(19), 9469–74.

Seguin-Orlando, A., Donat, R., Der Sarkissian, C., Southon, J., Theves, C., Manen, C. *et al.* 2021. Heterogeneous hunter-gatherer and steppe-related ancestries in Late Neolithic and Bell Beaker genomes from present-day France. *Current Biology* 31(5), 1072–83.

Shennan, S. 2018. *The first farmers of Europe: an evolutionary perspective.* Cambridge: Cambridge University Press.

Sheridan, J.A. 2007. From Picardie to Pickering and Pencraig Hill? New information on the 'Carinated Bowl Neolithic' in northern Britain. In A. Whittle and V. Cummings (eds), *Going over: the Mesolithic–Neolithic transition in north-west Europe*, 441–92. Proceedings of the British Academy 144. Oxford: Oxford University Press.

Sheridan, A. 2010. The Neolithization of Britain and Ireland: the 'big picture'. In B. Finlayson and G. Warren (eds), *Landscapes in transition*, 89–105. Oxford: Oxbow Books.

Sherratt, A. 1994. The transformation of early agrarian Europe: the later Neolithic and Copper Ages. In B. Cunliffe (ed.), *The Oxford illustrated prehistory of Europe*, 167–201. Oxford: Oxford University Press.

Sherratt, A. 2004. Fractal farmers: patterns of Neolithic origin and dispersal. In J. Cherry, C. Scarre and S. Shennan (eds), *Explaining social change*, 53–63. Cambridge: MacDonald Institute for Archaeological Research.

Soares, P., Achilli, A., Semino, O., Davies, W., Macaulay, V., Bandelt, H.-J. *et al.* 2010. The archaeogenetics of Europe. *Current Biology* 20, R174–83.

Soares, P., Ermini, L., Thomson, N., Mormina, M., Rito, T., Röhl, A. *et al.* 2009. Correcting for purifying selection: an improved human mitochondrial molecular clock. *American Journal of Human Genetics* 84, 740–59.

Tolan-Smith, C. 2008. Mesolithic Britain. In G. Bailey and P. Spikins (eds), *Mesolithic Europe*, 132–57. Cambridge: Cambridge University Press.

Torroni, A., Huoponen, K., Francalacci, P., Petrozzi, M., Morelli, L., Scozzari, R. *et al.* 1996. Classification of European mtDNAs from an analysis of three European populations. *Genetics* 144, 1835–50.

Torroni, A., Schurr, T.G., Cabell, M.F., Brown, M.D., Neel, J.V., Larsen, M. *et al.* 1993. Asian affinities and continental radiation of the four founding Native American mtDNAs. *American Journal of Human Genetics* 53(3), 563–90.

Vander Linden, M. 2016. Population history in third-millennium-BC Europe: assessing the contribution of genetics. *World Archaeology* 48, 714–28.

Wang, C.C., Reinhold, S., Kalmykov, A., Wissgott, A., Brandt, G., Jeong, C. *et al.* 2019. Ancient human genome-wide data from a 3000-year interval in the Caucasus corresponds with eco-geographic regions. *Nature Communications* 10(1), 590. https://doi.org/10.1038/s41467-018-08220-8.

Whittle, A. Healy, F. and Bayliss, A. 2011. *Gathering time: dating the early Neolithic enclosures of southern Britain and Ireland.* Oxford: Oxbow Books.

Wilson, J.F., Weiss, D.A., Richards, M., Thomas, M.G., Bradman, N. and Goldstein, D.B. 2001. Genetic evidence for different male and female roles during cultural transitions in the British Isles. *Proceedings of the National Academy of Sciences of the United States of America* 98, 5078–83.

Zvelebil, M. (ed.) 1986. *Hunters in transition: Mesolithic societies of temperate Eurasia and their transition to farming.* Cambridge: Cambridge University Press.

Zvelebil, M. 1995. Farmers our ancestors and the identity of Europe. In P. Graves-Brown, S. Jones and C. Gamble (eds), *Cultural identity and archaeology*, 145–66. London: Routledge.

Zvelebil, M. 2000. The social context of the agricultural transition in Europe. In C. Renfrew and K. Boyle (eds), *Archaeogenetics*, 57–79. Cambridge: McDonald Institute for Archaeological Research.

Zvelebil, M. 2001a. The agricultural transition and the origins of Neolithic society in Europe. *Documenta Praehistorica* 28, 1–26.

Zvelebil, M. 2001b. Demography and dispersal of early farming populations at the Mesolithic-Neolihic transition: genetic and linguistic implications. In P. Bellwood and C. Renfrew (eds), *Examining the language-farming dispersal hypothesis*, 379–94. Cambridge: McDonald Institute for Archaeological Research.

Zvelebil, M. and Dolukhanov, P. 1991. The transition to farming in eastern and northern Europe. *Journal of World Prehistory* 5, 233–78.

Chapter 3

Five challenges for an integrated archaeogenetic paradigm

Kristian Kristiansen

The increasing pace of ancient DNA research, especially since 2015, can be seen as part of the third science revolution in archaeology. I outline what I see as the five current principal challenges, covering sampling and collaborative ethics, in the hope of creating shared codes of conduct; definitions of terminology and context, to avoid cross-disciplinary misunderstandings; open access to all forms of big data; a need to shift from interdisciplinarity to transdisciplinarity; and the integration of the interpretation of genes and culture, to investigate respective admixture processes and to translate biological mating processes into rules of kinship and marriage. The study of environmental DNA (eDNA) is seen as part of the next steps forward, representing the second phase of the third science revolution in archaeology.

BACKGROUND: 10 YEARS AFTER THE THIRD SCIENCE REVOLUTION

The third science revolution in archaeology has now been ongoing for little more than 10 years, since the first human prehistoric genomes were published in 2010. However, it is only from about 2015 that developments in both sequencing capacity and an increasing number of prehistoric samples being analysed created a real breakthrough in our understanding of genetic results for European prehistory. This has been summarised in several popular syntheses (Reich 2018; Krause 2019), and raised critical debates over the implications of the new genetic results, and how to integrate them into an archaeological context (Kristiansen 2022). From that arises the prospect of a more integrated archaeogenetic approach based on a truly interdisciplinary or even a transdisciplinary integration between the two disciplines. However, to get there we need to be aware of some of the challenges ahead. Here I discuss what I consider to be the five major challenges, some well recognised, others less so.

TOWARD AN INTEGRATED ARCHAEOGENETIC PARADIGM

1. Sampling and collaborative ethics

This topic has risen to become a key issue, with papers discussing the demands that need to be fulfilled (Prendergast and Sawchuk 2018; Sirak and Sedig 2019; Alpaslan-Roodenberg 2021). How do we create a truly integrated collaborative sampling and project design, where sampling is done to support clearly formulated research questions, and where collaboration is real? The immediate answer of course is to invite all relevant disciplines on board when starting a new project, including sample providers. This latter group is highly diverse, and we encounter huge differences in different parts of the world.

To begin with we need to realise that archaeology is a discipline of destruction and selective preservation. Excavation means destroying the object of study, and in the process documenting as much as possible. Therefore, the history of archaeology has seen the establishment of written and unwritten rules of how to preserve through destruction; among the unwritten rules are the constant refinement of methods of documentation – from actual excavation methods to the preservation of documentation in archives, and objects in museums. Among the written rules are the legal frameworks that regulate the preservation of sites and monuments in the landscape, economic obligations to pay for rescue excavations when destruction is inevitable, and the legal framework for the operation of museums to store and present archaeological evidence for researchers and the public (Kristiansen 2009). Access to archaeological material for research also has a destructive side if one needs to sample objects for further scientific analysis, and this has been an ongoing practice since the beginnings of archaeology. However, with the advent of new scientific breakthroughs or revolutions in archaeology (Kristiansen 2014), the frequency of such sampling has multiplied: from pottery to metals in order to undertake various forms of isotope and lipid analyses; from animal, plant and human material to sample for radiocarbon dating; and various forms of strontium analyses.

Over the years codes of conduct, often unpublished, have been established for how and under which conditions sampling is allowed, just as protocols have been established, most clearly for sampling for radiocarbon dating, where only small samples are now needed (Sirak and Sedig 2019). However, the most recent scientific revolution, that of ancient DNA (hereafter aDNA) or palaeogenomics and archaeogenetics, has not yet seen the formulation of shared codes of conduct for collaboration between the archaeological and the scientific community, even if needs and principles have been demonstrated and discussed (Prendergast and Sawchuk 2018; Sirak and Sedig 2019) that can form the basis for future codes of conduct, preferably by archaeological societies such as EAA and SAA (Alpaslan-Roodenberg 2021). The highest quality aDNA research on archaeological samples is typically found when geneticists, curators of anthropological collections and archaeologists engage each other in close and equitable research collaborations. All partners are needed to fully take advantage of the information provided by aDNA sequencing. It is exactly in the interface between genetics and archaeology and anthropology that the most creative and novel research is born. The road towards this goal, however, is paved with problems of many kinds, some of which I shall now discuss.

2. Lost in translation: terminologies and contexts

What is in a word (terminology), and what is in a context? I propose that the answer to those questions demands a discussion of how archaeological contexts relate to the formation of culture, and the ways we label and interpret culture. Here archaeologists have recently provided some good case studies to support the notion that context is crucial for the interpretation of genetic data (Booth *et al.* 2021; Bloxam and Parker Pearson 2022).

However, the answer also relates to how we translate biological/genetic terminology into archaeological terminology, which represents another level of potential misunderstanding in debates, previously discussed by Sørensen (2017). More recently the problem has been re-emphasised by Alexandra Ion (in press). She states:

> *There might be two main challenges inherent to the fact that the data is very different in nature: (1) each discipline might have its own ontological reading of the studied object; (2) the scale the data operates on. For these reasons when different disciplines meet on the same territory either tensions or misunderstandings might arise (see article on terminology by Eisenmann et al. 2018). In the case of genetic analysis, osteology, cultural anthropology, isotope studies etc., each of them has their own ontological view ascribed to a person's identity.*

She rightly suggests that the impact of different ontologies has been somewhat overlooked: 'Surprisingly though, it seems that precisely this complex process of negotiation and of finding a "meta-language" is almost absent at present' (Ion 2019, 177, 189; see also Sørensen 2017 for earlier discussion). I venture to propose that right now we are in a phase where sometimes misunderstanding, even misrepresentation, of 'the other' has led to a series of partly unfounded critiques, or rather over-interpretations, of what new genetic results imply from both sides. It is in some measure due to the kind of misunderstanding that Ion ascribed to different meta-languages. Geneticists have a specific understanding of genetic admixture and change that cannot easily be translated into archaeological language without simplification. As a result, critical archaeologists have tended to overstate the negative interpretative implications or dangers of at least some genetic results, while some genetic papers on the contrary have tended to over-interpret their results in terms of archaeological and linguistic implications.

The first step forward is of course to identify those concepts and contexts that can lead to misunderstandings, to which also belongs the concept of 'ancestry' with very different meaning in genetics and archaeology. Booth (2020) addressed this issue in a recent discussion paper:

> *I think many population geneticists would argue that terms such as 'population' and 'ancestry' are not euphemisms for race, and do not represent attempts to sanitize racial groups. In the discussion of human genetic diversity, terms like 'population' and 'ancestry' represent a convenient way of talking about genetic structure (for an accessible summary see Birney et al. 2019). Genetic structure is defined by the genetic data and not by pre-existing population labels.*

Here we are at the root of some current misunderstandings, lost in translation from genetic to archaeological meta-language. When a genetic population for convenience is translated into an archaeological culture, such as Yamnaya or Corded Ware, it implies to many archaeologists an implicit correspondence between genes, culture, and ethnic identity, not least when further translated into popular dissemination. Therefore, utmost care and explanation are demanded when translating genetic and archaeological meta-language (Eisenmann *et al.* 2018). Consequently, neutral terms to characterise genetic admixture processes are now being employed when possible, such as steppe ancestry, Anatolian/farmer ancestry, western and eastern hunter-gatherer ancestry. Accordingly, a discussion about good practice for making interdisciplinary interpretations is mandatory, and for that, a historical perspective provides a useful background (Díaz-Andreu and Coltofean-Arizancu 2021).

However, the debate is continuing, as it has a much wider scope than archaeology and aDNA (see the most recent summary in Coop 2022).

3. Big data: towards open access

Another side of the third science revolution is its powerful use of Big Data. Once archaeological data entered the digitised world, it could be analysed and correlated with other types of data, such as the geodata forming the backbone of GIS (McCoy 2017), or environmental and genetic data (Roberts *et al.* 2018; Racimo *et al.* 2020). All published genetic data are stored in a global database. This implies that all new aDNA analyses can be compared to previous analyses, as well as to modern reference data. Old data can in this way be re-analysed with new methods, all of which is part of the rapid advance and strength of archaeogenetics. But how do we create open access archaeological databases to match those of aDNA? To be able to reproduce and re-use existing Big Data is a prerequisite for advancing archaeological data analysis to new levels, and to further advance interdisciplinarity. The potential of this has recently been demonstrated when the European Open Access database for pollen diagrams (Fyfe *et al.* 2009) was employed to compare changes in landscape openness between the Neolithic and Copper Age/Early Bronze Age with similar genetic changes based on aDNA. When radiocarbon dates were added it revealed major differences between Neolithic and Bronze Age migration patterns (Racimo *et al.* 2020).

So far, most archaeological Big Data are stored in national databases and are therefore of limited use. Thus, the full potential of archaeological Big Data has yet to be realised (Perry and Taylor 2018; Huggett 2020). However, lists of radiocarbon dates have been made publicly available in the journal *Radiocarbon* since 1959, and can thus be employed in more advanced research crosscutting national borders. Such research has already had a profound effect upon our understanding of prehistoric demography (Hinz *et al.* 2012; Shennan *et al.* 2013; Blanco-Gonzales *et al.* 2018; Roberts *et al.* 2019). Therefore, in our recently started ERC Synergy project, Corex, we are creating European-wide databases covering the period from 6000–500 cal BC (https://www.corex-erc.com). They include strontium isotopic samples from humans, archaeobotanical and osteological data from settlement contexts and archaeological burial contexts, just as we employ existing databases for European pollen diagrams and aDNA. The ultimate goal is to transform these research databases into open access databases for archaeological research.

Combining environmental, genetic and archaeological evidence to produce new integrated interpretations demands a new type of interdisciplinary practice, which in turn raises fundamental questions about how to balance such interpretations (Arponen *et al.* 2019a; 2019b; 2019c). It puts new demands on all participating parties, but of what kind?

4. From interdisciplinarity to transdisciplinarity

Liv Nilsson Stutz suggests that, in order to create a more productive environment for interdisciplinary collaboration, it is necessary to understand what it takes and that it represents a demanding process of increasing knowledge-sharing. She then suggests a three-phase knowledge-sharing process, moving from 'multidisciplinarity', through 'interdisciplinarity' toward 'transdisciplinarity' (Stutz 2016). She defines the different stages in the following way:

> *Multidisciplinarity* denotes a model where different disciplines, each providing its own perspective, collaborate by bringing their disciplinary expertise to bear on an issue;
> *Interdisciplinary* work denotes a higher level of integration by analysing, synthesising, and harmonising links between disciplines 'into a coordinated and coherent whole';
> *Transdisciplinarity*, even more integrated, creates a unity of intellectual frameworks beyond the disciplinary perspectives. Moving from inter- to trans-disciplinarity thus demands an open forum of intellectual reflection, and additional intellectual labour. It demands a wider context, including comparative knowledge of results from other disciplines. And that inevitably reduces the number of researchers who are capable and willing to provide that extra investment of labour in a new field where such interpretations for the foreseeable future will remain debatable. Until now the most productive way forward has been project teamwork, where archaeologists, geneticists and researchers from other relevant disciplines such as environmental science, historical linguistics and so on, work together, from formulating research goals through to final publication.

To situate the present debates, we need to understand the ultimate goal of transdisciplinarity. According to Liv Nilsson Stutz, it is a way of integrating all the different voices inside and outside academia that form our perceptions of the past – from cultural, critical heritage to the way we interpret evidence under a shared theoretical framework that understands the complicated processes of genetics and culture interactions – and which are able to situate the results in the present. We are certainly not there yet; rather we are in the middle phase where the two disciplines are grappling to create a shared understanding of genetic and archaeological evidence and their impact in the present. Here, archaeology comes with the burden of a long history of contested and sometimes politicised narratives of the past against a new genetic discipline of ancient DNA without such a historical burden. This imbalance has clearly shaped some of the debates about European prehistory (Frieman and Hofmann 2019).

5. Genes versus culture

This field of research is theoretically the most demanding and therefore also contested. Here I propose two themes for further examination:

1. How do genetic admixture processes relate to cultural admixture processes?
2. How do we translate biological mating processes into rules of kinship and marriage?

Genetic admixture processes versus cultural admixture processes. While genetic admixture processes are reasonably well understood, the same is not true of cultural admixture processes. There are several reasons for this; culture and its meanings are under-theorised and thus debated (Kristiansen 2022, 28–30). Therefore, to begin with we need to delineate and theorise what constitute cultural and ethnic identities (Jones 1997). Cultural identities and ethnicities are always formed in relation to and sometimes in opposition to other such identities (Barth 1969; Sahlins 2010). From this arises the theoretical paradox that, while cultures are seemingly autonomous and often studied as such, they are derived from larger 'global' processes of interlinked political economies, which fuel a process of identification with certain cultural and cosmological values and material expressions. They are part of a process of elite formation and elite control, in need of boundaries to exert its dominance by establishing a system of shared values. Over time, cultural identity may come to include other forms of identification; for example, language may lend to it a certain degree of relative autonomy. While nationalism may have taken on more sophisticated and penetrating means of identity formation during the late modern period, it is shaped by the very same processes that led to the emergence of regional identities in the Neolithic and Bronze Age. Those need therefore to be studied with due respect to these larger historical processes.

From a methodological point of view, boundary formation of various forms can often be demonstrated in the archaeological record, which define 'us' and 'them' (Hodder 1978; Burmeister and Müller-Schessel 2007). We may assume that complex societies produced more boundaries than less complex societies, internal as well as external. The definition of such boundaries in the archaeological record, however, is only a first step. Next follows the theoretical interpretation of the social and economic processes leading to such divisions in the material record. If they carry any weight, it must be possible to link them to the formation and reproduction of institutions.

Translating biological mating networks into rules of kinship and marriage. This field of research is entirely new, as we have not previously been able to characterise biological mating networks. But how do we move from the biological to the social world, and what is the relation – if any – between ethnic origins and blood ties, and what is the role of kinship in maintaining or changing such relationships? And how do we define kinship in relevant prehistoric terms (Booth *et al.* 2020)? Kinship institutions and their rules of marriage, inheritance, fosterage, adoption and so on represented the daily conduct of life within the tens of thousands of households that increasingly covered Europe during the Neolithic and later on during the Bronze Age. They are therefore fundamental to our understanding of the dynamics of social and economic reproduction in time and space. One of the most common principles of marriage in the anthropological literature is the matrilateral mother's brother's daughter cross-cousin marriage, or alternatively the patrilateral father's sister's daughter. It represents an interpersonal way to create alliances between lineages (Sahlins 1968, chapter 4). Thus, traditional marriage is not strictly personal but rather a marriage of families. In the words of Marshall Sahlins (1968, 10): 'kinship is a fundamental ground of peaceful human discourse. The wide extension of kinship idioms, relations, and groups in tribal societies represents another way to seek peace'.

However, to unravel marriage and kinship relations demands in-depth analyses of local community cemeteries, megaliths or groups of barrows (Cassidy *et al.* 2020; Mittnik *et al.* 2020; Sjögren *et al.* 2021; Fowler *et al.* 2022). It further demands a proper understanding of the vast corpus of kinship practices accumulated in social anthropology (Lévi-Strauss 1969) and in Indo-European studies (Olsen 2019; 2020) in order to translate biological mating patterns into rules of social kinship. It is, therefore, still a field of research in its infancy, but it represents a potential for archaeology to contribute new types of evidence to existing anthropological knowledge of kinship. As kinship institutions are integrated into larger networks, we may further assume that such case studies are valid for a region corresponding to the geographical origin of the analysed individuals. Even if that provides some ground for generalisation, we need many more in-depth local studies to provide larger spatial and temporal coverage than we have today, as we may assume that such institutions alter over time and may also display geographical variation.

FROM HERE ONWARDS: WHAT IS NEXT?

Even if environmental DNA was introduced 20 years ago by Eske Willerslev and his team (Willerslev *et al.* 2003), it is only now that we are capable of realising its full potential. This in turn will open up completely new doors to previously hidden genetic knowledge about daily life at prehistoric settlements. Sampling cultural layers and other settlement contexts will potentially reveal which plants, animals, pathogens were around, and possibly also human genomes. Over the past 20 years background reference libraries for the DNA identification of thousands of species have been built up, allowing the determination of plants, animals and pathogens from prehistoric settlement layers and sediments. Also, knowledge of what soil conditions – minerals and other materials – that favour DNA preservation has increased. However, human DNA has been less successfully identified, even if we can observe progress here (Vernot *et al.* 2021).

In our recently started Corex ERC Synergy project we shall employ eDNA from 40–50 prehistoric settlement sites from the period 6000–500 cal BC in temperate Europe, which will form a local community-based window to understand larger processes of change unveiled by Big Data (https://www.corex-erc.com). In this way eDNA holds the potential to provide a high-resolution window to living conditions at local sites, and it also holds a future potential to provide an alternative source of human DNA, that can balance the highly selective and limited number of prehistoric skeletons available for aDNA analysis. It will provide a richer prehistory, but also present new theoretical and not least methodological challenges of how to balance and integrate local and supra local processes of change. It will also provide a new way forward for sampling of human DNA, since settlement evidence represent a nearly unlimited resource, with excavations continuously providing new sampling contexts. Thus, we may now be entering a second phase of the third science revolution.

REFERENCES

Alpaslan-Roodenberg, S., Anthony, D., Babiker, H., Bánffy, E., Booth, T., Capone, P.A. *et al.* 2021. Ethics of DNA research on human remains: five globally applicable guidelines. *Nature* 599, 41–6.

Arponen, V.P.J., Dörfler, W., Feeser, I., Grimm, S., Groß, D., Hinz, M. *et al.* 2019a. Environmental determinism and archaeology: understanding and evaluating determinism in research design. *Archaeological Dialogues* 26, 1–9.

Arponen, V.P.J., Dörfler, W., Feeser, I., Grimm, S., Groß, D., Hinz, M. *et al.* 2019b. Two cultures in the times of interdisciplinary archaeology: a response to commentators. *Archaeological Dialogues*, 26, 19–24.

Arponen, V.P.J., Grimm, S., Käppel, L.L., Ott, K., Thalheim, B., Kropp, Y. *et al.* 2019c. Between natural and human sciences: on the role and character of theory in socio-environmental archaeology. *The Holocene* 29(10), 1671–6.

Barth, F. 1969. Introduction. In F. Barth (ed.), *Ethnic groups and boundaries: the social organization of culture difference*, 9–38. London: Allen & Unwin.

Blanko-Gonzales, A., Lillios, K.T., Lopez-Saez, J.A. and Drake, B.L. 2018. Cultural, demographic and environmental dynamics of the Copper and Early Bronze Age in Iberia (3300–1500 BC): towards an interregional multiproxy comparison at the time of the 4.2 ky BP Event. *Journal of World Prehistory* 31, 1–79.

Bloxam, A. and Parker Pearson, M. 2022. Funerary diversity and cultural continuity: the British Beaker phenomenon beyond the stereotype. *Proceedings of the Prehistoric Society*, doi:10.1017/ppr.2022.2.

Booth, T.J. 2019. A stranger in a strange land: a perspective on archaeological responses to the palaeogenetic revolution from an archaeologist working amongst palaeogeneticists. *World Archaeology* 51(4), 586–601.

Booth, T.J. 2020. Imagined biodeterminism? *Archaeological Dialogues* 27, 16–19.

Booth, T.J., Brück, J., Brace, S. and Barnes, I. 2021. Tales from the Supplementary Information: ancestry change in Chalcolithic–Early Bronze Age Britain was gradual with varied kinship organization. *Cambridge Archaeological Journal* 31, 379–400.

Bürmeister, S. and Müller-Schessel, N. (eds) 2007. *Soziale gruppen, Kulturelle Grenzen: die Interpretation sozialer Identitäten in der prähistorischen Archäologie*. Münster: Waxman.

Cassidy, L.M., Maolduin, R.O., Kador, T., Lynch, A., Jones, C., Woodman, P.C. *et al.* 2020. A dynastic elite in monumental Neolithic society. *Nature* 582(7812), 384–8.

Coop, G. 2022. Genetic similarity and genetic ancestry groups. *arXiv:2207.11595v1*.

Crema, E.R., Bevan, A. and Shennan, S. 2017. Spatio-temporal approaches to archaeological radiocarbon dates. *Journal of Archaeological Science* 87, 1–9.

Díaz-Andreu, M. and Coltofean-Arizancu, L. 2021. Interdisciplinarity and archaeology. a historical introduction. In L. Coltofean-Arizancu and M. Díaz-Andreu (eds), *Interdisciplinarity and archaeology: scientific interactions in nineteenth- and twentieth-century archaeology*, 1–21. Oxford: Oxbow Books.

Eisenmann, S., Bánffy, E., van Dommelen, P., Hofmann, K.P., Maran, J., Lazaridis, I. *et al.* 2018. Reconciling material cultures in archaeology with genetic data: The nomenclature of clusters emerging from archaeogenomic analysis. *Scientific Reports* 8. https://doi.org/10.1038/s41598-018-31123-z.

Fowler, C., Olalde, I., Cummings, V., Armit, I., Büster, L., Cuthbert, S., Rohland, N. *et al.* 2022. A high-resolution picture of kinship practices in an Early Neolithic tomb. *Nature* 601(7894), 584–7.

Frieman, C.J. and Hofmann, D. 2019. Present pasts in the archaeology of genetics, identity, and migration in Europe: a critical essay. *World Archaeology* 51(4), 528–45.

Furholt, M. 2018. Massive migrations? The impact of recent aDNA studies on our view of third millennium Europe. *European Journal of Archaeology* 21, 159–78.

Furholt, M. 2019. Re-integrating archaeology: a contribution to aDNA studies and the migration discourse on the 3rd millennium BC in Europe. *Proceedings of the Prehistoric Society* 85, 115–29.

Fyfe, R.M., de Beaulieu, J.L., Binney, H., Bradshaw, R.H.W., Brewer, S., Flao, A.L. *et al.* 2019. The European pollen database: past efforts and current activities. *Vegetation History and Archaeobotany* 18, 417–24.

Hinz, M., Feeser, I., Sjögren, K.-G. and Müller, J. 2012. Demography and the intensity of cultural activities: an evaluation of Funnel Beaker Societies (4200–2800 cal BC). *Journal of Archaeological Sciences* 39, 3331–40.

Hodder, I. (ed.) 1978. *The spatial organisation of culture*. London: Duckworth.

Huggett, J. 2020. Is big digital data different? Towards a new archaeological paradigm. *Journal of Field Archaeology* 45, 8–17.

Ion, A. 2019. Who are we as historical beings? Shaping identities in the light of the archaeogenetics 'revolution'. *Current Swedish Archaeology* 27, 11–36.

Ion, A. in press. Boundary objects, identities and archaeology. *Forum Kritische Archäologie.*

Johnson, K.M. and Paul, K.S. 2016. Bioarchaeology and kinship: integrating theory, social relatedness, and biology in ancient family research. *Journal of Archaeological Research* 24, 75–123.

Jones, S. 1997. *The archaeology of ethnicity: constructing identities in the past and the present.* London: Routledge.

Krause, J., with Trappe, T. 2019. *Die Reise unserer Gene: eine Geschichte über uns und unsere Vorfahren.* Berlin: Propyläen.

Kristiansen, K. 2008. The discipline of archaeology. In B. Cunliffe, C. Gosden and R.A. Joyce (eds), *The Oxford handbook of archaeology*, 1–46. Oxford: Oxford University Press.

Kristiansen, K. 2014. Towards a new paradigm? The third science revolution and its possible consequences in archaeology. *Current Swedish Archaeology* 22, 11–34.

Kristiansen, K. 2022. *Archaeology and the genetic revolution in European prehistory.* Cambridge: Cambridge University Press.

Lévi-Strauss, C. 1969. *The elementary structures of kinship.* Boston: Beacon Press.

McCoy, M.D. 2017. Geospatial big data and archaeology: prospects and problems too great to ignore. *Journal of Archaeological Science* 84, 74–94.

Mittnik, A., Massy, K., Knipper, C., Wittenborn, F., Friedrich, R., Pfrengle, S. *et al.* 2019. Kinship-based social inequality in Bronze Age Europe. *Science* 366, 731–4.

Nilsson Stutz, L. 2018. A future for archaeology: in defense of an intellectually engaged, collaborative and confident archaeology. *Norwegian Archaeological Review* 51, 48–56.

Olsen, B.A. 2019. Aspects of family structure among the Indo-Europeans. In B.A. Olsen, T. Olander and K. Kristiansen (eds), *Tracing the Indo-Europeans: new evidence from archaeology and historical linguistics*, 145–64. Oxford: Oxbow Books.

Olsen, B.A. 2020. Kin, clan and community in Proto-Indo-European. In B. Whitehead, B.A. Olsen and J. Jacquet (eds), *Kin, clan and community in Indo-European society*, 39–180. Copenhagen: Tusculanum Press.

Perry, S. and Taylor, J.S. 2018. Theorising the digital: a call to action for the archaeological community. In M. Matsumoto and E. Uleberg (eds), *Oceans of data: Proceedings of the 44th Conference on computer applications and quantitative methods in archaeology*, 11–22. Oxford: Archaeopress.

Prendergast, M.E. and Sawchuk, E. 2018. Boots on the ground in Africa's ancient DNA 'revolution': archaeological perspectives on ethics and best practices. *Antiquity* 92, 803–15.

Reich, D. 2018. *Who we are and how we got here: ancient DNA and the new science of the human past.* Oxford: Oxford University Press.

Roberts, C.N., Woodbridge, J., Palmisano, A., Bevan, A., Fyfe, R. and Shennan, S. 2019. Mediterranean landscape change during the Holocene: synthesis, comparison and regional trends in population, land cover and climate. *The Holocene* 29(5), 923–37.

Sahlins, M. 1968. *Tribesmen.* Englewood Cliffs, N.J.: Prentice Hall.

Sahlins, M. 1972. *Stone Age economics.* Chicago: Aldine Atherton.

Sahlins, M. 2010. The whole is a part: intercultural politics of order and change. In T. Otto and N. Bubandt (eds), *Experiments in holism: theory and practice in contemporary anthropology*, 102–26. Oxford: Wiley-Blackwell.

Shennan, S., Downey, S., Timpson, A., Edinborough, K., Colledge, S., Kerig, T., Manning, K. and Thomas, M.G. 2013. Regional population collapse followed initial agriculture booms in mid-Holocene Europe. *Nature Communications* 4, 2486.

Sirak, K.A. and Sedig, J.W. 2019. Balancing analytical goals and anthropological stewardship in the midst of the paleogenomics revolution. *World Archaeology* 51, 560–73.

Sjögren, K.-G., Olalde, I., Carver, S., Allentoft, M.E., Knowles, T., Kroonen, G. *et al.* 2021. Kinship and social organization in Copper Age Europe. a cross-disciplinary analysis of archaeology, DNA, isotopes, and anthropology from two Bell Beaker cemeteries. *PLoS One* 15(11): e0241278.

Sørensen, F. 2017. The two cultures and a world apart: archaeology and science at a new crossroads. *Norwegian Archaeological Review* 50(2), 101–15.

Willerslev, E., Hansen, A.J., Binladen, J., Brand, T.B., Gilbert, M.T.P., Shapiro, B. *et al.* 2003. Diverse plant and animal genetic records from Holocene and Pleistocene sediments. *Science* 300, 791–5.

Vernot, B., Zavala, E.I., Gómez-Olivencia, A., Jacobs, Z., Slon, V., Mafessoni, F. *et al.* 2021. Unearthing Neanderthal population history using nuclear and mitochondrial DNA from cave sediments. *Science* 372, eabf1667.

Chapter 4

Ancient genomics methodology and genetic insularity in Neolithic Europe

Bruno Ariano and Daniel G. Bradley

A question for ancient genomics in terms of reproductive networks is whether Neolithic seascapes were accelerants or retardants of genomic exchange. The standard canon of allele frequency-based genome analysis methods has shown conclusively that agriculture was spread via migration rather than acculturation, and throughout the Mediterranean and also across the British and Irish archipelago it is clear that sea corridors carried communities of farmers in initial colonisations. However, for the examination of subsequent networks among genomically similar Neolithic populations a more in-depth interrogation of genomic diversity is needed. This is provided by a next generation of analyses that consider similarity within and between genomes based on shared chunks of chromosomes. The detailed data required for these methods can be obtained by genome-wide imputation in a cost-effective leveraging of partially sequenced genomes. These genealogical approaches parse fine structure among European Neolithic genomes and unveil the retarding effects of seascapes for genetic relations, rather than their connectivities.

There have been recent informative reviews of ancient DNA methods (Orlando *et al.* 2021; Liu *et al.* 2022). Here we focus on two aspects: the approaches to enhancing endogenous DNA content to enable sequencing, and genome imputation to enable genealogical approaches to unveiling more detailed affinities among populations and individuals. We discuss our recent analysis of the European Neolithic as an illustration.

METHODS AND PROGRESS IN ANCIENT GENOMICS

With ancient specimens, both quantity and quality of retrieved DNA are lessened as a result of age-related lesions, exposure to soil chemistry, microbial challenge and high temperatures. The first decade or so of research on DNA from ancient specimens focused on mitochondrial genomes, which give higher chances of success on extraction but with obviously limited information content. Within its second decade, enabled by the emergence of massively parallelised high-throughput sequencing technologies, the field has decisively shifted to autosomal genome sequencing. However, even with successive technical advances, the cost of sequencing remains a limiting factor and maximising the yield of endogenous DNA is a key aim. This has been enhanced by three main developments: an appreciation of the different DNA preservation capacities of different bone elements; the use of bait capture techniques to concentrate targeted sequences; and more aggressive extraction using bleach to selectively remove environmental and contaminating DNA fractions. With choice of bone sample, density is a decisive factor. Gamba *et al.* (2014) first showed that the densest bone element, the petrous temporal, gave markedly superior yields to other bones and it has become the sample of choice. Cementum in teeth and dense regions of other bones can also perform well. It has been observed many times that, with well-preserved bones, the early problems of contamination from modern sources that plagued the field have simply been sidestepped by the quantitative analyses allowed by high-throughput data. Contamination persists but usually at such a minor fraction of total yield that essential analyses are unaffected.

Bait hybridisation capture uses synthesised RNA or DNA strands to bind to endogenous molecules and selectively concentrate them for sequencing (Avila-Arcos *et al.* 2011). It is a widely used and cost-effective approach with particular importance for poorly preserved specimens but has two limitations. First, it is most often an incomplete sampling of the genome (compared to more expensive whole genome shotgun sequencing), as the variable positions sequenced are usually pre-defined by the targets chosen. Second, the use of this intermediate selection step can lead to biases when using some platforms, which can affect important population genomic analyses (Rohland *et al.* 2022).

Preliminary bleach washing in extractions eliminates selectively the environmental fraction that constitutes the bulk of DNA retrieved from most bones. Sequencing this mixture of bacterial, fungal and other non-target species is a waste of resource. As endogenous DNA is more likely to be effectively embedded in the bone matrix than that of exogenous origin, it is more protected against the destructive action of the bleach (Korlević and Meyer 2019). Including this step often increases several-fold the relative yield of endogenous DNA and makes shotgun sequencing more affordable.

IMPUTATION

Notwithstanding notable exceptions where yield and budget allow deep sequencing, researchers usually have to contend with missing genotype information when analysing ancient samples. One approach is to read only one allele from the available aligned positions, that is, consideration of a pseudohaploid genome. However, autosomal genomes are of course diploid and this reduction, in addition to obviously halving the aspirational information within a genome, prevents the use of a range of advanced, informative analyses that use phased variation from all sister chromosomes. However, one increasingly utilised method to fill missing genotype information in ancient genomics is imputation. This takes advantage of linkage between neighbouring loci together with information from a reference panel of genomes to predict unknown genotypes from partial sequence input data (Pasaniuc *et al.* 2012). Several softwares operate to use known short haplotypes and recombination maps from well-characterised genomes of thousands of individuals to reconstruct the unknown genotype information in target genomes (Browning 2006; LI and Y 2006; Marchini *et al.* 2007). However, given the very large number of possible haplotype combinations involved, these methods usually require long computational times when imputing millions of diploid variants using hundreds of individuals. One solution is to reduce the number of haplotypes present in the reference dataset by selecting only individuals closer to the target genome. Also and importantly, recent algorithms such as that implemented in the programme GLIMPSE show markedly more efficient computation (Rubinacci *et al.* 2021).

Imputation has been successfully applied in ancient humans, first by Gamba and colleagues in 2014 (Gamba *et al.* 2014) to a time series of Hungarian genomes. Among other findings, this allowed the first demonstration that genetic diversity increased, as indicated by a lower fraction of the genome under runs of homozygosity (ROH) from hunter-gatherers through Neolithic to Bronze and Iron Age samples. Martiniano *et al.* (2017) imputed a larger set of ancient samples spanning from the Palaeolithic to the early medieval periods, investigating fine-population structure and phenotypic traits. Antonio *et al.* (2019) used the approach to investigate the fine-scale structure of genomes of people that lived in modern-day Italy between the Mesolithic and early modern periods. Thanks to the high resolution provided by the haplotype information the authors of this work could detect a range of ancestries present during the imperial era. More recently Cassidy *et al.* (2020), by applying the same methods, discovered that a Neolithic sample from Ireland came from first-order incestuous parentage, suggesting that he may have belonged to an elite dynasty. Imputation also enabled the observation of Irish Mesolithic ancestry within a single Neolithic individual (among 42 sampled), illustrating both the existence and limits of indigenous hunter-gatherer contribution to early farmer ancestry. Diploid imputed genotypes were also effectively used to investigate the expansion of Viking populations from Scandinavia to Europe (Margaryan *et al.* 2020). Lastly, our recent work expanded the range of samples imputed to also include SNP-captured samples giving in total >300 ancient highly covered diploid genomes (Ariano *et al.* 2022). In this work we investigated population structure, population size and inbreeding for populations ranging from Palaeolithic to Neolithic periods. In particular, by using diploid imputed data for 258 Neolithic individuals, this work highlighted the effects of geography that shaped the genetic architecture of ancient Europe.

HAPLOTYPE-BASED ESTIMATION OF AFFINITY USING A GENEALOGICAL APPROACH

When two individuals share a recent common ancestor, chromosome chunks or shared haplotypes, termed 'identical by descent' (IBD), can be observed as having been passed to them through the separating generations (Browning 2008; Browning and Browning 2010). We can consider the affinities between genomes as a compendium of chunk genealogies, giving a rich well of inference. The size and quantity of these IBD segments can be used in genomics to investigate and distinguish affinities at different time-depths stretching from familial kinship (longer stretches of shared genome) to population-level relationship through to separations of thousands of years (resulting in shorter segments). For example, first cousins are approximately 25% IBD, with an average length of segments of 25 centiMorgans (approximately 25 million nucleotide bases) (Thompson 2013). After the detection of IBD segments from dense diploid genotype data other tools can be used

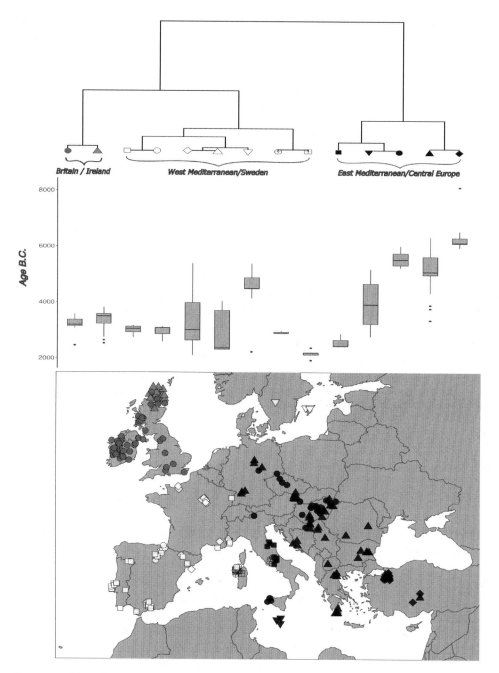

Figure 4.1. FineSTRUCTURE (Lawson et al. *2012) analysis estimating clusters of European Neolithic genomes and phylogenetic relationships among them. Based on Chromopainter-calculations of chromosome chunk sharing among individuals, this is adapted from Ariano* et al. *(2022) and shows the grouping of samples into geographically and temporally consistent clusters.*

to infer kinship or to estimate population size (Manichaikul *et al.* 2010; Browning and Browning 2015). For example, Williams and colleagues recently developed a series of tools that help in understanding how IBD segments pattern can be used to infer genealogies (https://hapi-dna.org). In another example Belbin and colleagues used IBD to discover a variant associated with short stature that was present in high frequency in Puerto Rican individuals due to a founding population event (Belbin *et al.* 2017). The power of analysis of chunk ancestries using the Chromopainter and Finestructure methods were instrumental in the first effective parsing of the diverse ancestries of British people with an immediate ancestry from the island (Lawson *et al.* 2012; 2015).

In a recent example of application to ancient genomes, Margaryan *et al.* (2020) analysed IBD segments among 298 imputed Viking-period genomes to parse their genetic affinities. These included evidence for Danish ancestry in English samples, Swedish influx in the Baltic, and Norwegian dissemination around the Atlantic sphere in Ireland, Iceland and Greenland. More recently, we (Ariano *et al.* 2022) applied similar methods to 278 ancient Neolithic Europeans to disentangle a genetic structure shaped by barriers and maritime cabotage (Fig. 4.1).

This approach showed that European Neolithic individuals could be sorted into geographically and temporally coherent groups defined on their shared genealogy of segments. At a higher level of branching, the primary division is between east and west Europe, and then between continental populations and those of Britain and Ireland. The latter gives some indication of the influence of sea barriers in forming this structure; differentiation along the Mediterranean is another. Two islands also show some distinction. Maltese Neolithic samples form a small cluster. Interestingly, the only division that emerges within Britain and Ireland is that between a cluster of genomes that predominate in Orkney and those of both mainland islands.

CHUNK GENEALOGY AND DEMOGRAPHY

When a population is restricted in size, there is a tendency for enhanced sharing of genome chunks. Simply, within such a group because opportunities for outbreeding in its past were limited, the genealogical loops in shared ancestry tend to be more numerous and more recent. This manifests in data in two ways, increased sharing between individuals in a sample (IBD) and sharing between the maternally and paternally derived chromosomes within an individual manifesting as runs of homozygosity (ROH; Fig. 4.2).

ROH segments can be used to infer the size of a population and also to investigate inbreeding events that happened in the genealogy of an individual. As for IBD, the quantity and length of the ROH segments are important to understand the relatedness between the parents of an inbred organism. For example, Yengo and colleagues have used the pattern of ROH segments to investigate inbreeding in approximately 450,000 modern individuals in the UK Biobank dataset (Yengo *et al.* 2019). This showed that approximately 1 out of 3652 individuals of UK origin were from parents who were at least second-degree related. Imputation has allowed the discovery of inbreeding in ancient times. Cassidy *et al.* (2020) discovered a high quantity of long ROH segments in a Neolithic Irish individual: the offspring of a union between first-degree relatives.

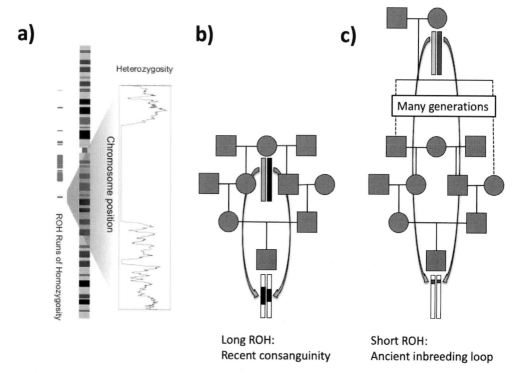

Figure 4.2. Runs of homozygosity. These are identified as runs of genomic sequence where heterozygosity falls to zero, implying a common ancestry for the male and female parental chromosomes. As inherited chunks of chromosomes are disrupted by recombination through time, long ROH (b) are indicative of recent inbreeding loops, while short ROH (c) are the result of more ancient common ancestries. As such loops are more likely in smaller mating networks, the extent of ROH informs on effective population size.

The presence of short ROH segments informs on population history rather than immediate familial relationships. The levels of ROH have been shown to decline through time from higher levels in Palaeolithic and Mesolithic hunter-gatherers, through Neolithic and Bronze Age populations in Europe. This was noted in the first imputed data set (Gamba *et al.* 2014), then more markedly by Jones *et al.* (2015) with publication of Upper Palaeolithic Europeans. Both Irish and Japanese ancient hunter-gatherers show enhanced ROH profiles, presumably because of demographic effects in either their colonisation of those islands or subsequently restricted population sizes (Cassidy *et al.* 2020; Cooke *et al.* 2021).

Recently, developing a novel approach, Ringbauer *et al.* (2021) detected stretches of homozygous genomes in ancient human genomes without requiring an imputation step. This allowed the authors to investigate inbreeding in 1785 ancient humans, comprehensively describing the decline of ROH (and consequently increase in effective population size) with time across multiple regions, with the highest drop reported in the transition between Mesolithic and Neolithic periods. Figure 4.3 shows ROH calculated for ancient European

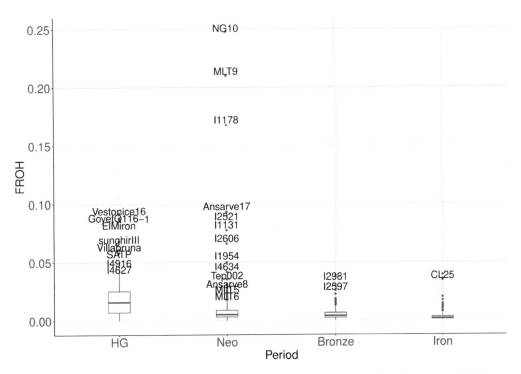

Figure 4.3. Fraction of European genomes under runs of homozygosity (FROH) in different periods. Hunter-gatherer (HG) individuals have a distribution of higher FROH, and this declines through time, consistent with higher effective population size. Each period has outliers, notably the Neolithic where several individuals with consanguineous ancestry have been identified.

genomes using our imputation pipeline. It illustrates the broad trend. Ancient hunter-gatherers have higher proportions of their genomes where parental genomes shared identical chunks. However, this only rarely manifests as an outlying large ROH burden from a degree of recent familial inbreeding; the highest ROH observed are in several Neolithic samples. The inbreeding loops in European hunter-gatherers are the result of deeper coalescences denoting a limited overall reproductive population network size, but not one where consanguineous union was the norm.

Recently, we discovered the second most inbred prehistoric genome yet reported, a Neolithic Maltese who was likely the result of a union of second-degree relatives (Fig. 4.3: MLT9) (Ariano *et al.* 2021). This individual was one of three genomes recovered from the Xaghra Circle hypogeum where the other two (Fig. 4.3: MLT5, MLT6) also showed high levels of ROH. However, these latter involved shorter shared chunks, at a level more reminiscent of earlier European hunter-gatherers, and indicated a restricted ancestral mating network rather than more immediate inbreeding. Both IBD (Browning and Browning 2015) and ROH (Fernandes *et al.* 2021) may be used to estimate effective population size and for the three Maltese individuals we estimated this to be small at 400–600. This matches (within a couple of multiples) the estimated carrying capacity of

Neolithic Gozo (French *et al.* 2020, 258) but more importantly indicates they are drawn from a population without substantial external influx within their recent ancestry. This was a striking illustration of genomic insularity and is mirrored in other data. The second most restricted population signal in the Neolithic sample came from remains in the Tomb of the Eagles at Isbister in Orkney. This is perhaps surprising given the cultural flourishing of Orkney and undoubted long-range contacts in this period (Edmonds 2019). However, population restriction is echoed in a later Orcadian Bronze Age signal (at Links of Noltland) which estimated an effective population size of only a few hundred (Dulias *et al.* 2022). Ringbauer *et al.* (2021) have also noted a coincidence of high ROH levels and island contexts.

WERE NEOLITHIC SEAWAYS HIGHWAYS?

An important archaeological question is whether the seascapes of prehistory need be regarded as barriers or rather, as evidenced for example by the rapid westward spread of agricultural lifeways along the Mediterranean littoral and also myriad material culture networks, should be more correctly seen as corridors facilitating exchange (Rainbird 2007; Cherry and Leppard 2014). Despite obvious difficulties in maritime transportation, domestic animals appear in Cyprus *c.* 10,600 years ago (Vigne *et al.* 2012), only very shortly after their initial capture for management on the Near Eastern mainland.

A consequent question for ancient genomics in terms of reproductive networks is whether Neolithic seascapes were accelerants or retardants of genomic exchange. The parsing of fine structure among European Neolithic genomes unveils some effects of seascapes in shaping the ancient genetic geography of the continent. Some island communities (Malta, Orkney, Gotland) show elevated levels of ROH or within-site IBD, suggesting that their mating networks were limited, probably influenced by their maritime environment. They also show reduced levels of imported ancestral admixtures relative to the mainland. Both Malta and Sardinia have been shown to have persisting balances of Neolithic and European hunter-gatherer ancestry despite the dissemination of a resurgence in western hunter-gatherer ancestry experienced across mainland Europe (Fernandes *et al.* 2020; Marcus *et al.* 2020; Ariano *et al.* 2022). The Bronze Age genomic turnover in Orkney differs dramatically from that of mainland Britain with a persistence of local Y-chromosome haplotypes (Fernandes *et al.* 2020; Marcus *et al.* 2020; Dulias *et al.* 2022).

The power of haplotype-based analysis, parsing relatedness within and between genomes considering contiguous chunks of sequence, has allowed striking illustrations of genomic insularity in the European Neolithic.

ACKNOWLEDGEMENTS

Bruno Ariano and Daniel Bradley were funded by Science Foundation Ireland/Health Research Board/Wellcome Trust Biomedical Research Partnership Investigator Award No. 205072, 'Ancient Genomics and the Atlantic Burden'.

REFERENCES

Antonio, M.L., Gao, Z., Moots, H.M., Lucci, M., Candilio, F., Sawyer, S. *et al.* 2019. Ancient Rome: a genetic crossroads of Europe and the Mediterranean. *Science* 366(6466), 708–14.

Ariano, B., Mattiangeli, V., Breslin, E.M., Parkinson, E.W., McLaughlin, T.R., Thompson, J.E. *et al.* 2022. Ancient Maltese genomes and the genetic geography of Neolithic Europe. *Current Biology*, 2668–2680.e6. doi:10.1016/j.cub.2022.04.069.

Avila-Arcos, M.C., Cappellini, E., Romero-Navarro, J.A., Wales, N., Moreno-Mayar, J.V., Rasmussen, M. *et al.* 2011. Application and comparison of large-scale solution-based DNA capture-enrichment methods on ancient DNA. *Scientific Reports* 1, 74.

Belbin, G.M., Odgis, J., Sorokin, E.P., Yee, M.-C., Glicksberg, B.S., Gignoux, C.R. *et al.* 2017. Genetic identification of a common collagen disease in Puerto Ricans via identity-by-descent mapping in a health system. *eLife*, 6. doi:10.7554/eLife.25060.

Browning, S.R. 2006. Multilocus association mapping using variable-length Markov chains. *American Journal of Human Genetics* 78 (6), 903–13.

Browning, S.R. 2008. Estimation of pairwise identity by descent from dense genetic marker data in a population sample of haplotypes. *Genetics* 178(4), 2123–32.

Browning, S.R. and Browning, B.L. 2010. High-resolution detection of identity by descent in unrelated individuals. *American Journal of Human Genetics* 86(4), 526–39.

Browning, S.R. and Browning, B.L. 2015. Accurate non-parametric estimation of recent effective population size from segments of identity by descent. *American Journal of Human Genetics* 97(3), 404–18.

Cassidy, L.M., Maolduin, R.O., Kador, T., Lynch, A., Jones, C., Woodman, P.C. *et al.* 2020. A dynastic elite in monumental Neolithic society. *Nature* 582(7812), 384–8.

Cherry, J.F. and Leppard, T.P. 2014. A little history of Mediterranean island prehistory. In A.B. Knapp and P. Van Dommelen (eds), *The Cambridge prehistory of the Bronze and Iron Age Mediterranean*, 10–24. Cambridge: Cambridge University Press.

Dulias, K., Foody, M.G.B., Justeau, P., Silva, M., Martiniano, R., Oteo-Garcia, G. *et al.* 2022. Ancient DNA at the edge of the world: continental immigration and the persistence of Neolithic male lineages in Bronze Age Orkney. *Proceedings of the National Academy of Sciences of the United States of America* 119(8): e2108001119. https://doi.org/10.1073/pnas.2108001119.

Edmonds, M. 2019. *Orcadia: land, sea and stone in Neolithic Orkney.* London: Head of Zeus.

Fernandes, D.M., Mittnik, A., Olalde, I., Lazaridis, I., Cheronet, O., Rohland, N. *et al.* 2020. The spread of steppe and Iranian-related ancestry in the islands of the western Mediterranean. *Nature Ecology & Evolution* 4(3), 334–45.

Fernandes, D.M., Sirak, K.A., Ringbauer, H., Sedig, J., Rohland, N., Cheronet, O. *et al.* 2021. A genetic history of the pre-contact Caribbean. *Nature* 590(7844), 103–10.

French, C., Hunt, C.O., Grima, R., McLaughlin, R., Stoddart, S. and Malone, C. 2020. *Temple landscapes: fragility, change and resilience of Holocene environments in the Maltese Islands.* Cambridge: McDonald Institute for Archaeological Research.

Gamba, C., Jones, E., Teasdale, M., McLaughlin, R., Gonzalez-Fortes, G., Mattiangeli, V. *et al.* 2014. Genome flux and stasis in a five millennium transect of European prehistory. *Nature Communications* 5, 21 October 2014, doi: 10.1038/ncomms6257.

Jones, E.R., Gonzales-Fortes, G., Connell, S., Siska, V., Eriksson, A., Martiniano, R. *et al.* 2015. Upper Palaeolithic genomes reveal deep roots of modern Eurasians. *Nature Communications* 6, 8912.

Korlević, P. and Meyer, M. 2019. Pretreatment: removing DNA contamination from ancient bones and teeth using sodium hypochlorite and phosphate. In B. Shapiro, A. Barlow, P. Heintzman, M. Hofreiter, J. Paijmans and A. Soares (eds), *Ancient DNA, Methods in Molecular Biology, vol 1963*, 15–19. New York: Humana Press.

Lawson, D.J., Hellenthal, G., Myers, S. and Falush, D. 2012. Inference of population structure using dense haplotype data. *PLoS Genetics* 8(1), e1002453.

Leslie, S., Winney, B., Hellenthal, G., Davison, D., Boumertit, A., Day, T. *et al.* 2015. The fine-scale genetic structure of the British population. *Nature* 519(7543), 309–14.

Liu, Y., Bennett, E.A. and Fu, Q. 2022. Evolving ancient DNA techniques and the future of human history. *Cell* 185(15), 2632–5.

LI and Y 2006. Mach 1.0: rapid haplotype reconstruction and missing genotype inference. *American Journal of Human Genetics* 79, 2290.

Manichaikul, A., Mychaleckyj, J.C., Rich, S.S., Daly, K., Sale, M and Chen, W.-M. 2010. Robust relationship inference in genome-wide association studies. *Bioinformatics* 26(22), 2867–73.

Marchini, J., Howie, B., Myers, S., McVean, G. and Donnelly, P. 2007. A new multipoint method for genome-wide association studies by imputation of genotypes. *Nature Genetics* 39(7), 906–13.

Marcus, J.H., Posth, C., Ringbauer, H., Lai, L., Skeates, R., Sidore, C. *et al.* 2020. Genetic history from the Middle Neolithic to present on the Mediterranean island of Sardinia. *Nature Communications* 11(1), 939.

Margaryan, A., Lawson, D.J., Sikora, M., Racimo, F., Rasmussen, S., Moltke, I. *et al.* 2020. Population genomics of the Viking world. *Nature* 585(7825), 390–6.

Martiniano, R., Cassidy, L.M., Ó'Maoldúin, R., McLaughlin, R., Silva, N.M., Manco, L. *et al.* 2017. The population genomics of archaeological transition in west Iberia: investigation of ancient substructure using imputation and haplotype-based methods. *PLoS Genetics* 13(7), e1006852.

Orlando, L., Allaby, R., Skoglund, P., Sarkissian, C., Stockhammer, P.W., Avila, M. *et al.* 2021. Ancient DNA analysis. *Nature Reviews Methods Primers* 1(1), 1–26.

Pasaniuc, B., Rohland, N., McLaren, P.J., Garimella, K., Zaitlen, N., Li, H. *et al.* 2012. Extremely low-coverage sequencing and imputation increases power for genome-wide association studies. *Nature Genetics* 44(6), 631–5.

Rainbird, P. 2007. *The archaeology of islands.* Cambridge: Cambridge University Press.

Ringbauer, H., Novembre, J. and Steinrücken, M. 2021. Parental relatedness through time revealed by runs of homozygosity in ancient DNA. *Nature Communications* 12(1), 5425.

Rohland, N., Mallick, S., Mah, M., Maier, R., Patterson, N. and Reich, D. 2022. Three reagents for in-solution enrichment of ancient human DNA at more than a million SNPs. *bioRxiv.* doi:10.1101/2022.01.13.476259.

Rubinacci, S., Ribeiro, D., Hofmeister, R. and Delaneau, O. 2021. Efficient phasing and imputation of low-coverage sequencing data using large reference panels: *Nature Genetics* 53, 120–126

Thompson, E.A. 2013. Identity by descent: variation in meiosis, across genomes, and in populations. *Genetics* 194(2), 301–26.

Vigne, J.-D., Briois, F., Zazzo, A., Willcox, G., Cucchi, T. Thiébault, S. *et al.* 2012. First wave of cultivators spread to Cyprus at least 10,600 y ago. *Proceedings of the National Academy of Sciences of the United States of America* 109(22), 8445–9.

Yengo, L., Wray, N.R. and Visscher, P.M. 2019. Extreme inbreeding in a European ancestry sample from the contemporary UK population. *Nature Communications* 10(1), 3719.

Chapter 5

Reconstructing the genealogical relationships of hunter-gatherers and farmers

Leo Speidel

In this chapter, I give an overview of a new set of statistical tools that promise to extract more information than previously possible from ancient DNA data to infer key historical events. I demonstrate these techniques in an application to data from the European Neolithic and beyond and show that we can learn about a broad range of phenomena of the past, ranging from natural selection, to quantifying genetic structure, and tracing a mutation rate change that occurred in ancestors of Neolithic farmers.

MAKING SENSE OF GENETIC VARIATION TO LEARN ABOUT OUR HISTORY

Recent years have increasingly seen ancient humans being sequenced at scale, enabling us to directly observe genetic variation of the past and how it compares to the present. Our goal is to learn about key historical events from such data, by using statistical approaches to decipher the patterns in genetic variation that are left behind.

Historical events, such as mixture events of previously distinct groups, adaptation to changing lifestyles and environments through natural selection, or more fundamental changes in the molecular processes that generate mutation or impact on the ways in which these are passed on to offspring, affect genetic variation in subtly different ways. As multiple processes act on our genomes simultaneously, making sense of genetic variation is not an easy task. However, the ever-increasing numbers of sequenced individuals, and a long history of statistical and mathematical models in genetics, help us in this endeavour.

Ancient DNA (hereafter aDNA) has played a particularly important role in exploring historical civilisations, how they interacted and how they relate to people today. Without aDNA, we relied on extrapolating from the genomes of present-day people into the past, and in many cases, it was not possible to identify clearly the historical groups that make-up present-day populations. By providing us with direct snapshots of the past, aDNA has led to remarkable discoveries about past migrations and mixtures (Skoglund and Mathieson 2018).

In this chapter, we will look at a new set of statistical tools that promise to extract more information than previously possible from aDNA data to infer key events in our history. We do this by building genealogical trees that describe how individuals from different time periods are genetically related to each other. These genealogical trees also allow us to extrapolate further into the past where sequence data are sparse. While still in its infancy, this new set of statistical tools promises to give us a more detailed and complete picture of our genetic past and should lead to better inferences about how humans have evolved and interacted with one another over millennia.

THE GENETIC FAMILY TREES THAT RELATE EVERYONE TO EVERYONE

To understand the link between historical events and how they affect genetic variation, it is useful to think about how we are all genetically related to each other. Genealogical trees, which can be thought of as genetic family trees, connect us through common ancestors back in time. In these trees, lineages merge back in time until we reach a single common ancestor, typically around a million years in the past. Any evolutionary forces affecting genetic variation do so by impacting upon these underlying genealogical trees. For instance, positive selection will change the shape of these trees such that lineages carrying the advantageous allele have more offspring. Population bottlenecks will force all lineages to go through a limited number of ancestors, resulting in a burst of coalescences at the time of the bottleneck. Therefore, if only we knew these tree relationships, we would obtain a much more direct way to make inferences about past events.

These genealogical tree relationships differ in different parts of the genome. The reason for this is best described in the example of siblings (Fig. 5.1a). In siblings, different parts of the genome derive from different grandparents. This is because we pass on a single set of chromosomes to our offspring, which consists of a random mixture of our maternal and paternal chromosomes, created through a process called recombination. As a consequence, in some parts of the genome, the most recent genetic common ancestor of siblings is their immediate parent, but in other parts of the genome siblings are genetically unrelated, and their most recent common ancestor could go back hundreds of thousands of years in the past (Fig. 5.1a). For a sample of unrelated individuals, we obtain millions of distinct tree relationships across the whole genome, each following a different path through ancestors; this collection of trees provides us with a rich description of ancestral relationships.

In Figure 5.1b, I plot a genealogical tree in the SLC24A5 gene constructed using a tool called Relate (Speidel *et al.* 2019). We highlight a mutation that is strongly associated with lighter skin pigmentation (Mallick *et al.* 2013). This mutation has been shown to be under strong positive selection and is carried by nearly all present-day individuals with European ancestries (Mallick *et al.* 2013; Fan *et al.* 2016). Alongside modern-day individuals from the Simon's Genome Diversity dataset (Mallick *et al.* 2016), the tree also contains a high-coverage western hunter-gatherer and early Neolithic farmer (Lazaridis *et al.* 2014), an early Neolithic Iranian farmer (Broushaki *et al.* 2016), a Yamnaya individual (de Barros Damgaard *et al.* 2018), a high-coverage Denisovan (Meyer *et al.* 2012), and a Neanderthal individual (Prüfer *et al.* 2017). We can see that the height of this tree exceeds one million years, indicating that genetic variation can in principle tell us about historical events up to millions of years in the past.

This tree describes a locus under strong positive selection in West Eurasians, evident by the fact that the most recent common ancestor of all West Eurasians is less than 100,000 years old in this tree. In contrast, in a random part of the genome, this ancestor

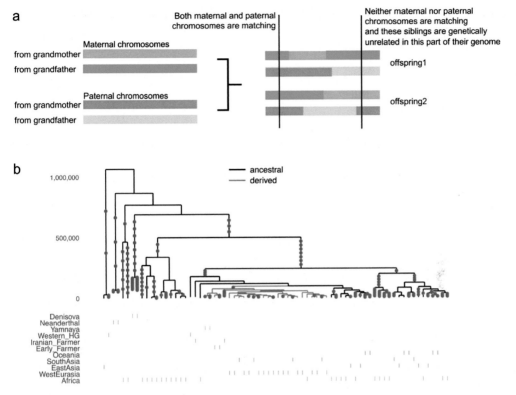

Figure 5.1. a) A schematic of how recombination breaks up parental chromosomes when they are passed on to the next generation. Siblings, as a result, are genetically closely related in some parts of their genomes and are unrelated in others. b) A genealogical tree at a locus in the SLC24A5 gene, showing how modern-day and ancient individuals are related to each other in this part of the genome. Lineages carrying an allele associated with lighter skin pigmentation are highlighted in red.

is typically 10 times older. We see that groups not experiencing selection at this locus, such as East Asians and Africans, have a much older common ancestor. Perhaps contrary to expectation, this tree does not cleanly separate global groups. This is because present-day groups emerged recently compared to the time-depths of this tree, and lineages that are older than the split time of these groups are no longer associated with the group labelling at the bottom of the tree. A consequence is that many mutations are shared across populations and only differ in their respective frequencies.

HOW DO WE INFER GENEALOGICAL TREES?

Mathematical models for describing how we expect genealogical trees to look have existed for many decades (Kingman 1982; Hudson and Kaplan 1985; Griffiths and Marjoram 1997), and have been fundamental to many, if not most, of the methods we use in population genetics. These models have also been instrumental in phylogenetics and the reconstruction of trees of non-recombining genetic material such as mitochondrial DNA (Drummond and Rambaut 2007). However, it remained challenging to use these models to infer unknown whole-genome genealogies.

A major challenge is that it is not possible to observe directly where recombination has happened. Instead, these sites have to be located by looking at patterns in mutation sharing across individuals. Doing this in a principled statistical way for any meaningful number of samples is computationally unfeasible (Griffiths and Marjoram 1996). Until recently, genealogical inference has therefore remained unsolved even for moderate sample sizes, but new methods have now made it possible to infer genealogical trees (Rasmussen *et al.* 2014), including for many thousands or more samples (Kelleher *et al.* 2019; Speidel *et al.* 2019; Zhang *et al.* 2021). This advance is primarily based on finding new ways to approximate the otherwise computationally difficult problem of making exact statistical inference and introducing computational shortcuts that are founded on principled ideas.

While still in their infancy, genealogy-based methods are promising because they extract, in principle, as much information about the past as possible from genetic data, provided that we can infer these trees accurately and without bias. Similar to aDNA, they provide snapshots of genetic variation of the past by extrapolating from the present day (or from sequenced ancient individuals). This also makes genealogies an ideal framework for combining modern and aDNA samples in a principled way.

To demonstrate how genealogical inference works, I will use the example of Relate (Speidel *et al.* 2019), a tool that we developed for inference of such trees for many thousands of individuals. This and other tools have been widely applied across species, adapted to work with aDNA (Schaefer *et al.* 2021; Speidel *et al.* 2021; Wohns *et al.* 2022), and have led to many downstream tools that utilise these trees for studying population structure, admixture and selection (Stern *et al.* 2019; 2021; Ralph *et al.* 2020; Fan *et al.* 2022).

EACH MUTATION INDICATES THE EXISTENCE OF A BRANCH

So how do mutations and their sharing patterns tell us about the tree structure and timings of local genealogical trees? It is easiest to first think of an easier case, namely if there was no recombination and hence only a single tree describing the ancestry of our sample. The main assumption we and others make is that every mutation happened only once in history. In other words, at any position in the genome, there is either one or no mutation to be observed, and any mutation can be traced to a single event. This assumption is known as the infinite-sites assumption (Kimura 1969) and justified by the fact that the mutation rate is low in humans, so that repeat mutations are rare. If every mutation is unique and in the absence of sequencing errors, we can see that every mutation indicates exactly the existence of one branch, namely a branch for which the descendant set exactly matches the carriers of this mutation. If we have enough mutations, we can therefore exactly reconstruct the tree-like relationship of our sample. Once the tree structure is resolved, we can date branches by mapping mutations on to the corresponding branches with matching descendant sets. Assuming a known mutation rate, we can then rescale branches such that they reflect the number of mutations occurring on them.

DETECTING RECOMBINATION

With recombination, a different tree describes the relationships of our sample in different regions of the genome, but we do not know where these tree relationships change. We therefore rely on noticing that mutations start to contradict each other and become inconsistent with a single tree. For example, a partial overlap in carriers of mutations is impossible without recombination and is therefore sufficient to conclude that there has been at least one event between such mutations (Hudson and Kaplan 1985). Not all recombination events are detectable. We are only able to detect events that are sufficiently tagged by flanking mutations to cause contradictions. In addition, some recombination events do not cause contradictions in sharing patterns and are therefore invisible to us.

Once we have decided where breakpoints happen, we can then go back to the no recombination case and construct local genealogies. In practice, we use statistical approaches that somewhat account for the uncertainty in where recombination occurs.

APPLICATIONS TO NEOLITHIC EUROPE AND BEYOND

The promise of genealogy-based inference is threefold. First, these methods should have increased statistical power, allowing us to detect patterns in the data that we may not be able to detect with more conventional approaches. Secondly, all inferences are derived from a single reconstruction of history, and different inferences we derive should therefore be self-consistent and more easily comparable, aiding interpretability. Finally, these trees naturally incorporate ancient samples of different ages.

Here I look at two applications of genealogies to genomes from ancient Europe (Speidel *et al.* 2021). First, we use genealogies to quantify population structure. We demonstrate that genealogies are able to quantify how long ago such structure may have arisen. Secondly, we use genealogies to quantify a mutation rate pulse, probably occurring in ancestors of early Anatolian farmers, and demonstrate that genealogies can be used to study a multitude of processes impacting upon genetic variation.

GENEALOGIES CAN ACCURATELY QUANTIFY RECENT POPULATION STRUCTURE

Population structure reflects systematic differences in the ways in which individuals are related to each other, and has been shown to exist at very fine scales in present-day people, such as almost at county-level resolution in some regions of Britain (Leslie *et al.* 2015). To demonstrate that genealogy-based inference can accurately detect recent population structure where more conventional approaches would struggle to do so, we first use a simulated example where the true underlying population history is known.

We adapt the simulation used in Fan *et al.* (2022), which simulates 25 populations arranged in a 5 times 5 grid (Fig. 5.2b). These populations derive from a common ancestral population 100 generations ago (less than 3000 years ago). Migration between neighbouring grid cells is allowed at a rate of 1% per generation, and the diploid population sizes in each of the 25 populations is set to 500, and 10,000 in the ancestral population. From this simulation, we obtain data emulating sequencing data from 50 individuals (two individuals per population).

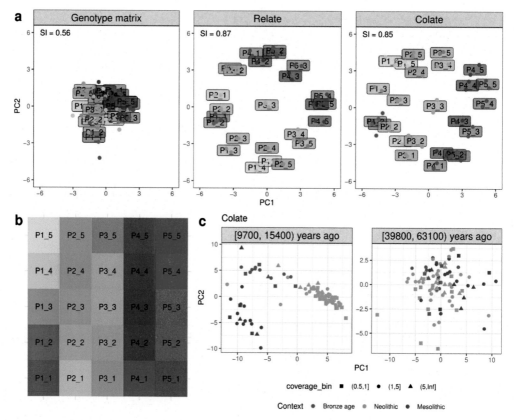

Figure 5.2. a) Genetic structure quantified in three different ways. Left panel shows the first two principal components (PCs) of a matrix storing pairwise differences between individuals. Middle panel shows the first two PCs of a matrix storing pairwise coalescence rates in the past 100 generations inferred using Relate. Right panel is analogous to the middle panel but inferred using Colate. Colours shown are according to the grid-like underlying structure in the simulations, shown in b. c) First two PCs of coalescence rates calculated for real ancient data of individuals from the European Mesolithic, Neolithic and Bronze Age. The PCs are calculated for two periods.

Additionally, we sample 100 individuals from the ancestral population, which can be thought of as a closely related outgroup.

In Figure 5.2a, we quantify structure in three different ways and calculate a separation index (SI), which indicates how well groups are separated; this index ranges from 0.5 (poor separation) to 1.0 (good separation) (Fan *et al.* 2022).

First, to establish a baseline for how difficult it is to detect population structure in this example, we quantify structure without using genealogies. We calculate the number of pairwise genetic differences between all pairs of the 50 individuals. We visualise this matrix using a technique called principal component analysis (PCA). A PCA finds the two dimensions that best describe the matrix, allowing us to visualise the patterns it contains with ease. We can see that while there is perhaps some agreement with the grid-like organisation of these populations, it does so not very convincingly (SI = 0.56).

Secondly, we build genealogical trees for these 50 individuals using Relate and calculate the average relatedness of pairs of samples in the past 100 generations. Technically, we do this by calculating the rate of coalescence in this time period averaged across the whole genome. Again visualising this matrix using a PCA, we now clearly recover the grid-like organisation of these populations (SI = 0.87). An added benefit is that we can tweak how much into the past we want to measure this relatedness, which can be used as an estimate for how long ago these populations emerged.

Finally, we quantify structure in a related but slightly different way. We use a method called Colate (Speidel *et al.* 2021), which we designed to work on ancient genomes sequenced to low coverage. For low-coverage samples, it is not possible to build genealogical trees directly, since we are not able to determine their genomes with confidence. To apply Colate, we first build a genealogy for the 100 outgroup individuals, which we assume are sequenced to high coverage. In practice, these outgroup individuals could be a large-scale dataset of present-day people. We then use this reference genealogy to calculate relatedness in the past 100 generations between all pairs of target individuals (the 50 individuals in 25 populations) using Colate. As for Relate, we recover a grid-like structure, indicating increased power compared to the first approach in Figure 5.2a (SI = 0.85).

Application of Colate to data from the European Mesolithic, Neolithic and Bronze Age is shown in Figure 5.2c. We visualise two time periods. Around 10,000 years ago, we detect known genetic structure differentiating hunter-gatherers from early farmers and later Bronze Age people (Lazaridis *et al.* 2014). More than 40,000 years ago, this structure largely disappears. The structure we observe around 10,000 years ago with Colate looks comparable to that obtained with conventional approaches (Lazaridis *et al.* 2014). The likely reason for not observing finer-scale structure at this point is that we currently lack the sample size to identify finer-scale structure within each respective time period and geographic region. To what extent such structure existed, for instance during the Neolithic, is subject to further study.

TRACING A MUTATION RATE PULSE IN ANCIENT EUROPE

Temporal changes in fundamental biological processes, such as the rate at which mutations occur, can leave traces in the variation patterns that we observe. Genealogies allow us to measure the mutation rate easily because we can simply count how many mutations occur in any time period. Using this, we can identify a pulse in the mutation rate of the triplet TCC mutating towards TTC, first identified by Kelley Harris (2015; Harris and Pritchard 2017). This pulse is absent from present-day groups outside West and South Eurasia and therefore appears to have occurred in an ancestor of these groups but not of other global populations. It appears that the driver of this pulse was temporal and is no longer present in people today (Harris and Pritchard 2017; Speidel *et al.* 2019).

To pinpoint its origin, we quantified this pulse in ancient individuals (Fig. 5.3a). Our analysis suggests that the pulse was already carried by early Anatolian farmers (*e.g.* Bon002) (Kılınç *et al.* 2016), as well as western hunter-gatherers (*e.g.* Bichon) (Jones *et al.* 2015), eastern hunter-gatherers (Sidelkino) (de Barros Damgaard *et al.* 2018), and Caucasus hunter-gatherers (Satsurblia) (Jones *et al.* 2015), who were living around 10,000 years ago.

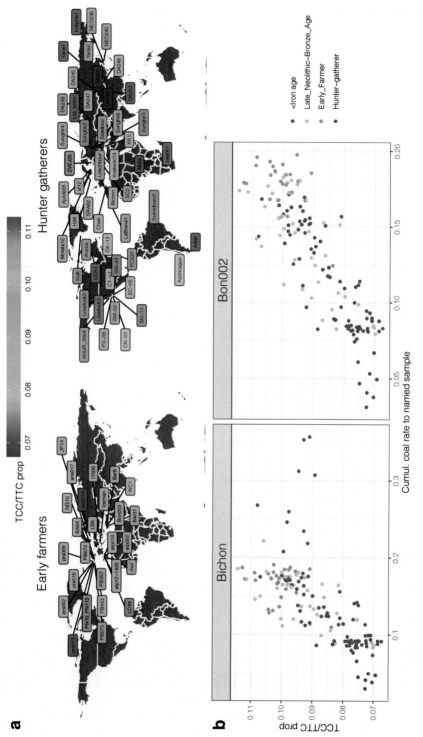

Figure 5.3. a) Map showing strength of the TCC/TTC mutation rate pulse in ancient people, grouped into early farmers and hunter-gatherers. A larger TCC/TTC proportion indicates a stronger pulse. b) Strength of TCC/TTC in individuals plotted against how closely they are related to a western hunter-gatherer (left) and an early Anatolian farmer (right).

Assuming a single origin, this suggests that a group ancestral to all West Eurasian hunter-gatherers of this time is the origin for this pulse. The signal appears absent from earlier hunter-gatherers, such as Sunghir3 (Sikora *et al.* 2017) and Kostenki14 (Seguin-Orlando *et al.* 2014). Overall, the pulse is stronger in early Neolithic farmers, and correlates remarkably well with overall genetic relatedness to an Anatolian farmer (Fig. 5.3b). This may indicate a dilution of this ancestry in other hunter-gatherer groups or directional migration of ancestors of Anatolian farmers into other hunter-gatherer groups across Europe, predating the spread of farming.

We do in fact detect signals consistent with potential bidirectional migration between ancestors of Anatolian farmers and other hunter-gatherer groups in our genealogical trees (Speidel *et al.* 2022). However, the detailed genetic relationship among West Eurasian hunter-gatherer groups in the Late Palaeolithic is currently not fully understood. One candidate group that may be the missing link between these groups is the Dzudzuana Cave individuals, a group living in the Caucusus around 26,000 years ago (Lazaridis *et al.* 2018). These are thought to be closely related to later Anatolians and have links to other hunter-gatherer groups across Europe. A related possibility is also an increase in migrations during the Bølling-Allerød interstadial, a brief warming period following the Last Glacial Maximum in Europe (Fu *et al.* 2016). Ancient DNA data are currently sparse in this time period and it remains to be seen whether further advances in statistical analyses and new aDNA data can shed light on how these hunter-gatherer groups relate to each other.

DISCUSSION

In this chapter, I introduced recent advances that have enabled us to infer genealogies for large datasets including modern and ancient genomes. While still in their infancy, they have already proven to be a powerful framework for shedding light on a broad range of evolutionary events that have usually been done using separate tools. These include the inference of population structure, demographic history, admixture, positive selection and mutation rate changes.

The framework presented is promising because it aims to reconstruct our genetic past to the best achievable resolution and therefore maximise the information we can extract from genetic data. There are, however, limitations in our ability to do this. A fundamental limitation, for instance, is that for many parts of the genome, we are unable to fully resolve genealogical trees with high confidence. This is because recombination occurs at a comparable frequency to mutation, such that some lineages in the trees will end up with no mutations evidencing it. Since this limitation is fundamental to the way in which we inherit DNA and is not solved by increased data or better methods, it is important to construct trees that are unbiased in unresolved parts of the trees – something towards which we have put a lot of care when developing Relate but which may still be imperfect in some cases. A strength of Relate and similar methods such as tsinfer is that they are built on few assumptions, reflected in the fact that they have been applied successfully across species with different evolutionary parameters including in humans, canids (Bergström *et al.* 2022), plants (Kreiner *et al.* 2022), and fish (Matschiner *et al.* 2022). These tools are particularly well suited to combining data from larger numbers of samples and will benefit from the ever-increasing numbers of aDNA data becoming available.

ACKNOWLEDGEMENTS

I thank Clare West for helpful comments and acknowledge support provided through a Sir Henry Wellcome Postdoctoral fellowship [220457/Z/20/Z].

REFERENCES

Bergström, A., Stanton, D.W.G., Taron, U.H., Frantz, L., Sinding, M.-H. S., Ersmark, E. *et al.* 2022. Grey wolf genomic history reveals a dual ancestry of dogs. *Nature* 607(7918), 313–20.

Broushaki, F., Thomas, M.G., Link, V., López, S., van Dorp, L., Kirsanow, K. *et al.* 2016. Early Neolithic genomes from the eastern Fertile Crescent. *Science* 353(6298), 499–503.

de Barros Damgaard, P., Martiniano, R., Kamm, J., Moreno-Mayar, J.V., Kroonen, G., Peyrot, M. *et al.* 2018. The first horse herders and the impact of early Bronze Age steppe expansions into Asia. *Science* 360(6396), eaar7711.

Drummond, A.J. and Rambaut, A. 2007. BEAST: Bayesian evolutionary analysis by sampling trees. *BMC Evolutionary Biology* 7, 214.

Fan, C., Mancuso, N. and Chiang, C.W.K. 2022. A genealogical estimate of genetic relationships. *American Journal of Human Genetics* 109(5), 812–24.

Fan, S., Hansen, M.E.B., Lo, Y. and Tishkoff, S.A. 2016. Going global by adapting local: a review of recent human adaptation. *Science* 354(6308), 54–9.

Fu Q., Posth C., Hajdinjak M., Petr M., Mallick S., Fernandes D. *et al.* 2016. The genetic history of Ice Age Europe. *Nature* 534(7606), 200–5.

Griffiths, R.C. and Marjoram, P. 1996. Ancestral inferences from samples of DNA sequences with recombination. *Journal of Computational Biology: A Journal of Computational Molecular Cell Biology* 3, 479–502.

Griffiths, R.C. and Marjoram, P. 1997. An ancestral recombination graph. In P. Donnelly and S. Tavaré (eds), *Progress in population genetics and human evolution*, 257–70. New York: Springer.

Harris, K. 2015. Evidence for recent, population-specific evolution of the human mutation rate. *Proceedings of the National Academy of Sciences of the United States of America* 112, 3439–44.

Harris, K. and Pritchard, J. 2017. Rapid evolution of the human mutation spectrum. *eLife* 6, e24284.

Hudson, R.R. Kaplan, N.L. 1985. Statistical properties of the number of recombination events in the history of a sample of DNA sequences. *Genetics* 111, 147–64.

Jones, E.R., Gonzalez-Fortes, G., Connell, S., Siska, V., Eriksson, A., Martiniano, R. *et al.* 2015. Upper Palaeolithic genomes reveal deep roots of modern Eurasians. *Nature Communications* 6(1), 8912.

Kelleher, J., Wong, Y., Wohns, A. W., Fadil, C., Albers, P.K. and McVean, G. 2019. Inferring whole-genome histories in large population datasets. *Nature Genetics* 51(9), 1330–8.

Kimura, M. 1969. The number of heterozygous nucleotide sites maintained in a finite population due to steady flux of mutations. *Genetics* 61, 893.

Kingman, J.F.C. 1982. On the genealogy of large populations. *Journal of Applied Probability* 19, 27–43.

Kılınç, G.M., Omrak, A., Özer, F., Günther, T., Büyükkarakaya, A.M., Bıçakçı, E. *et al.* 2016. The demographic development of the first farmers in Anatolia. *Current Biology: CB* 26(19), 2659–66.

Kreiner, J.M., Sandler, G., Stern, A.J., Tranel, P.J., Weigel, D., Stinchcombe, J.R. and Wright, S.I. 2022. Repeated origins, widespread gene flow, and allelic interactions of target-site herbicide resistance mutations. *eLife*, 11. https://doi.org/10.7554/eLife.70242

Lazaridis, I., Patterson, N., Mittnik, A., Renaud, G., Mallick, S., Kirsanow, K. *et al.* 2014. Ancient human genomes suggest three ancestral populations for present-day Europeans. *Nature* 513(7518), 409–13.

Lazaridis, I., Belfer-Cohen, A., Mallick, S., Patterson, N., Cheronet, O., Rohland, N. *et al.* 2018. Paleolithic DNA from the Caucasus reveals core of West Eurasian ancestry. *bioRxiv:*10.1101/423079.

Leslie, S., Winney, B., Hellenthal, G., Davison, D., Boumertit, A., Day, T. *et al.* 2015. The fine-scale genetic structure of the British population. *Nature* 519(7543), 309–14.

Mallick, C.B., Iliescu, F.M., Möls, M., Hill, S., Tamang, R., Chaubey, G. *et al.* 2013. The light skin allele of SLC24A5 in South Asians and Europeans shares identity by descent. *PLoS Genetics* 9, e1003912.

Mallick, S., Li, H., Lipson, M., Mathieson, I., Gymrek, M., Racimo, F. *et al.* 2016. The Simons Genome Diversity Project: 300 genomes from 142 diverse populations. *Nature* 538(7624), 201–6.

Matschiner, M., Barth, J.M.I., Tørresen, O.K., Star, B., Baalsrud, H.T., Brieuc, M.S.O., Pampoulie, C., Bradbury, I., Jakobsen, K.S. and Jentoft, S. 2022. Supergene origin and maintenance in Atlantic cod. *Nature Ecology & Evolution* 6(4), 469–81.

Meyer, M., Kircher, M., Gansauge, M.-T., Li, H., Racimo, F., Mallick, S. *et al.* 2012. A high-coverage genome sequence from an archaic Denisovan individual. *Science* 338(6104), 222–6.

Prüfer, K., De Filippo, C., Grote, S., Mafessoni, F., Korlević, P., Hajdinjak, M. *et al.* 2017. A high-coverage Neandertal genome from Vindija Cave in Croatia. *Science* 358(6363), 655–8.

Ralph, P., Thornton, K. and Kelleher, J. 2020. Efficiently summarizing relationships in large samples: a general duality between statistics of genealogies and genomes. *Genetics* 215(3), 779–97.

Rasmussen, M.D., Hubisz, M.J., Gronau, I. and Siepel, A. 2014. Genome-wide inference of ancestral recombination graphs. *PLoS Genetics* 10, e1004342.

Schaefer, N.K., Shapiro, B. and Green, R.E. 2021. An ancestral recombination graph of human, Neanderthal, and Denisovan genomes. *Science Advances* 7(29). https://doi.org/10.1126/sciadv.abc0776.

Seguin-Orlando, A., Korneliussen, T.S., Sikora, M., Malaspinas, A.-S., Manica, A., Moltke, I. *et al.* 2014. Genomic structure in Europeans dating back at least 36,200 years. *Science* 346(6213), 1113–18.

Sikora, M., Seguin-Orlando, A., Sousa, V.C., Albrechtsen, A., Korneliussen, T., Ko, A. *et al.* 2017. Ancient genomes show social and reproductive behavior of early Upper Paleolithic foragers. *Science* 358(6363), 659–62.

Skoglund, P. and Mathieson, I. 2018. Ancient genomics of modern humans: the first decade. *Annual Review of Genomics and Human Genetics* 19(1), 381–404.

Speidel, L., Cassidy, L., Davies, R.W., Hellenthal, G., Skoglund, P. and Myers, S.R. 2021. Inferring population histories for ancient genomes using genome-wide genealogies. *Molecular Biology and Evolution* 38(9), 3497–511.

Speidel, L., Forest, M., Shi, S. and Myers, S.R. 2019. A method for genome-wide genealogy estimation for thousands of samples. *Nature Genetics* 51(9), 1321–9.

Stern, A.J., Speidel, L., Zaitlen, N.A. and Nielsen, R. 2021. Disentangling selection on genetically correlated polygenic traits via whole-genome genealogies. *American Journal of Human Genetics* 108(2), 219–39.

Stern, A.J., Wilton, P.R. and Nielsen, R. 2019. An approximate full-likelihood method for inferring selection and allele frequency trajectories from DNA sequence data. *PLoS Genetics* 15(9), e1008384.

Wohns, A.W., Wong, Y., Jeffery, B., Akbari, A., Mallick, S., Pinhasi, R., Patterson, N., Reich, D., Kelleher, J. and McVean, G. 2022. A unified genealogy of modern and ancient genomes. *Science* 375(6583), eabi8264.

Zhang, B.C., Biddanda, A. and Palamara, P.F. 2021. Biobank-scale inference of ancestral recombination graphs enables genealogy-based mixed model association of complex traits. *bioRxiv* 2021.11.03.466843). https://doi.org/10.1101/2021.11.03.466843

Chapter 6

Ancient DNA of Near Eastern populations: the knowns and the unknowns

Eva Fernández-Domínguez

Human archaeogenetics have had a prominent role in the understanding of the biological processes underlying the emergence of agriculture in south-west Asia and the mechanisms involved in their spread into Europe. Genome-wide ancient human DNA data show that a strong genetic substructure existed among the first farming populations of the Fertile Crescent (c. 8000 cal BC). This suggests multiple origins of farming and a local evolution of farmer groups from preceding hunter-gatherer populations with limited gene flow at the onset of the Neolithic. To date, the available Neolithic palaeogenomic data indicate a mainly Anatolian origin for the continental route of the Neolithic expansion, punctuated by local episodes of admixture with local hunter-gatherer groups. According to other lines of evidence, an earlier parallel, sea-mediated expansion from the Levantine and Anatolian coasts cannot be discarded. While ancient DNA has been instrumental in deciphering phenomena of gene-flow among these first farming communities, very little information is available on the social structure and low-scale population movements of these first farmers. Despite recent advances in sampling strategies and genotyping methods, obtaining quality data from ancient Near Eastern samples is still challenging. A multidisciplinary approach including archaeological, anthropological, spatial, chronological and isotopic data could help in filling in the gaps and complementing the still scarce available genomic data.

FIRST FARMERS

A pivotal change in humankind was the shift from a hunter-gatherer to a farming and herding lifestyle 12,000 years ago. This process, known as the 'Neolithic transition', was first initiated by human populations inhabiting a strip of land in south-west Asia known as the 'Fertile Crescent', a region extending from the Sinai Peninsula in the south up to the eastern fringe of the Taurus in the north and the Zagros mountains in the east (Fig. 6.1). Within this region, three interconnected cultural provinces representing different environmental entities and with different trajectories in the adoption and dispersal of Neolithic practices can be distinguished; the *southern Levant* stretches from the Sinai Peninsula up to the Damascus basin, the *northern Levant* extends from this point up to the Taurus and Zagros mountains, and the *eastern Fertile Crescent* or *Zagros* region includes the Zagros mountain-chain and the hilly flanks of western Iran and eastern Iraq. Cyprus is also often included as part of the Levant province due to cultural similarities and chronological synchronicity. While often included as part of the Fertile Crescent, central and western Anatolia represent the initial dispersion of the Neolithic rather than its development *in situ* (Goring-Morris and Belfer-Cohen 2013).

Concomitant with the development of new subsistence practices through the domestication of cereal and animal species were population growth, increase in sedentism and the appearance of the first cities. It is also during this period that characteristic forms of funerary and ritual behaviour became widespread mainly in the western part of the Fertile Crescent, such as the special burial treatment devoted to human skulls, through their modification, plastering or deposition in distinctive places (Bienert 1991). Wall paintings and clay or plaster figurines were other forms of cultural or ritual expression of these first farming societies (Verhoeven 2002). In the Zagros and Anatolia, the emphasis was put on monumentality, with the erection of sculpted pillars and free-standing figures (Asouti 2007). Pottery, one of the main markers of the 'Neolithic package' that expanded from the Near East into Europe, appears in the Near East 3000 years after the start of the Neolithic in the 7th millennium cal BC (Price 2000).

The Neolithic transition in south-west Asia was a slow process that took millennia to complete, built upon the traditions of preceding Late Epipalaeolithic groups (*c.* 13–11ky cal BC) who actively and systematically had already started to modify their local environments. The transformations giving rise to the emergence of a productive economy should be therefore understood in the context of changing climatic and environmental conditions at the end of the Pleistocene with the Younger Dryas cold climatic event (*c.* 10.8–9.6ky cal BC), followed by temperature and rainfall increase at the start of the Holocene (Goring-Morris and Belfer-Cohen 2014). In the southern Levant Late Epipalaeolithic Natufian groups had an economy mainly based on foraging but that had already started to experiment and harvest wild cereals. Some of these groups also showed early signs of sedentism, living in partially subterraneous circular structures (pit-houses), and burying their dead inside or next to their houses, a tradition that would continue in the oldest stages of the Neolithic in the region (Bar-Yosef and Belfer-Cohen 1991; Belfer-Cohen and Bar-Yosef 2002; Goring-Morris and Belfer-Cohen 2013). In the northern Levant and south-eastern Anatolia sedentary forager groups also start to establish towards the end of the Natufian period (Belfer-Cohen and Bar-Yosef 2002).

The PPNA (pre-pottery Neolithic A) represents the earliest stage of the Neolithic in south-west Asia during the 9th and first half of the 8th millennium cal BC. While practising crop cultivation, most PPNA communities were still reliant on animal hunting and gathering for survival. These groups were mainly sedentary and, as their predecessors, also inhabited circular semi-subterranean houses. Public buildings with a probable ritual function are also documented in most sites (Belfer-Cohen and Bar-Yosef 2002). In the southern Levant, the PPNA seems to be tightly connected culturally with the Natufian world (Belfer-Cohen and Goring-Morris 2010).

In the archaeological record, the PPNA phase is succeeded by the pre-pottery Neolithic B (PPNB), which spans from the second half of the 8th to the first half of the 7th millennium cal BC and is subdivided into three or four phases: the Early PPNB, the Middle PPNB, the Late PPNB, and the Final PPNB or PPNC. It is during the PPNB period that agricultural and husbandry practices become the main way of subsistence of human communities. In the whole Fertile Crescent a steep demographic increase is observed during the course of the PPNB, as attested by the emergence of mega-sites or large villages which, in some cases, reach 10–14 ha in size, exceeding the dimensions of the largest PPNA/Natufian sites by one order of magnitude (Kadowaki 2012). During the PPNB there is also a change in house architecture and the round, small subterranean PPNA structures are replaced by large square pluricellular houses (Goring-Morris and Belfer-Cohen 2013). Human burials during this period are often found inside or at the porch of the houses, marking a connection between the living and the dead, and human skulls are often given a differential funerary treatment, being deposited (and sometimes accumulated) in distinctive spaces, painted and covered with plaster (Kuijt *et al.* 2011). For some scholars, the homogeneity of cultural traits observed across the whole of the Levant and part of Anatolia during this period supports the notion of a PPNB civilisation, *koine* or 'interaction sphere' (Bar-Yosef and Belfer-Cohen 1989), while others stress the existence of regional differentiation (Asouti 2007).

Already documented during the PPNA, the PPNB also saw an increase of the complexity of trading networks of goods like obsidian or stone beads, extending throughout the Levant, south-eastern and central Anatolia. The existence of these extensive communication webs would have allowed the exchange of ideas, resources and perhaps also genes among human groups, being instrumental in the success of the Neolithic revolution (Ibáñez *et al.* 2015). While in some sites of the southern Levant the PPNB gave way to a transitional phase between the aceramic and the ceramic Neolithic, the PPNC, most villages experienced a hiatus in their occupation at the end of the PPNB, a phenomenon known as the 'PPNB collapse'. Different reasons have been proposed to explain the widespread abandonment of sites during this period: a shift in settlement patterns leading to relocation of human communities, a rapid climate deterioration (8.2ky event), local overexploitation of resources, disease or tensions between neighbouring communities (Bar-Yosef 2001).

The pre-pottery Neolithic (PPN) period is succeeded by the pottery Neolithic (PN). From this moment onwards there is an emergence of regionally distinct cultural units and pottery starts to be produced. It is at this point during the early 7th millennium cal BC that the 'Neolithic package' spreads into Europe.

Several developments in the techniques of genetic analysis during the mid-1980s led to the emergence of the ancient DNA (aDNA) discipline (Higuchi *et al.* 1984). One of the multiple methodological applications within the scope of this plural science is 'archaeogenetics' (Renfrew and Boyle 2000). Through the genetic analysis of skeletal elements of humans and animals that lived hundreds or thousands of years ago, this sub-discipline can address fundamental questions on population origins, population admixture and biological relationships within burials or settlements.

In the following sections of this chapter the knowns and the unknowns in ancient human DNA research in south-west Asia will be presented and discussed. Methodological challenges and limitations of this approach will be highlighted and the state-of-the-art of aDNA research in the first Neolithic Near Eastern communities will be summarised and the evidence revisited in the light of the following research questions:

1. What was the relationship of the first Neolithic Near Eastern communities with their preceding Epipalaeolithic groups?
2. How mobile were these first farmers? Did mobility, gene-exchange and population aggregation play a role in the formation of the first mega-sites?
3. Were the populations within the PPNB interaction sphere genetically homogeneous?

4. Was there a local population replacement after the 'PPNB collapse'?
5. How did the Neolithic expand into Europe? Was it a movement of people, ideas or both?
6. What is the main ancestry source for the spread of the Neolithic into Europe? Is there a single ancestry source?
7. Do the economic, cultural and demographic changes observed in the archaeological record translate into changes of social organisation? Can we investigate these using aDNA?

The chapter will conclude with a reflection on what has been achieved so far and, in the opinion of the author, which steps could be taken to gain a more nuanced approach to the study of the world's first farming societies.

METHODOLOGICAL CHALLENGES AND RECENT TECHNICAL DEVELOPMENTS

The analysis of aDNA from human populations from the early Neolithic in south-west Asia has been hindered by a poor molecular preservation of human remains. Long-term DNA survival in skeletal elements is strongly influenced by environmental conditions during and after deposition such as temperature, pH, humidity or oxygen availability. Among these, the fossil 'thermal history', which accounts for both the mean temperature and temperature fluctuations that it has endured up to its analysis, has been demonstrated to have a major effect on DNA degradation through depurination leading to strand fragmentation (Smith *et al.* 2003). The warm climate of the Near East, combined sometimes with detrimental post-excavation storage conditions, poses a major difficulty for the recovery of informative DNA fragments. As a result, modern Near Eastern populations have been used as a proxy for early Neolithic groups from the same region until very recently (Richards *et al.* 2000; Haak *et al.* 2010; Soares *et al.* 2010). This approach is, however, problematic, as recent ancient works have shown us that the genetic composition of human populations around the globe has changed substantially in the last five millennia (Haak *et al.* 2015).

Three main technological breakthroughs have made it possible to overcome these challenges, at least to some extent, in order to access genetic information from key but climatically challenging areas such as the Near East. The first of these was the development of a new strategy of DNA replication and sequencing, known as 'Next Generation Sequencing'. In contrast with its technical predecessors PCR and Sanger Sequencing, NGS does not target discrete regions of the genome in independent reactions but allows for the simultaneous recovery of all the existing DNA fragments in the extraction pool. Developed by Margulies *et al.* (2005), this technique was used for the first time in the ancient DNA field in 2006 to sequence mammoth DNA and quickly replaced traditional genotyping methods in the study of human aDNA (Poinar *et al.* 2006; Sánchez-Quinto *et al.* 2012). The second game-changer was the development of custom DNA 'enrichment' or 'capture' strategies that simultaneously select the desired fractions of the genome, substantially bringing down analytical costs. Among these, the '1240k capture system', an in-solution DNA capture panel implemented in 2015 by the Harvard lab (Fu *et al.* 2013; Haak *et al.* 2015; Mathieson *et al.* 2015), has been extensively applied to the study of Neolithic and pre-Neolithic populations. This method allows the simultaneous selection of 1,240,000 neutral positions across the human genome that are variable across human populations and its study has shown to be enough to uncover major population substructure and to infer events of past population admixture. The last relevant breakthrough was the discovery that the DNA contained within the *pars petrosa* of the skull temporal bone is particularly resilient to long-term environmental degradation, providing between four to 16 times more endogenous aDNA than teeth and between 100 and 200 times more than any other skeletal element (Gamba *et al.* 2014; Pinhasi *et al.* 2015).

In a six-year timespan, the combination of these three technological developments has enabled the unlocking of crucial genomic information from the first farmers of different regions of the Fertile Crescent. Figure 6.1 shows the location of Epipalaeolithic and Neolithic archaeological sites from the Fertile Crescent and Anatolia that have provided genetic information so far. As can be appreciated in the figure, the chronological and geographical representation is still scarce and patchy, and key regions within the northern Levant such as the middle Euphrates valley are almost unexplored.

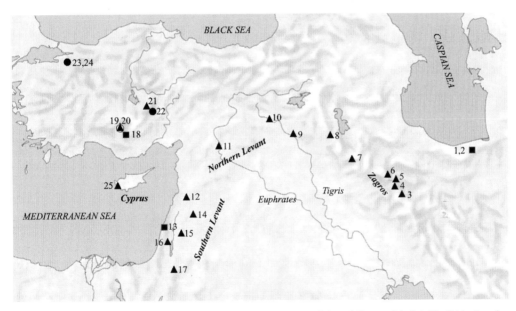

Figure 6.1. Location of pre-Neolithic (squares), Pre-pottery (triangles) and Pottery (circles) Neolithic sites that have provided ancient DNA data in the Near East. * All individuals radiocarbon dated, **Some individuals radiocarbon dated. 1: Hotu Cave (9100–8600 cal BC), Belt Cave (12000–8000 cal BC), 3: Tepe Guran (6700–5500 cal BC), 4: Tepe Abdul Hosein (8200–7700 cal BC)*, 5: Ganj Dareh (7461–7076 cal BC)**, 6: Wehmeh Cave (7461–7076 cal BC)*, 7: Bestansur (8000–7000 cal BC), 8: Shanidar (8200–7900 cal BC)**, 9: Nemrik 9 (9500–8000 cal BC), 10: Bonçuklu Tarla (9000–8500 cal BC), 11: Tell Halula (7500–7300 cal BC), 12: Tell Ramad (7300–6650 cal BC), 13: Raqefet Cave (12000–9500 cal BC)**, 14: Kfar HaHoresh (7728–7588 cal BC)*, 15: 'Ain Ghazal (8300–6700 cal BC)**, 16: Motza (7300–6200 cal BC), 17: Ba'ja (7100–6700 cal BC), 18: Pinarbaşi (13629–13308 cal BC)*, 19: Bonçuklu Höyük (8212–7600 cal BC)**, 20: Çatalhöyük (7035–6075 cal BC), 21: Aşıklı Höyük (8225–7475 cal BC)*, 22: Tepecic-Çiftlik Höyük (6570–6072 cal BC)*, 23: Barcın Höyük (6500–6007 cal BC)**, 24: Menteşe Höyük (6400–5600 cal BC), 25: Kyssonerga-Mylouthia (8300–7000 cal BC).

THE LAST HUNTER-GATHERERS AND THE FIRST FARMERS OF SOUTH-WEST ASIA

As detailed above, before the transition to farming, south-west Asia was populated by local Epipalaeolithic groups with a predominantly hunter-gatherer economy. While the available archaeological evidence points towards a gradual adoption of a production economy by some of these groups, the roles of human mobility and gene-flow in the emergence of agriculture have been a matter of discussion among scholars for decades.

In recent years, different ancient DNA works have addressed this issue, focusing on the genetic analysis of the last hunter-gatherers and the first farmers of the main domestication centres: the southern Levant (Lazaridis *et al.* 2016; 2022a; Feldman *et al.* 2019), the northern Levant/Upper Mesopotamia (Fernández *et al.* 2014; Lazaridis *et al.* 2022a) and the Zagros region (Broushaki *et al.* 2016; Gallego-Llorente *et al.* 2016; Narasimhan *et al.* 2019; Allentoft *et al.* 2022; Lazaridis *et al.* 2022a), alongside secondary areas of Neolithisation such as central/western Anatolia (Kılınç *et al.* 2016; Feldman *et al.* 2019; Lazaridis *et al.* 2022a) and Cyprus (Lazaridis *et al.* 2022a). The pre-Neolithic genetic background (whole genome data and/or mitochondrial DNA) is represented by just 11 individuals: eight Natufians from Raqefet cave in Israel, two Epipalaeolithic hunter-gatherers from Belt cave and Hotu Cave in Iran and one from Pinarbaşi in central Anatolia. In the southern Levant, the Neolithic background is represented by 16 individuals: 14 from Jordan from the PPNB and PPNC levels of 'Ain Ghazal (n=13) and the Late PPNB in Baja (n=1) and two from the PPNB levels from Kfar HaHoresh and Motza in Israel. In northern Mesopotamia, so far just three individuals belonging to the PPNB period have provided whole-genome data, one from Bonçuklu Tarla in south-eastern Turkey and two from Nemrik 9 in northern Iraq, but mitochondrial DNA data from 15 individuals are also available from the Middle PPNB levels of Tell Halula and Tell Ramad in modern Syria. The pre-pottery Neolithic of the eastern Fertile Crescent is represented by 10 individuals from Ganj Dareh, three from Tepe Abdul Hossein, one from Wehmet Cave and three from Tepe Guran in the central Zagros in Iran, and four from Bestansur (8000–7000 cal BC) and three from Shanidar cave (*c.* 8300–7900 cal BC) in the northern Zagros region of Iraq. Outside of the Fertile Crescent in central Anatolia genetic data from the first farmers are available from 17 PPNB individuals, nine from Bonçuklu and eight from Aşıklı Höyük. In Cyprus, genetic profiles have been obtained from three PPNB individuals from Kissonerga-Mylouthkia. Dates and site locations can be found in Figure 6.1.

Whole-genome data of the first Near Eastern farmers show a profound regional genetic structure and overall genetic continuity with preceding Epipalaeolithic groups, which account for 75–90% of their respective ancestries. Three main genetic clusters can be distinguished across the region. In the southern Levant, a *Levantine ancestral component* is maximised in Natufian groups and early (PPNB) Neolithic farmers from Jordan and Israel. Epipalaeolithic hunter-gatherers and early farmers from the eastern Fertile Crescent show a distinct, divergent *Iranian genetic profile*, which is also maximised in Caucasus hunter-gatherers. Similarly, Anatolian pre-ceramic farmers derive most of their ancestry from the Pinarbaşi Epipalaeolithic hunter-gatherer. In sum, all these findings support the idea that the development of agriculture was driven by genetically different hunter-gatherer groups that inhabited the Levant, the Zagros and Anatolia and shared technological innovations (see references above, and Feldman *et al.* 2021 for a synthesis).

The three northern Mesopotamian PPNB individuals from the upper Tigris cluster closer to the individuals from the Zagros, indicating the presence of a high proportion of Iranian-like ancestry in them. Their ancestry profiles can be modelled, however, as a mixture of Iranian and Anatolian-like ancestries (Lazaridis *et al.* 2022a). The lack of pre-Neolithic genetic data from this region prevents making inferences regarding the origins of this ancestry profile and specifically, whether it was already present in preceding Natufian/Epipalaeolithic groups or originated in a different region of the Fertile Crescent.

Archaeological evidence supports an exogenous origin rather than a local development of the Neolithic in Cyprus. Evidence for the pre-Neolithic occupation of Cyprus is scarce and limited to a few enclaves that show no obvious continuity with the well-documented and widespread pre-ceramic sites. The first Neolithic settlements in Cyprus, Asprokremnos and Klimonas, date to the PPNA and are contemporaneous to Late PPNA and PPNA–PPNB transition sites in the Levant. Direct parallels in architecture and material culture have been drawn between these early Neolithic sites in Cyprus and some sites in the Middle Euphrates, which suggests that the island was most likely colonised by groups of pre-ceramic farmers from the northern Levant (Vigne *et al.* 2009). The available genetic data from Neolithic Cyprus are restricted to three individuals found in commingled contexts in the PPNB site of Kissonerga-Mylouthkia and show a predominantly Anatolian-related ancestry, suggestive of an Anatolian origin. The depositional context of these individuals is, however, rather unusual, as instead of being formally buried, they were placed in water wells close to the sea. This atypical mortuary practice raises the question of whether these individuals are representative of the general PPNB population in Cyprus, or constitute an outlier (Peltenburg 2003; Lazaridis *et al.* 2022b).

GENE-FLOW AMONG FIRST FARMERS

A detailed analysis of the genomic structure of these first farming populations revealed that despite deriving most of their ancestry from their hunter-gatherer predecessors, they also received variable levels of gene-flow from neighbouring groups.

PPNB populations from the southern Levant derive part of their ancestry (25%) from Anatolian-like farming populations. This 'excess' of Anatolian ancestry is not present in the Natufian group, which suggests that it was acquired through admixture at the first stages of development of the Neolithic (Lazaridis *et al.* 2016; 2022a; Feldman *et al.* 2019). While the ancestry profiles of PPNB farmers from central Anatolia (Bonçuklu and Aşıklı Höyük) show they mainly descend from local Epipalaeolithic individuals, different levels of additional 'Iranian' and 'Levantine-like' ancestries have also been detected, indicating that they received additional gene-flow from a population or populations carrying these ancestries around the time of the adoption of agriculture (Feldman *et al.* 2019; Lazaridis *et al.* 2022a). These two population groups can be effectively modelled as a mixture of the local Epipalaeolithic hunter-gatherer (Pinarbaşi) and Mesopotamian PPNB individuals, which supports the hypothesis that the 'donor population' could have been the Mesopotamian group itself or a close population with a similar genetic profile (Lazaridis *et al.* 2022a).

Later Anatolian populations belonging to the Ceramic horizon display 6 to 23% extra Levantine ancestry, which indicates post-PPNB gene-flow into Anatolia (Feldman *et al.* 2019; Lazaridis *et al.* 2022a). This ancestry could be traced back to southern Levantine-like populations or could have also been introduced by other unsampled Levantine populations, for example from the middle Euphrates region, from which whole genome data have not been recovered yet (Lazaridis *et al.* 2022a).

It is not until the Chalcolithic/Late Neolithic period (*c.* 6ky cal BC) that this genetic differentiation observed among first farmer groups of south-west Asia starts to decrease as a result of increased gene-flow among populations (Skourtanioti *et al.* 2020; Lazaridis *et al.* 2022b). During this period a genetic gradient of decreasing Anatolian ancestry and increasing Iran/Caucasus ancestry can be observed between western Anatolia to the Caucasus and Iran. This cline, indicative of extensive population admixture across these regions, is maintained throughout the Chalcolithic and the Bronze Age. In contrast, populations of the northern Levant experienced a post-Neolithic increase of south-Levantine and Iran/Caucasus related ancestries, through multiple gene-flow events from different sources or, alternatively, from northern Mesopotamia (Skourtanioti *et al.* 2020).

POPULATION SOURCES OF THE EUROPEAN NEOLITHIC

From the Near East the Neolithic spread into Europe around the 7th millennium cal BC, reaching first the Aegean coast and then diffusing across continental and Mediterranean Europe. Multiple ancient DNA studies have shown that early farmers across Europe carry ancestry from north-western Anatolian Pottery Neolithic populations, thus supporting the view that the Neolithic diffusion was mediated by ceramic farming groups of Anatolian origin. The same ancestry source is present, albeit in different proportions, in early farming groups from the Balkans (Gamba *et al.* 2014; Haak *et al.* 2015a; Hervella *et al.* 2015; Szécsényi-Nagy *et al.* 2015; Mathieson *et al.* 2018), central Europe (Brandt *et al.* 2013; Lazaridis *et al.* 2014; Haak *et al.* 2015; Mathieson *et al.* 2015), Scandinavia (Mittnik *et al.* 2018), southern France and Iberia (Olalde *et al.* 2015; 2019; Rivollat *et al.* 2020) and Britain (Brace *et al.* 2019). As these first farmers moved around the landscape, they also interacted with local hunter-gatherer populations in different regions, creating different genetic profiles in different parts of Europe (Mathieson *et al.* 2018; Rivollat *et al.* 2020; Allentoft *et al.* 2022).

However, a few individuals that are not consistent with descending from the same source population as other European farmers have also been reported: four from Diros and Franchthi Cave in the Greek Peloponnese (*c.* 4000 cal BC), one from Krepost in Bulgaria (5718–5626 cal BC) belonging to the Karanovo Neolithic cultural complex (Mathieson *et al.* 2018), and 10 early Neolithic individuals from central Italy from Grotta Continenza and Ripabianca di Monterado (*c.* 6000–5000 cal BC) (Antonio *et al.* 2019). In addition to ancestry from north-west Anatolian farmers, these individuals carry an excess of 'Iranian ancestry', suggesting that they descend from a different source population than other early Neolithic individuals in Europe. The earliest described sources with this ancestry profile in the Near East can be found in Anatolian Ceramic sites such as

Tepeçik Çiftik and Kumtepe (Mathieson *et al.* 2018), but origins in unsampled regions from northern Levant cannot be discarded. While the exact origin of this ancestry is still unknown, these results constitute direct evidence that more than one population source was involved in the spread of the Neolithic from south-west Asia into Europe. Similarities in mitochondrial DNA haplotype and haplogroup composition between *c.* 8000 cal BC farmers from the middle Euphrates valley and the Damascus basin in the northern Levant and modern Cyprus have also suggested an early colonisation of the island by PPNB farmers from the Levant, in agreement with archaeological evidence (Fernández *et al.* 2014). While the only whole-genome PPN data from Cyprus available to date indicate an Anatolian origin of the tested individuals, as pointed out before the particularities of their burial arrangement cast doubts on their representativity for the whole PPNB horizon in the island (Lazaridis *et al.* 2022a).

To understand the extent to which Near Eastern populations other than Anatolia contributed to the genetic pool of the first farmers, it would be essential to examine genome-wide data of early Neolithic individuals from the Aegean and the Adriatic. In the case of Cyprus, the genetic analysis of individuals from archaeological sites with clear archaeological parallels with Levantine pre-pottery groups will be key to fully assessing the origins of the first farmers that colonised the island.

ANCIENT DNA AND SOCIAL ORGANISATION OF THE FIRST FARMING COMMUNITIES

The transition from a forager to a productive economy alongside the increase in sedentism and the emergence of the first cities in south-west Asia was accompanied by a major restructuring of social roles in early Neolithic groups. As individual workloads increased, so did competition for land-access and resources. Living in permanent structures in densely occupied settlements would have added to these tensions.

Traditionally, the study of societal changes associated with the adoption of agriculture has been approached through the analysis of settlement architecture, material culture and mortuary practices, drawing occasional ethnographic parallels with modern hunter-gatherer or farming societies. Comparatively, less emphasis has been devoted to the direct analysis of the skeletal remains. A key question is the role played by biological kin in the organisation of these first farming societies and how and if it was reflected in their funerary practices. Across the PPNA, PPNB and Pottery Neolithic periods in most of the Levant and Anatolia individuals were buried beneath the floor of the houses while they were still in use, providing a link between the living and the dead. Houses were often rebuilt, and new buildings placed above the old ones. By examining the role of kin in these societies an answer can be provided to questions such as:

1. Were these groups endogamic and, to what extent?
2. Were societies articulated around nuclear, extended families or unrelated cooperative groups?
3. Were houses inhabited by families or non-family related individuals?

4. Were the inhabitants of different rebuilt levels of the same house biologically connected?
5. What was the relationship between intra-mural burials and those in public structures?

The analysis of dental and skeletal epigenetic traits suggests that both endogamic (Alt *et al.* 2013) and exogamic (Alt *et al.* 2015) mating systems might have been common among certain early farming communities, but the evidence is limited to just a few sites. The study of isotopes of diet (C, N) and mobility (Sr, O) in Neolithic and pre-Neolithic groups has also a great potential to identify dietary differences within the same household and evaluate intra- and inter-site individual mobility to detect differences in mobility patterns, but the available data from the Near East are still very limited (Pearson *et al.* 2015; 2021; Santana *et al.* 2021).

The refinement of methods of estimation of biological relatedness or kinship from low-coverage human genomes offers a unique opportunity to approach these questions empirically (Kuhn and Jakobsson 2015; Fernandes *et al.* 2021). To date, the data are limited to three studies and five archaeological sites, but this is expected to increase in the following years. The first attempt to reconstruct family relationships among first farming communities focused on the mtDNA analysis of individuals from intra-mural house contexts in the Middle PPNB site of Tell Halula, Syria. Shared mitochondrial haplotypes were identified both among different rebuilt phases of the same house and across neighbouring houses from the same and different archaeological phases. These results suggest a homogeneous population structure, but the study has a limited resolution, as only short mitochondrial DNA fragments could be recovered with the techniques available at the time (Fernández *et al.* 2008).

A similar approach using full genomes alongside uniparental markers was employed (Chyleński *et al.* 2019; Yaka *et al.* 2021) to decipher biological kinship patterns in two 9th-millennium PPNB central Anatolian sites, Bonçuklu and Aşıklı Höyük and three PN sites from the 8th–6th millennia cal BC in central (Çatalhöyük and Tepecik-Çiftlik) and north-western Anatolia (Barcın Höyük). The majority of individuals that provided usable genetic data in the pre-ceramic sites (nine in Bonçuklu and five in Aşıklı Höyük) had relatives within the same house or in neighbouring houses, but others were not biologically related to analysed members of the same house. In the two ceramic sites, genetic data could be obtained mostly from non-adult individuals (14 in Çatalhöyük, 23 in Barcın Höyük and five in Tepecik-Çiftlik). Contrary to their predecessor PPNB groups, the presence of relatives within co-burials and neighbouring buildings in these sites was rare. In Çatalhöyük and Tepecik-Çiftlik only one pair of first-degree relatives were found within the same building, while in Barcın two pairs of related individuals were found in separate houses in close proximity. Overall, these results support the notion that at the early stages of the Neolithic in Anatolia genetic relatedness played a role in household composition. Later ceramic households, however, do not seem to be organised around biological kinship according to the gathered data. The limited biomolecular preservation of the human remains, which allowed for the recovery of genetic information of just 20% of the sampled individuals and the differential biomolecular preservation of adults and subadults, prevents us from drawing more general conclusions about the funerary practices of these groups and by extension, about aspects of their social organisation.

THE UNKNOWNS AND MOVING FORWARD

As detailed in the previous sections, the analysis of ancient DNA from Near Eastern populations has helped to clarify essential questions on the emergence and dispersal of agriculture in the region by clarifying the biological relationship between farmers and foragers, identifying major gene-flow events from different population groups, pinpointing the source(s) of origin of the Neolithic spread in Europe and investigating the role of biological kinship in the social organisation of the first farming societies.

The poor preservation of human remains in the area and the difficulty to access, export and study material in 'politically sensitive' areas has greatly limited the resolution of some of these studies. For example, the inference of population admixture relies on the availability of high-quality coverage genomes to act as proxies of population groups carrying a particular genetic signature. While current methods are sufficient to distinguish between the main 'ancestry components' of a given past population, the population sources, timings and processes that gave rise to a particular genetic profile are still difficult to ascertain without a good chronological and geographical representation of the data. In the case of the Fertile Crescent, an obvious gap is the lack of genomic information of Epipalaeolithic/Natufian and PPN individuals from the northern Levant, a key region in the emergence, consolidation and spread of agricultural practices.

Except for Anatolia, where data from Epipalaeolithic, Pre-ceramic and Ceramic sites are available from a handful of locations, ancient DNA from chronological transects spanning the transition to agriculture is not yet available for south-west Asia. This information is essential to answer questions of genetic continuity and gene-flow at a regional scale. The transition to the PPN to the PN in the Levant and the eastern Fertile Crescent and the population implications of the 'PPNB collapse' are other unknowns that will only be able to be resolved through dense sampling across different archaeological phases of the same site or region.

Apart from the difficulties associated with the access to samples and the technical limitations in the recovery of Neolithic Near Eastern aDNA, there are other reasons that could be holding back the advancement in the knowledge of the genetic composition of the first Near Eastern farmers. On one hand, there is a generalised lack of transparency in sample processing and back-up sample storage in ancient DNA laboratories. Genetic data outputs are stored in public repositories such as Genbank (Clark *et al.* 2016) or ENA (European Nucleotide Archive) (Leinonen *et al.* 2011) and are freely available to download. Negative and sample screening results below the threshold for analysis, however, are often not disclosed. In a similar way, once skeletal samples are processed, most labs retain remains for safety or future analysis. A simple initiative such as the public disclosure of all the studied samples and DNA screening results would be very effective to avoid resampling, boost collaboration, inform sampling strategies and better understand differential preservation across sites and regions in the Near East. On the other hand, engagement with other disciplines is still limited. In a region that has proven particularly harsh for DNA preservation, a multidisciplinary approach including archaeological, anthropological, spatial, chronological and isotopic data could help in filling in the gaps and complementing the still scarce available genomic data.

ACKNOWLEDGEMENTS

The author would like to express her gratitude to the Leverhulme Trust for funding her research on ancient human Near Eastern Neolithic DNA through the Research Project 'What's in a house? Exploring the kinship structure of the world's first houses'.

REFERENCES

Allentoft, M.E., Sikora, M., Refoyo-Martínez, A., Irving-Pease, E.K., Fischer, A., Barrie, W. *et al.* 2022. Population genomics of Stone Age Eurasia. *bioRxiv* preprint, 1–71. https://doi.org/10.1101/2022.05.04.490594.

Alt, K.W., Benz, M., Müller, W., Berner, M.E., Schultz, M., Schmidt-Schultz, T.H., Knipper, C., Gebel, H.-G.K., Nissen, H.J. and Vach, W. 2013. Earliest evidence for social endogamy in the 9,000-year-old-population of Basta, Jordan. *PLoS One* 8. doi:10.1371/journal.pone.0065649.

Alt, K.W., Benz, M., Vach, W., Simmons, T.L. and Goring-Morris, A.N., 2015. Insights into the social structure of the PPNB Site of Kfar HaHoresh, Israel, based on dental remains. *PLoS One* 10, e0134528. doi:10.1371/journal.pone.0134528

Antonio, M.L., Gao, Z., Moots, H.M., Lucci, M., Candilio, F., Sawyer, S. *et al.* 2019. Ancient Rome: a genetic crossroads of Europe and the Mediterranean. *Science* 366, 708–714.

Asouti, E. 2007. Beyond the Pre-Pottery Neolithic B interaction sphere. *Journal of World Prehistory* 20, 87–126.

Bar-Yosef, O., 2001. From sedentary foragers to village hierarchies: the emergence of social institutions. In W.G. Runciman (ed.), *The origin of human social institutions*, 1–38. London: British Academy.

Bar-Yosef, O. and Belfer-Cohen, A. 1989. The Levantine 'PPNB' interaction sphere. In I. Hershkowitz (ed.), *People and culture in change*, 59–72. Oxford: British Archaeological Reports.

Bar-Yosef, O. and Belfer-Cohen, A. 1991. From sedentary hunter-gatherers to territorial farmers in the Levant. In S.A. Gregg (ed.), *Between bands and states*, 181–202. Carbondale: Centre for Archaeological Investigations.

Belfer-Cohen, A. and Bar-Yosef, O. 2002. Early sedentism in the Near East. A bumpy ride to village life. In I. Kuijt (ed.), *Life in Neolithic farming communities: social organization, identity and differentiation, fundamental issues in archaeology*, 19–38. New York: Kluwer Academic Publishers.

Belfer-Cohen, A. and Goring-Morris, A. 2010. The initial Neolithic of the Near East: Why is it so difficult to deal with the PPNA? *Journal of the Israel Prehistoric Society* 40, 1–18.

Bienert, H.-D. 1991. Skull cult in the prehistoric Near East. *Journal of Prehistoric Religion* 5, 9–23.

Brace, S., Diekmann, Y., Booth, T.J., Dorp, L. van, Faltyskova, Z., Rohland, N. *et al.* 2019. Ancient genomes indicate population replacement in Early Neolithic Britain. *Nature Ecology & Evolution* 3, 765–71.

Brandt, G., Haak, W., Adler, C.J., Roth, C., Szecsenyi-Nagy, A., Karimnia, S. *et al.* 2013. Ancient DNA reveals key stages in the formation of Central European mitochondrial genetic diversity. *Science* 342, 257–61.

Broushaki, F., Thomas, M.G., Link, V., López, S., Dorp, L. van, Kirsanow, K. *et al.* 2016. Early Neolithic genomes from the eastern Fertile Crescent. *Science* aaf7943. doi:10.1126/science.aaf7943.

Chyleński, M., Ehler, E., Somel, M., Yaka, R., Krzewińska, M., Dabert, M., Juras, A. and Marciniak, A. 2019. Ancient mitochondrial genomes reveal the absence of maternal kinship in the burials of Çatalhöyük people and their genetic affinities. *Genes* 10, 207.

Clark, K., Karsch-Mizrachi, I., Lipman, D.J., Ostell, J., Sayers, E.W., 2016. GenBank. *Nucleic Acids Research* 44, D67–D72.

Feldman, M., Fernández-Domínguez, E., Reynolds, L., Baird, D., Pearson, J., Hershkovitz, I. *et al.* 2019. Late Pleistocene human genome suggests a local origin for the first farmers of central Anatolia. *Nature Communications* 10, 1218.

Feldman, M., Gnecchi-Ruscone, G.A., Lamnidis, T.C. and Posth, C. 2021. Where Asia meets Europe – recent insights from ancient human genomics. *Annals of Human Biology* 48, 191–202.

Fernandes, D.M., Cheronet, O., Gelabert, P. and Pinhasi, R. 2021. TKGWV2: an ancient DNA relatedness pipeline for ultra-low coverage whole genome shotgun data. *Scientific Reports* 11, 21262.

Fernández, E., Ortiz, J.E., Torres, T., Pérez-Pérez, A., Gamba, C., Tirado, M., Baeza, C., López-Parra, A.M., Turbón, D., Anfruns, J., Molist, M. and Arroyo-Pardo, E. 2008. Mitochondrial DNA genetic relationships at the ancient Neolithic site of Tell Halula. *Forensic Science International: Genetics Supplement Series* 1, 271–3.

Fernández, E., Pérez-Pérez, A., Gamba, C., Prats, E., Cuesta, P., Anfruns, J., Molist, M., Arroyo-Pardo, E. and Turbón, D. 2014. Ancient DNA analysis of 8000 B.C. Near Eastern farmers supports an Early Neolithic pioneer maritime colonization of mainland Europe through Cyprus and the Aegean Islands. *PLoS Genetics* 10, e1004401. doi:10.1371/journal.pgen.1004401.

Fu, Q., Meyer, M., Gao, X., Stenzel, U., Burbano, H.A., Kelso, J. and Pääbo, S. 2013. DNA analysis of an early modern human from Tianyuan Cave, China. *Proceedings of the National Academy of Sciences of the United States of America* 110, 2223–7.

Gallego-Llorente, M., Connell, S., Jones, E.R., Merrett, D.C., Jeon, Y., Eriksson, A. *et al.* 2016. The genetics of an early Neolithic pastoralist from the Zagros, Iran. *Scientific Reports* 6, 31326.

Gamba, C., Jones, E.R., Teasdale, M.D., McLaughlin, R.L., Gonzalez-Fortes, G., Mattiangeli, V. *et al.* 2014. Genome flux and stasis in a five millennium transect of European prehistory. *Nature Communications* 5, 5257.

Goring-Morris, A. and Belfer-Cohen, A. 2013. Houses and households: a Near Eastern perspective. In D. Hofmann and J. Smyth (eds), *Tracking the Neolithic house in Europe: sedentism, architecture and practice*, 19–44. Springer: New York.

Goring-Morris, A.N. and Belfer-Cohen, A. 2014. The southern Levant (Cisjordan) during the Neolithic period. In A.E. Killebrew and M. Steiner (eds), *The Oxford Handbook of the archaeology of the Levant: c. 8000–332 BCE*, 141–63. Oxford: Oxford University Press.

Haak, W., Balanovsky, O., Sanchez, J.J., Koshel, S., Zaporozhchenko, V., Adler, C.J. *et al.* 2010. Ancient DNA from European Early Neolithic farmers reveals their Near Eastern affinities. *PLoS Biology* 8, e1000536. doi:10.1371/journal.pbio.1000536.

Haak, W., Lazaridis, I., Patterson, N., Rohland, N., Mallick, S., Llamas, B. *et al.* 2015. Massive migration from the steppe was a source for Indo-European languages in Europe. *Nature* 522, 207–11.

Hervella, M., Rotea, M., Izagirre, N., Constantinescu, M., Alonso, S., Ioana, M., Lazăr, C., Ridiche, F., Soficaru, A.D., Netea, M.G. and de la Rua, C. 2015. Ancient DNA from South-East Europe reveals different events during Early and Middle Neolithic influencing the European genetic heritage. *PLoS One* 10, e0128810. doi:10.1371/journal.pone.0128810.

Higuchi, R., Bowman, B., Freiberger, M., Ryder, O.A. and Wilson, A.C. 1984. DNA sequences from the quagga, an extinct member of the horse family. *Nature* 312, 282–4.

Ibáñez, J.J., Ortega, D., Campos, D., Khalidi, L. and Méndez, V. 2015. Testing complex networks of interaction at the onset of the Near Eastern Neolithic using modelling of obsidian exchange. *Journal of the Royal Society Interface* 12. doi:10.1098/rsif.2015.0210.

Kadowaki, S., 2012. A household perspective towards the Pre-Pottery Neolithic to Late Neolithic cultural transformation in the Southern Levant. *Orient* 47, 3–28.

Kılınç, G.M., Omrak, A., Özer, F., Günther, T., Büyükkarakaya, A.M., Bıçakçı, E., Baird, D. *et al.* 2016. The demographic development of the first farmers in Anatolia. *Current Biology* 26, 2659–66.

Kuhn, J.M.M. and Jakobsson, M. 2015. Estimating genetic kin relationships in prehistoric populations. *PLoS One* 13, 21.

Kuijt, I., Guerrero, E., Molist, M. and Anfruns, J. 2011. The changing Neolithic household: household autonomy and social segmentation, Tell Halula, Syria. *Journal of Anthropological Archaeology* 30, 502–22.

Lazaridis, I., Patterson, N., Mittnik, A., Renaud, G., Mallick, S., Kirsanow, K. *et al.* 2014. Ancient human genomes suggest three ancestral populations for present-day Europeans. *Nature* 513, 409–13.

Lazaridis, I., Nadel, D., Rollefson, G., Merrett, D.C., Rohland, N., Mallick, S. *et al.* 2016. Genomic insights into the origin of farming in the ancient Near East. *Nature* 536, 419–24.

Lazaridis, I., Alpaslan-Roodenberg, S., Acar, A., Açıkkol, A., Agelarakis, A., Aghikyan, L. *et al.* 2022a. Ancient DNA from Mesopotamia suggests distinct Pre-Pottery and Pottery Neolithic migrations into Anatolia. *Science* 377, 982–7.

Lazaridis, I., Alpaslan-Roodenberg, S., Acar, A., Açıkkol, A., Agelarakis, A., Aghikyan, L. *et al.* 2022b. The genetic history of the Southern Arc: a bridge between West Asia and Europe. *Science* 377, eabm4247. doi:10.1126/science.abm4247.

Leinonen, R., Akhtar, R., Birney, E., Bower, L., Cerdeno-Tárraga, A., Cheng, Y. *et al.* 2011. The European Nucleotide Archive. *Nucleic Acids Research* 39, D28–D31.

Margulies, M., Egholm, M., Altman, W.E., Attiya, S., Bader, J.S., Bemben, L.A. *et al.* 2005. Genome sequencing in microfabricated high-density picolitre reactors. *Nature* 437, 376–80.

Mathieson, I., Lazaridis, I., Rohland, N., Mallick, S., Patterson, N., Roodenberg, S.A. *et al.* 2015. Genome-wide patterns of selection in 230 ancient Eurasians. *Nature* 528, 499–503.

Mathieson, I., Alpaslan-Roodenberg, S., Posth, C., Szécsényi-Nagy, A., Rohland, N., Mallick, S. *et al.* 2018. The genomic history of southeastern Europe. *Nature* 555, 197–203.

Mittnik, A., Wang, C.-C., Pfrengle, S., Daubaras, M., Zariņa, G., Hallgren, F. *et al.* 2018. The genetic prehistory of the Baltic Sea region. *Nature Communications* 9, 1–11.

Narasimhan, V.M., Patterson, N., Moorjani, P., Rohland, N., Bernardos, R., Mallick, S. *et al.* 2019. The formation of human populations in south and central Asia. *Science* 365, eaat7487. doi:10.1126/science.aat7487.

Olalde, I., Schroeder, H., Sandoval-Velasco, M., Vinner, L., Lobón, I., Ramirez, O. *et al.* 2015. A common genetic origin for early farmers from Mediterranean Cardial and Central European LBK cultures. *Molecular Biology and Evolution* msv181. doi:10.1093/molbev/msv181.

Olalde, I., Mallick, S., Patterson, N., Rohland, N., Villalba-Mouco, V., Silva, M. *et al.* 2019. The genomic history of the Iberian peninsula over the past 8000 years. *Science* 363, 1230–4.

Pearson, J., Lamb, A., Evans, J.A., Engel, C., Russell, N., Somel, M., Van Neer, W. and Wouters, W. 2021. Multi-isotope evidence of diet (carbon and nitrogen) and mobility (strontium) at Neolithic Çatalhöyük. In I. Hodder (ed.), *Peopling the landscape of Çatalhöyük: reports from the 2009–2017 seasons*, 217–44. London: British Institute at Ankara.

Pearson, J.A., Bogaard, A., Charles, M., Hillson, S.W., Larsen, C.S., Russell, N. and Twiss, K. 2015. Stable carbon and nitrogen isotope analysis at Neolithic Çatalhöyük: evidence for human and animal diet and their relationship to households. *Journal of Archaeological Science* 57, 69.

Peltenburg, E. (ed.) 2003. *Colonisation and settlement of Cyprus: investigations at Kissonerga-Mylouthkia 1976–1996. Lemba Archaeological Project, Cyprus: 3.* Sävedalen: Paul Forlag Astroms.

Pinhasi, R., Fernandes, D., Sirak, K., Novak, M., Connell, S., Alpaslan-Roodenberg, S. *et al.* 2015. Optimal ancient DNA yields from the inner ear part of the human petrous bone. *PLoS One* 10, e0129102. doi:10.1371/journal.pone.0129102.

Poinar, H.N., Schwarz, C., Qi, J., Shapiro, B., Macphee, R.D.E., Buigues, B. *et al.* 2006. Metagenomics to paleogenomics: large-scale sequencing of mammoth DNA. *Science* 311, 392–4.

Price, T.D. 2000. Europe's first farmers: an introduction. In T.D. Price (ed.), *Europe's first farmers*, 1–18. Cambridge: Cambridge University Press.

Renfrew, A.C. and Boyle, K. (eds) 2000. *Archaeogenetics: DNA and the population prehistory of Europe.* Cambridge: McDonald Institute for Archaeological Research.

Richards, M., Macaulay, V., Hickey, E., Vega, E., Sykes, B., Guida, V. *et al.* 2000. Tracing European founder lineages in the Near Eastern mtDNA pool. *American Journal of Human Genetics* 67, 1251–76.

Rivollat, M., Jeong, C., Schiffels, S., Küçükkalıpçı, İ., Pemonge, M.-H., Rohrlach, A.B. *et al.* 2020. Ancient genome-wide DNA from France highlights the complexity of interactions between Mesolithic hunter-gatherers and Neolithic farmers. *Science Advances* 6, eaaz5344. doi:10.1126/sciadv.aaz5344.

Sánchez-Quinto, F., Schroeder, H., Ramirez, O., Avila-Arcos, M.C., Pybus, M., Olalde, I. et al. 2012. Genomic affinities of two 7,000-year-old Iberian hunter-gatherers. *Current Biology: CB.* doi:10.1016/j.cub.2012.06.005.

Santana, J., Millard, A., Ibáñez-Estevez, J.J., Bocquentin, F., Nowell, G., Peterkin, J., Macpherson, C., Muñiz, J., Anton, M., Alrousan, M. and Kafafi, Z. 2021. Multi-isotope evidence of population aggregation in the Natufian and scant migration during the early Neolithic of the Southern Levant. *Scientific Reports* 11, 11857. doi:10.1038/s41598-021-90795-2.

Skourtanioti, E., Erdal, Y.S., Frangipane, M., Balossi Restelli, F., Yener, K.A., Pinnock, F. *et al.* 2020. Genomic history of Neolithic to Bronze Age Anatolia, Northern Levant, and Southern Caucasus. *Cell* 181, 1158–75.

Smith, C.I., Chamberlain, A.T., Riley, M.S., Stringer, C. and Collins, M.J. 2003. The thermal history of human fossils and the likelihood of successful DNA amplification. *Journal of Human Evolution* 45, 203–17.

Soares, P., Achilli, A., Semino, O., Davies, W., Macaulay, V., Bandelt, H.-J., Torroni, A. and Richards, M.B. 2010. The archaeogenetics of Europe. *Current Biology: CB* 20, R174-83.

Szécsényi-Nagy, A., Brandt, G., Haak, W., Keerl, V., Jakucs, J., Möller-Rieker, S. *et al.* 2015. Tracing the genetic origin of Europe's first farmers reveals insights into their social organization. *Proceedings of the Royal Society of London B: Biological Sciences* 282, 20150339. doi:10.1098/rspb.2015.0339.

Verhoeven, M. 2002. Ritual and ideology in the Pre-Pottery Neolithic B of the Levant and southeast Anatolia. *Cambridge Archaeological Journal* 12, 233–58.

Vigne, J.-D., Zazzo, A., Saliège, J.-F., Poplin, F., Guilaine, J. and Simmons, A. 2009. Pre-Neolithic wild boar management and introduction to Cyprus more than 11,400 years ago. *Proceedings of the National Academy of Sciences of the United States of America* 106, 16135–8.

Yaka, R., Mapelli, I., Kaptan, D., Doğu, A., Chyleński, M., Erdal, Ö.D. *et al.* 2021. Variable kinship patterns in Neolithic Anatolia revealed by ancient genomes. *Current Biology* 31, 2455–68.

Chapter 7

Farmer-forager interactions in the Iron Gates: new insights and new dilemmas

Maxime N. Brami and Yoan Diekmann

Early farmers in Europe are known to have migrated from Anatolia and the Aegean basin. The latest ancient DNA and archaeological studies indicate that there were significant biological and cultural interactions between the Neolithic incomers and indigenous Mesolithic communities, including adoption of local subsistence and burial practices by migrant farmers and their offspring in places like the Danube's Iron Gates. However, the evidence for foragers becoming farmers is more equivocal, hinging on the interpretation of a handful of archaeological sites including Lepenski Vir.

INTRODUCTION

Ancient DNA (hereafter aDNA) has been used to create new narratives about the movement and mixtures of peoples during the Neolithic at varying scales (Furholt 2021). A well-founded concern is that prehistory is being hastily rewritten as a deep history of mass migrations, with 'pots' and 'people' inextricably linked together, as was the case in the heyday of culture-historical archaeology (Heyd 2017). Some aDNA studies have nonetheless begun to explore more detailed relationships at the smaller scale of particular contexts, such as individual graves and cemeteries (for Neolithic Anatolia and south-east Europe, see for example, de Becdelièvre *et al.* 2020; Yaka *et al.* 2021; Brami *et al.* 2022). Here we illustrate how aDNA can be used at the individual site level, together with the archaeology, to generate new ideas and promote new dialogues about a region of enormous importance for our understanding of the European Neolithic.

Lepenski Vir is widely examined as part of the Iron Gates Mesolithic–Neolithic transition but has also received an unusual amount of attention as an individual settlement site (see Borić 2016; Bonsall and Boroneanţ 2018 for recent overviews of the archaeological record). It is currently the only site in inland Europe with credible support for an *in situ* transition from Mesolithic to Neolithic lifeways (Shennan 2018). Elsewhere, agriculture and related innovations, such as pottery and early village societies, are thought to have been introduced fully-fledged by migrant farmers, who derived almost all of their ancestry from populations established in Anatolia and the Aegean basin (hereafter described as 'Aegeans') since at least the 7th millennium cal BC (Hofmanová *et al.* 2016; Kılınç *et al.* 2016; Mathieson *et al.* 2018; Feldman *et al.* 2019; Marchi *et al.* 2022). Evidence for interaction between farmers and foragers during the early Neolithic period in inland Europe is similarly limited to a handful of sites, which show either a tiny Mesolithic contribution to the local Neolithic gene pool (Lipson *et al.* 2017; Mathieson *et al.* 2018; Nikitin *et al.* 2019) or intriguing patterns of parallel occupation without an outright shift in food production (Bollongino *et al.* 2013).

Long viewed as an atypical Mesolithic site, Lepenski Vir has, in recent years, produced compelling evidence for genetic and cultural interactions between foragers and Aegean first farmers (Hofmanová 2017; Mathieson *et al.* 2018; Borić 2019; Hofmanová *et al.* 2022; Marchi *et al.* 2022). To date, patterns of hybridity observed at the site have been primarily explained as Neolithic women marrying into a Mesolithic group (Borić and Price 2013), a scenario that does not sit well with the genetic evidence (Brami *et al.* 2022; Hofmanová *et al.* 2022). This article revisits evidence for interaction between early farmers and foragers in the Iron Gates, during the so-called 'Mesolithic–Neolithic transition' phase of Lepenski Vir, demonstrating how aDNA alters the interpretation of these interactions to a far greater extent than currently accepted in the literature.

NEOLITHIC DISPERSALS AND THE IRON GATES MESOLITHIC

Ever since Gordon Childe's *Danube in Prehistory* (Childe 1929), the Neolithic expansion in inland Europe has been primarily regarded as a 'riverine' phenomenon (Whittle and Bickle 2014 and references therein). The distribution of the first farming communities in southeast Europe generally follows fertile river valleys and watercourses, the Danube being the most significant European highway. Given their geographical situation, the Iron Gates – referring to the 134 km-long stretch of the Danube that connects the central European Pannonian basin with the Wallachian steppes, today's border between Serbia and Romania – appear to have been an important gateway for farming dispersals (Fig. 7.1). Lined by high mountains on both sides, there was limited hinterland for cereal agriculture and the main way through the gorge was via the river.

A remarkable Mesolithic/Neolithic phenomenon flourished in this environment, with over 450 burials containing the remains of over 700 individuals recovered at over 50 caves and open-air sites, including Lepenski Vir, Padina, Schela Cladovei and Vlasac (Bonsall and Boroneanţ 2018). Iron Gates foraging communities appear to have taken advantage of seasonal fish migrations from the Black Sea to settle down, on a semi-permanent basis, on the banks of the river, from *c.* 7600 cal BC onwards (Bonsall 2008). Stable isotope studies conducted since the mid-1990s on skeletons from the Iron Gates indicate a shift from aquatic to mixed aquatic/terrestrial (plant- or animal-based) food webs in some humans buried at Lepenski Vir and other Iron Gates sites starting *c.* 6200 cal BC (Bonsall *et al.* 1997).

The early change in human isotopic signatures is puzzling, given the absence of domesticates in the Iron Gates before *c.* 5900 cal BC (sheep/goat, cattle and pig) (Borić and Dimitrijević 2007). While isotopic changes may simply reflect different foraging practices, the most parsimonious explanation for this shift is that individuals with a terrestrial diet were raised as farmers outside the gorge, as indicated by their 'non-local' strontium isotope signature (Borić and Price 2013). Alternatively, cereals could have been obtained from communities outside the gorge. Small-scale plant and/or animal husbandry in the hillsides and adjoining valleys remains theoretically possible.

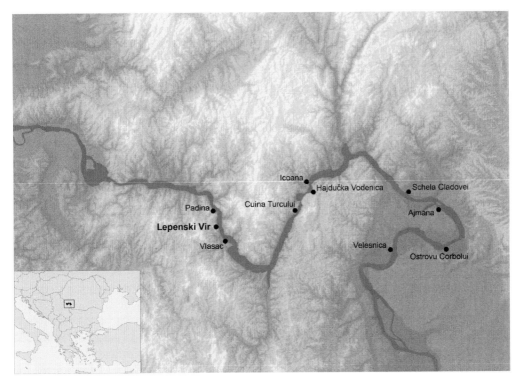

Figure 7.1. Map of the Iron Gates with the location of key Mesolithic and Neolithic sites including Lepenski Vir; topographic map © EuroGeographics.

NEOLITHIC WOMEN JOINING A MESOLITHIC VILLAGE? MODELLING SEX, SOCIETY AND AGRICULTURE AT LEPENSKI VIR

First used as a burial location in the 10th millennium cal BC, Lepenski Vir was re-settled *c*. 6200 cal BC after a hiatus of several hundred years, at the time of the arrival of agriculture in the central Balkans (Krauß *et al.* 2018; Porčić *et al.* 2020). At the peak of occupation, during the 'Mesolithic–Neolithic transition' phase (Borić 2016), *c*. 6200–5900 cal BC, clusters of elaborate houses with trapezoidal red limestone floors were built according to an apparently predetermined plan on the banks of the Danube and lower terraces of the Koršo mountain. Adults, children and neonates were buried both inside and outside these houses, often in extended supine position, as described by Dušan Borić (2016) in his *Deathways at Lepenski Vir*. Spectacular stone carvings in the form of human heads with fish-like features found deposited on floors of abandoned houses date to this period.

While few today would describe the Mesolithic–Neolithic transition at Lepenski Vir as autochthonous, the assumption remains that the site began life as a Mesolithic fishing village, which later adopted aspects of Neolithic lifeways through interaction with farming communities outside the Iron Gates gorge. A scenario involving Neolithic women marrying into a Mesolithic community was first outlined in 2013, somewhat cautiously, as a way to explain the arrival of isotopically 'non-local' individuals at the site (Borić and Price 2013). The anthropological sexing information on which this premise was based has since been genetically revisited (Hofmanová *et al.* 2022):

> *Of 10 nonlocal individuals [...] at Lepenski Vir, all but one burial [...] are females or possible females. This pattern could be interpreted as suggesting a reciprocal mating network between the Danube Gorges foragers and the earliest farming communities in the surrounding areas (Borić and Price 2013, 3302).*

Following the publication of four genomes from Lepenski Vir in 2018 (Mathieson *et al.* 2018), three of which (two adult females and one child) showed significant Aegean ancestry proportions (>90%), a broader claim was made regarding 'women and material goods' being exchanged and 'trigger[ing] the burst of cultural and symbolic creativity found at Lepenski Vir' (Borić *et al.* 2018, 11).

Although sweeping changes at Lepenski Vir, including the abandonment of the trapezoidal houses, suggest that farmers subsequently dominated (*c.* 5900–5500 cal BC), farmers and foragers are considered to have lived together harmoniously during the transitional period (*c.* 6200–5900 cal BC). Much depends on the interpretation of Lepenski Vir as a settled fishing village welcoming a few non-natives, who were integrated into existing 'patrilocal' mating networks. However, the abrupt construction of the village at Lepenski Vir after a long hiatus, *c.* 6200 cal BC, has long raised questions about the Mesolithic background of the Neolithic occupation (Borić 2007). Although this scenario is compelling, does it withstand detailed scrutiny?

Assuming that Neolithic women joined an established Mesolithic community, and that their arrival initiated the process of Neolithic transition at Lepenski Vir, one would expect the following to be true:

- Predominance of females among incomers (consequently, admixture was sex-biased, *i.e.* predominantly male foragers mated with female farmers)
- Dominance of the forager culture at the site
- Adoption of farming practices by foragers.

MIGRANT FEMALES OR MIGRANT FAMILIES?

Ancient DNA analyses have now offered fresh perspectives on these questions, adding further dimensions that interact with, enrich and unsettle long-standing archaeological interpretations of Lepenski Vir as a Mesolithic village in the process of transition to agriculture. Genomic and mitochondrial sequences from 96 Iron Gates Mesolithic/ Neolithic individuals, including 34 at Lepenski Vir alone, provide unprecedented insights into this region's complex population history, indicating that two populations lived side by side and sporadically admixed at places like Lepenski Vir (González-Fortes *et al.* 2017; Hofmanová 2017; Mathieson *et al.* 2018; Hofmanová *et al.* 2022; Marchi *et al.* 2022).

Local Iron Gates hunter-gatherers (hereafter 'Iron Gates HGs') were joined around 6200 cal BC by people who traced their ancestry back to Anatolia and the Aegean

Basin. Indeed, some of the individuals identified genetically as Aegeans (Lepenski Vir, Burials 82, 122) have produced $\delta^{15}N$ values (respectively 11.2‰ and 9.5‰: Borić and Price 2013; Jovanović *et al.* 2019) that are consistent with a mixed or terrestrial C_3 plant food diet. New research indicates that newcomers were men, women and children born to immigrant parents. Among those individuals that show no admixture with Iron Gates HGs in a two-population qpAdm model (Brami *et al.* 2022), four are genetically male (Lepenski Vir Burials 61, 73, 82, 122) and two are female (Burials 17, 54e).

With regard to the Aegean males, at least one is definitely associated with the Mesolithic–Neolithic transition phase at Lepenski Vir. This is Burial 122, consisting of the stray skull without a mandible of an adolescent (15–18 years old), deposited in between the superimposed floors of trapezoidal houses 47 and 47', at the centre of the settlement (Marchi *et al.* 2022). Burial 61 provides another interesting case. This child, *c.* 8 years old, genetically male, has been reported in the literature as 'admixed', with a Y haplogroup (R1b) hinting at an Iron Gates hunter-gatherer contribution on the male side (Mathieson *et al.* 2018). Yet over 90% of his ancestry derives from the Aegean gene pool. This new evidence suggests that Aegean families settled at Lepenski Vir and raised their children there, occasionally admixing with Iron Gates HGs, who were also buried at the site (Burial 91).

Ancestry proportion estimates on the X chromosome and the autosomes for published Balkan Neolithic individuals indicate no sex-specific patterns (Mathieson *et al.* 2018, 201) and thus do not rule out a near-equal ratio of males and females from hunter-gatherer and farmer populations engaged in mating. At Lepenski Vir, likewise, admixture patterns are not consistent with exclusively Iron Gates HG males mating with Aegean females or exclusively Aegean males with Iron Gates HG females (Brami *et al.* 2022).

LOCAL FISHERFOLK PREFERENTIALLY BURIED AT THE PERIPHERY OF THE VILLAGE?

Lepenski Vir is one of the oldest settlements in inland Europe with elaborate residential architecture and complex sequences of human burials. Almost the entire surface area of the prehistoric site (*c.* 2500 m^2) was excavated from 1965 to 1970 by Dragoslav Srejović, in advance of the construction of the Đerdap I dam, allowing for detailed spatial analysis of the distribution of the burials across the settlement and beyond, in what has been described as a 'cemetery' on the western edge of the village (Srejović 1972, 140–1). Interestingly, Aegean incomers and their descendants, such as those discovered in Burials 122, 54e and 61 (respectively carrying K, J and H haplogroups), were closely associated with sequences of trapezoidal houses. Some Aegeans were also found as disarticulated remains outside or in between houses (Burial 82).

By contrast, individuals genetically closest to Iron Gates HGs (Burials 91, 27a, 27d) were all buried outside the space of habitation in large multi-inhumation pits during the transitional phase (Brami *et al.* 2022). These stacked burials, located just outside the horseshoe-shaped settlement 'shelf' identified by Srejović (1972), mainly in the upper terrace overlooking the site, have long been identified as an unusual feature of the Lepenski Vir occupation (see Radovanović 2000; Borić 2016). Borić (2016, 189–200), who devotes a separate section of his book to 'primary burials outside of trapezoidal buildings and in pits', described these features as 'point[ing] to a preference for peripheral parts of the settlement [… I]n three locations successive burials were recorded in the same place, with significant damage made to older primary inhumations through the interment of new burials or practices of secondary exhumation and manipulation of skeletal elements from primary burials'.

Mitochondrial information available for 20 individuals from the transitional phase indicates that those carrying U5 haplogroups were, with one exception, all buried some distance away from trapezoidal houses in the upslope area at the rear of the village (Fig. 7.2). U5 is generally seen as a marker for European hunter-gatherers before the arrival of the first farmers (Bramanti *et al.* 2009). Indeed, only one of 96 individuals from Anatolia and the Aegean Basin (*c.* 9500–5500 cal BC) has produced a U5 mitochondrial haplogroup (Brami *et al.* 2022, Electronic Supplementary Material), whereas most European hunter-gatherers belong to the U5 clade (Lazaridis *et al.* 2014).

In the same period, Aegean incomers and Iron Gates HGs thus appear to have buried their dead largely separately, suggesting differences in status between the two groups or cultural practices linked to ethnic identity. Intriguingly, some of the incomers (Burials 54e, 61) were buried like the locals in extended supine position parallel to the Danube with the head pointing downstream (Borić 2016). Distinctive burial practices between the two groups thus do not perfectly match the genetic evidence. This 'mosaic' pattern in burial traditions (de Becdelièvre *et al.* 2020), which could be described as syncretic behaviour, may not necessarily indicate assimilation of Aegeans into a 'dominant' Mesolithic society (*contra* Borić 2019, 43). Cultural hybridity rarely reflects a single identity (Hayden 2002, 215). Competitive interactions between the two groups are just as likely to have led to elements of the Mesolithic culture being adopted and transformed by Neolithic incomers. The latter did not merely introduce agriculture at Lepenski Vir but also appear to be the main inhabitants of the settlement with houses. Later in the sequence, *c.* 5900 cal BC, all burials were in contracted position on one side, as was customary among early Neolithic societies in Anatolia and south-east Europe (Brami 2017).

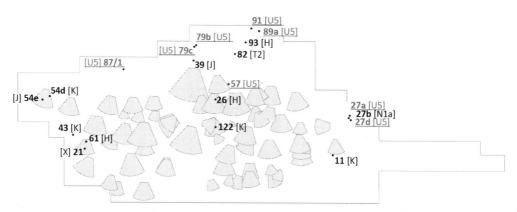

Figure 7.2. Spatial distribution of previously reported Lepenski Vir burials sampled for aDNA analysis during the Mesolithic–Neolithic transition phase (c. 6200–5900 cal BC). Trapezoidal house floors are indicated. Most of the individuals with a U5 mitochondrial haplogroup, i.e. typical of European hunter-gatherers, are buried outside the space of habitation in large multi-inhumation pits.

FARMERS ADOPTING FORAGING PRACTICES, BUT FORAGERS NOT BECOMING FARMERS?

With regard to subsistence, there is evidence of adaptation to the Iron Gates environment. Despite Lepenski Vir's location by the Danube, one of the main corridors of Neolithic expansion in Europe, the site never truly featured a Neolithic, *i.e.* food-producing, economy, due to the availability of fish as a perennial source of food and the lack of hinterland for cereal agriculture. Evidence for animal domesticates is similarly limited, found only during the latest phase of occupation at the site (Bökönyi 1970). Individuals with lower $\delta^{15}N$ values, who resemble farmers isotopically, either grew up elsewhere or acquired crops from farming communities outside the Iron Gates gorge and raised their children as fisherfolk (de Becdelièvre *et al.* 2020). Hence, for instance, the elevated $\delta^{15}N$ values observed in Burial 61 ($\delta^{15}N=16.1‰$), an Aegean child, genetically male, who interestingly was buried at the rear of House 40, underneath a fish statue known as 'Sirena' (Bonsall *et al.* 2008).

The picture is remarkably one-sided. Individuals assigned to the U clade, who presumably descended from Iron Gates hunter-gatherer populations (or at least had hunter-gatherer or admixed mothers), all show elevated $\delta^{15}N$ isotopic signatures consistent with fishing activities (Fig. 7.3). Thus, the onus was on farmers to adopt foraging practices

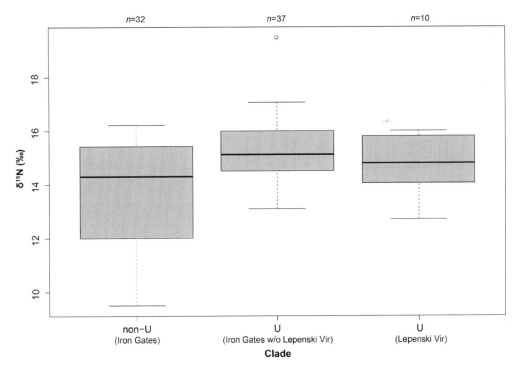

Figure 7.3. Distribution of median $\delta^{15}N$ values for Iron Gates individuals assigned to U and non-U mitochondrial clades. Any $\delta^{15}N$ value above 10‰ is likely to indicate some intake of aquatic proteins. Individuals from Lepenski Vir carrying a U haplogroup show no major shift to a terrestrial diet. See de Becdelièvre et al. (2020, fig. 2.5) for a fuller overview of the stable isotopic evidence in relation to mitochondrial haplogroups.

(de Becdelièvre *et al.* 2020), rather than the opposite. Assimilation of farmers into a foraging community is still a distinct possibility, but the conservativeness of Iron Gates HGs, who showed no inclination to relinquish their mode of subsistence and practices, speaks against a local transition to agriculture. Archaeology's reliance on indirect proxies, such as burial practices and material culture to determine 'identity' (*e.g.*, Chapman 2020), may obscure the more clear-cut economic and demographic processes observed with aDNA and stable isotope data.

In sum, the case for foragers becoming farmers at Lepenski Vir is thin if not absent. It is not even clear that those descended from Iron Gates HGs lived in the trapezoidal houses or had access to cereal plant-food – the only forager who seemingly changed diet during his lifetime (Burial 7/I-a) remains unsequenced (Bonsall and Boroneanţ 2018, 274).

DISCUSSION AND OUTLOOK

Although the expansion of the 'Neolithic' across continental Europe may seem obvious, we have barely begun to consider how Neolithic communities expanded at a local level. Such an expansion must have entailed setting up new permanent settlements within the territories of established hunter-gatherer groups, and finding ways to manage this encroachment successfully. Not only were the inhabitants of Lepenski Vir joined by a few incomers from the Aegean basin, as reported in the literature (Borić and Price 2013; Borić 2019), but these new people were also relatively numerous from the start of the transitional phase when elaborate trapezoidal houses were constructed (*c.* 6200–5900 cal BC).

We find no evidence of strict patrilocal residence practices at Lepenski Vir, or at least can reject a scenario in which only Neolithic women married into a Mesolithic group. This argument is based on few but significant observations, such as the almost equal representation of males and females with an Aegean background in our samples, as well as the presence of young children (Burial 61), who show no or limited admixture with Iron Gates HGs and must therefore be born to immigrant parents – suggesting relocation of entire Aegean families to the site (Brami *et al.* 2022). Some of the genetically identified newcomers were buried inside early trapezoidal houses, which may therefore have been their homes. Iron Gates HGs, on the other hand, appear to have been preferentially buried at the periphery of the village, in the rear upslope area, with limited access to terrestrial food resources, possibly cereals. At present, there is no conclusive evidence of their becoming farmers, and their participation as community members (of the village with houses) remains uncertain. Due caution is needed owing to limited sample size.

Our results highlight the dangers of relying on type sites such as Lepenski Vir to understand the transition from Mesolithic to Neolithic economies in south-east Europe. If the forager culture appears to be ubiquitous at Lepenski Vir, it was because incoming Aegean farmers adjusted their subsistence to the local environment, and adopted practices and aspects of traditions that were encountered locally. The fact that Iron Gates HGs maintained separate habitation, burial and dietary practices at the site speaks against a local adoption of agriculture. We might speculate that Lepenski Vir served as a staging post or gateway community controlling access through the Iron Gates gorge. Dragoslav Srejović, in his original description of the site, imagined Lepenski Vir to have centred around a 'marketplace' (Srejović 1974, 366). Latest aDNA and stable isotope results confirm that the site was an important place for cultural and biological interactions right at the outset of agricultural expansion in a frontier region.

Ancient DNA research cannot provide final 'answers' to questions about the past, specifically the Mesolithic–Neolithic transition in the Iron Gates. It uses new techniques and approaches (direct biomarkers of mobility and migration) to approach questions that have traditionally been answered archaeologically. These new techniques may seem invasive and alien, unsettling and intruding on long-standing archaeological interpretations and discussions. However, in our search to understand the past, they offer important new tools and perspectives.

ACKNOWLEDGEMENTS

We are grateful to Katie Meheux for helpful suggestions on an earlier version of this manuscript. Maxime Brami was supported by an Individual Fellowship from the H2020 Marie Skłodowska-Curie Actions (793893).

REFERENCES

Bökönyi, S. 1970. Animal remains from Lepenski vir. *Science* 167(3926), 1702–4.

Bollongino, R., Nehlich, O., Richards, M.P., Orschiedt, J., Thomas, M.G., Sell, C., Fajkosová, Z., Powell, A. and Burger, J. 2013. 2000 years of parallel societies in Stone Age central Europe. *Science* 342(6157), 479–81.

Bonsall, C. 2008. The Mesolithic of the Iron Gates. In G. Bailey and P. Spikins (eds), *Mesolithic Europe*, 238–79. Cambridge: Cambridge University Press.

Bonsall, C. and Boroneanţ, A. 2018. The Iron Gates Mesolithic – a brief review of recent developments. *L'Anthropologie* 122, 264–80.

Bonsall, C., Lennon, R., McSweeney, K., Stewart, C., Harkness, D., Boroneanţ, V., Bartosiewicz, L., Payton, R. and Chapman, J. 1997. Mesolithic and early Neolithic in the Iron Gates: a palaeodietary perspective. *Journal of European Archaeology* 5, 50–92.

Bonsall, C., Radovanović, I., Roksandic, M., Cook, G., Higham, T. and Pickard, C. 2008. Dating burial practices and architecture at Lepenski Vir. In C. Bonsall, V. Boroneanţ and I. Radovanović (eds), *The Iron Gates in prehistory: new perspectives*, 175–204. Oxford: Archaeopress.

Borić, D. 2007. Mesolithic-Neolithic interactions in the Danube Gorges. In J.K. Kozłowski and M. Nowak (eds), *Mesolithic-Neolithic interactions in the Balkans and in the Middle Danube Basin*, 31–45. Oxford: Archaeopress.

Borić, D. 2016. *Deathways at Lepenski Vir: patterns in mortuary practice*. Belgrade: Serbian Archaeological Society.

Borić, D. 2019. Lepenski Vir chronology and stratigraphy revisited. *Starinar* 69, 9–60.

Borić, D. and Dimitrijević, V. 2007. When did the 'Neolithic package' reach Lepenski Vir? Radiometric and faunal evidence. *Documenta Praehistorica* 34, 53–71.

Borić, D., French, C. and Dimitrijević, V. 2008. Vlasac revisited: formation processes, stratigraphy and dating. *Documenta Praehistorica* 35, 261–87.

Borić, D., Higham, T., Cristiani, E., Dimitrijević, V., Nehlich, O., Griffiths, S., Alexander, C., Mihailović, B., Filipović, D., Allué, E. and Buckley, M. 2018. High-resolution AMS dating of architecture, boulder artworks and the transition to farming at Lepenski Vir. *Scientific Reports* 8, 14221.

Borić, D. and Price, T.D. 2013. Strontium isotopes document greater human mobility at the start of the Balkan Neolithic. *Proceedings of the National Academy of Sciences of the United States of America* 110(9), 3298–303.

Bramanti, B., Thomas, M.G., Haak, W., Unterlaender, M., Jores, P., Tambets, K. *et al.* 2009. Genetic discontinuity between local hunter-gatherers and central Europe's first farmers. *Science* 326(5949), 137–40.

Brami, M.N. 2017. *The diffusion of Neolithic practices from Anatolia to Europe: a contextual study of residential construction, 8,500–5,500 BC cal.* Oxford: British Archaeological Reports.

Brami, M., Winkelbach, L., Schulz, I., Schreiber, M., Blöcher, J., Diekmann, Y. and Burger, J. 2022. Was fishing village of Lepenski Vir built by Europe's first farmers? *Journal of World Prehistory* 35, 109–33.

Chapman, J. 2020. *Forging identities in the prehistory of Old Europe: dividuals, individuals and communities, 7000–3000 BC.* Leiden: Sidestone Press.

Childe, V.G. 1929. *The Danube in prehistory.* Oxford: Clarendon Press.

de Becdelièvre, C., Jovanović, J., Hofmanová, Z., Goude, G. and Stefanović, S. 2020. Direct insight into dietary adaptations and the individual experience of Neolithisation: comparing subsistence, provenance and ancestry of Early Neolithic humans from the Danube Gorges c. 6200–5500 cal BC. In K.J. Gron, L. Sørensen and P. Rowley-Conwy (eds), *Farmers at the frontier: a pan-European perspective on Neolithisation*, 45–75. Oxford: Oxbow Books.

Feldman, M., Fernández-Domínguez, E., Reynolds, L., Baird, D., Pearson, J., Hershkovitz, I. *et al.* 2019. Late Pleistocene human genome suggests a local origin for the first farmers of Central Anatolia. *Nature Communications* 10(1), 1218.

Furholt, M. 2021. Mobility and social change: understanding the European Neolithic period after the archaeogenetic revolution. *Journal of Archaeological Research* 29, 481–535.

González-Fortes, G., Jones, E.R., Lightfoot, E., Bonsall, C., Lazăr, C., Grandal-d'Anglade, A. *et al.* 2017. Paleogenomic evidence for multi-generational mixing between Neolithic farmers and Mesolithic hunter-gatherers in the Lower Danube Basin. *Current Biology* 27(12), 1801–1810.e10.

Heyd, V. 2017. Kossinna's smile. *Antiquity* 91, 348–59.

Hofmanová, Z. 2017. *Palaeogenomic and biostatistical analysis of ancient DNA data from Mesolithic and Neolithic skeletal remains.* Doctoral dissertation, Johannes Gutenberg University Mainz. https://d-nb.info/113609640X/34.

Hofmanová, Z., Kreutzer, S., Hellenthal, G., Sell, C., Diekmann, Y., Díez-Del-Molino, D. *et al.* 2016. Early farmers from across Europe directly descended from Neolithic Aegeans. *Proceedings of the National Academy of Sciences of the United States of America* 113(25), 6886–91.

Hofmanová, Z., Reyna-Blanco, C.S., de Becdelièvre, C., Schulz, I., Blöcher, J., Jovanović, J. *et al.* 2022. Between fishing and farming: palaeogenomic analyses reveal cross-cultural interactions triggered by the arrival of the Neolithic in the Danube Gorges. *BioRxiv.* https://doi.org/10.1101/2022.06.24.497512.

Jovanović, J., de Becdelièvre, C., Stefanović, S., Živaljević, I., Dimitrijević, V. and Goude, G. 2019. Last hunters–first farmers: new insight into subsistence strategies in the Central Balkans through multi-isotopic analysis. *Archaeological and Anthropological Sciences* 11(7), 3279–98.

Kılınç, G.M., Omrak, A., Özer, F., Günther, T., Büyükkarakaya, A.M., Bıçakçı, E. *et al.* 2016. The demographic development of the first farmers in Anatolia. *Current Biology: CB* 26(19), 2659–66.

Krauß, R., Marinova, E., De Brue, H. and Weninger, B. 2018. The rapid spread of early farming from the Aegean into the Balkans via the Sub-Mediterranean-Aegean Vegetation Zone. *Quaternary International* 496, 24–41.

Lazaridis, I., Patterson, N., Mittnik, A., Renaud, G., Mallick, S., Kirsanow, K. *et al.* 2014. Ancient human genomes suggest three ancestral populations for present-day Europeans. *Nature* 513, 409–13.

Lipson, M., Szécsényi-Nagy, A., Mallick, S., Pósa, A., Stégmár, B., Keerl, V. *et al.* 2017. Parallel palaeogenomic transects reveal complex genetic history of early European farmers. *Nature* 551, 368–72.

Marchi, N., Winkelbach, L., Schulz, I., Brami, M., Hofmanová, Z., Blöcher, J. *et al.* 2022. The genomic origins of the world's first farmers. *Cell.* https://doi.org/10.1016/j.cell.2022.04.008.

Mathieson, I., Alpaslan-Roodenberg, S., Posth, C., Szécsényi-Nagy, A., Rohland, N., Mallick, S. *et al.* 2018. The genomic history of southeastern Europe. *Nature 555*, 197–203.

Nandris, J.G. 1988. The earliest European plaster pyrotechnology: the red floors of Lepenski Vir. *Rivista Di Archeologia* 12, 14–15.

Nikitin, A.G., Stadler, P., Kotova, N., Teschler-Nicola, M., Price, T.D., Hoover, J., Kennett, D. J., Lazaridis, I., Rohland, N., Lipson, M. and Reich, D. 2019. Interactions between earliest Linearbandkeramik farmers and central European hunter gatherers at the dawn of European Neolithization. *Scientific Reports* 9(1), 19544.

Porčić, M., Blagojević, T., Pendić, J. and Stefanović, S. 2020. The Neolithic Demographic Transition in the central Balkans: population dynamics reconstruction based on new radiocarbon evidence. *Philosophical Transactions of the Royal Society of London. Series B, Biological Sciences.* https://doi.org/10.1098/rstb.2019.0712.

Radovanović, I. 2000. Houses and burials at Lepenski Vir. *European Journal of Archaeology* 3, 330–49.

Shennan, S. 2018. *The first farmers of Europe: an evolutionary perspective.* Cambridge: Cambridge University Press.

Srejović, D. 1972. *Europe's first monumental sculpture: Lepenski Vir.* London: Thames and Hudson.

Srejović, D. 1974. Lepenski Vir, Yugoslavia: the first planned settlement in Europe. *Ekistics: Reviews on the Problems and Science of Human Settlements* 38(228), 364–7.

Whittle, A. and Bickle, P. (eds) 2014. *Early farmers: the view from archaeology and science.* Oxford: The British Academy.

Yaka, R., Mapelli, I., Kaptan, D., Doğu, A., Chyleński, M., Erdal, Ö.D. *et al.* 2021. Variable kinship patterns in Neolithic Anatolia revealed by ancient genomes. *Current Biology* 31(11), 2455–2468.e18.

Chapter 8

A glance at early Neolithic south-east and central Europe – as reflected by archaeological and archaeogenetic data

Eszter Bánffy

Focusing on Early Neolithic continental Europe, I present new archaeological results in comparison to similarly recent ancient DNA and stable isotope studies. I address various scenarios from one region in the Balkans and another in northern Germany, before zooming in on the eastern and western parts of the Carpathian basin: the last region with direct Balkan migrant groups and the first region with a growing local contribution as well as genetic influx. These examples show that there are possibilities to reconcile aDNA data with the archaeological record, as well as some contradictions, but above all they highlight the extremely high diversity of the Neolithic transition.

INTRODUCTION

I am going to attempt to give a brief sketch for the continental European Neolithic of how archaeological and archaeogenetic data relate to each other. I choose to focus on the beginnings: the Neolithic transition and the first few centuries of food-productive, sedentary life. With the examples selected, I aim to show that neither the thesis of a 'wave of advance' (Ammerman and Cavalli-Sforza 1984) nor a clear-cut dichotomy (as suggested by many authors) between hunter-gatherer and farmer existence can be supported.

As has become clear, the 'DNA revolution' and sister methods within molecular bioarchaeology are pivotal in the history of archaeology, brilliant tools that give us formerly unthinkable aspects to study, and indeed insights of which Neolithic population groups themselves may have not been aware at all. Their genetic ancestry alone would not have basically influenced their personhood and group identity. Yet genomic composition, Sr, N or O isotope results or oral microbiomes could have – sometimes more directly, sometimes in quite a hidden way – an influence on the cultural and social character of communities. Shared ancestry might go with similar subsistence strategies, leading for example to similar oral microbiomes or cultural traits. These chosen identities might, over time, also lead to marriage ties within a given group. Thus, the picture from such data and analyses needs to be compared with archaeological evidence for material culture, landscape choice, settlement pattern and importantly, contact and exchange networks; networks are especially important to compare with bioarchaeological patterns.

It is now a fact that periods like the Neolithic transition and the early Neolithic are firmly bound up with migration. Yet there is a major *caveat*. While comparing archaeological and aDNA data, it is important to do so without falling into the trap of previous cultural-historical migration theories. Neolithic archaeological and bioarchaeological patterns were arguably fluid, constantly shaping and re-shaping; this perspective is the main difference between 21st-century trajectories and earlier, static, migrationist theories (Furholt 2017; Frieman and Hofmann 2019).

First, we need to note the importance of terms such as 'the Neolithic transition' or 'the Neolithic lifestyle'. The advent of the Neolithic in Europe, as elsewhere globally, marked a profound transformation in human history, a major historical turn with many facets, but all with similar outcomes: a sedentary and food-producing Europe. Research on the archaeology of the European Neolithic transition is still rather split; it either consists of individual case studies (a bottom-up approach) or tries to find a generalising explanation for the whole historical process, assuming a fairly uniform transformation. Bioarchaeological data, if used cautiously, have the potential to cause a step-change here.

Most probably, for a range of different reasons, domestication of cereals and animals began at several distinct spots in between the Levant and the Zagros, in the 11th–9th millennia cal BC. The food-producing lifestyle spread soon towards Anatolia. To the best of our present knowledge, the process of Neolithisation was neither an 'invention', nor a single 'innovation', but rather a slowly emerging phenomenon moulded by the consequences (or side-effects) of meaningful choices of social practices, experimenting with domestication and the impact of all these in the cognitive sphere of communities. The pace of changes accelerated towards the last centuries of the transition (Watkins 2018). People's choices must have been influenced by climate change and demographic booms and busts, and motivated by risk-taking and exploiting opportunities, as well as perhaps the desire for higher prestige and other ideologies. (Better said, the process probably involved a combination of these elements.) Due to the sometimes patchy, mosaic-like and often highly diverse local variants of the transition, only a few common, ubiquitous traits of Neolithisation can be identified. Yet, ultimately, the changes proved to be irreversible (Robb 2013).

Outside of the primary, Near Eastern area, the Neolithisation process was also dependent on two factors: migrants arriving, and the choices of local foragers to adapt or refuse (or a blend of these). While it has long been clear that farming as a system was brought to Europe from outside, a dichotomy of migration versus adaptation has accompanied research on the Neolithic transition. Studying different find types also causes divergent views on the migration-adaptation dichotomy; arguments for migration in the culture-historical tradition were mainly based on pottery-making that spread from the south-east – while lithic experts were advocates of autochthonous development, due to local sources and continuing flint-knapping traditions. Evidence for population growth immediately following the introduction of the Neolithic into the Balkans also suggests migration (Bocquet-Appel *et al.* 2012). In the beginning, the 'revolutionary' molecular biological analyses put the Neolithic transition in the spotlight; now, a series of new results, coming from novel methods, need to be reconciled with the aforementioned traditional archaeological evidence.

I shall start with a case study from south-east Europe, from the Balkan-Danubian route of the spread of farming, which has a scant Mesolithic presence. My next case study is the Polish and German Plain, with a belated and longer-lasting turn and masses of surviving and flourishing forager communities. Then, I shall focus on the Carpathian basin, the region which seems to be the decisive zone where the ratio of migrants from the Balkans and cooperating local foragers turned. The new formation born here, the Linear Pottery culture (LBK), spread rapidly to large parts of continental Europe in the second half of the 6th millennium cal BC. The LBK helped to define the 5th millennium and had a strong impact until the advent of the 4th millennium; thus, there are ties with the first farming groups arriving in south-east Britain around that time. I shall try to highlight various processes that made the Neolithic lifestyle irreversible in the end, but above all, I would like to give some thoughts about people, encounters and mobility.

Farming was first introduced to south-east Europe in the mid-7th millennium cal BC and was associated with migrants arriving ultimately from Anatolia. Mathieson *et al.* (2018) have shown that the first farmers dispersed with limited hunter-gatherer admixture, yet some of their early groups were exceptions. This patchy, sporadic genetic mixture in the Balkans becomes more and more frequent and intensive, going northwards.

THE BALKANS

My first case study involves regions where the sporadic Mesolithic presence can surely not be ascribed to gaps in research (Fig. 8.1). It seems that there may have been some 'niches' with more concentrated settlement; apart from the Aegean, there are concentrations in the Trieste karstic regions with many caves, a similar landscape in Montenegro, and certainly, the most researched and well-known region, the Danube Gorges along both its Serbian and Romanian banks. There seems to be a sparsely occupied region in the central Balkans that became one of the centres of the first farmers upon their arrival.

From all these settlement concentrations, recent genetic and stable isotope analyses surprisingly show that the difference between the stereotypes of mobile hunters and foragers versus sedentary farmers in fact becomes blurred. Taking landscape use and archaeological remains, strontium isotope analyses for the mobility of humans and domesticated animals together, they all speak for more sedentary hunter-gatherers and more mobile first farmers than previously acknowledged (Borić and Price 2013; Price 2021).

Evidence from the Vrbička cave and at Crvena Stijena (Borić *et al.* 2021) and also from the lowland Kula site (Živaljević *et al.* 2017; 2021) shows that diachronic changes in food resource exploitation were determined by the character of the landscape and soil offering food resources, rather than the nature of the site being 'Mesolithic' or 'Neolithic'. That is, Kula lies in an open landscape that proved to be more suitable for animal husbandry and it continued to be in use also, most likely due to its long-term importance, as a fishing spot in the Early Neolithic. Similarly, at Danube Gorges sites, the diet remains largely based on the consumption of aquatic resources both before and after the Mesolithic–Neolithic transition. This was probably a result of favourable environmental conditions for such

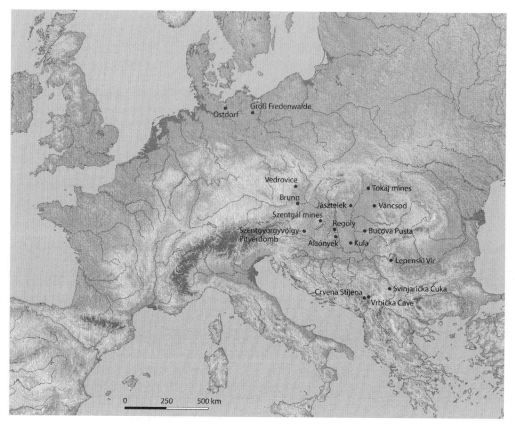

Figure 8.1. The main sites mentioned in the text (source: author and RGK: Oliver Wagner).

resources, but also of dietary practices inherited from earlier Mesolithic communities. A recent study shows that the incomer farmer ancestry became dominant over the native Mesolithic ancestry by the early 6th millennium cal BC (Brami *et al.* 2022).

From food perspectives, it seems that ecological conditions, local traditions and economic innovations interacted in various ways to shape the complex and multi-faceted Neolithisation process. DNA found in archaeological dental calculus proves that the introduction of farming in southern Europe did not significantly alter the oral microbiomes of local forager groups; thus, the basic food sources may not have undergone major changes (Ottoni *et al.* 2021). The macrobotanical analysis came to a similar conclusion. It appears that more or less the same 'set' of taxa were consistently in use through the Late Mesolithic and Early Neolithic, suggesting an unchanged availability of the (local) resources, as well as continuity of the 'gathering aspect' of subsistence strategy over a period of more than a thousand years (Marinova *et al.* 2013).

In the central Balkans, the next small insight is a genuine migrant farmers' settlement, along the river Morava. In the extended, classical and late Starčevo site of Svinjarička Čuka, the remains of buildings with upright walls were found. The site is rich in pottery, lithics and other finds, and yet it cannot be stated that its people were fully sedentary (Horejs *et al.* 2019). While all kinds of cereals and domesticated animals were attested, larger amounts of wild-gathered plants and bones of hunted game were also present. The recent scrutiny of comparative and multidisciplinary analyses should shed light on stages of 'becoming sedentary', at around 5600 cal BC.

Approaching the northern frontiers of the Balkans, a stark wave of intruding early farmers into the Carpathian basin and introducing the full Neolithic would be expected. Yet Körös sites in the Serbian Banat like Bucova Puszta show a different picture. Here rather we find nutrition strategies adapted to the riverine environment: an overwhelmingly 'Mesolithic' aquatic diet, at least as based on the remains of a child from the late Körös phase (*c.* 5600 cal BC). Were the inhabitants adaptable hunter-gatherers keeping some domesticates but basically sticking with their old traditions? Based on the full Körös context, they might rather be first farmers adapting to local circumstances (Krauß *et al.* 2018).

THE NORTH GERMAN PLAIN

A brief look at the other side of continental Europe offers a different picture. The transition not only takes place almost two millennia later, but the further north we look, the more visible the local foragers' participation becomes. In the north, skeletons even amidst Neolithic contexts are often genetically heterogeneous, having both Neolithic and local forager ancestry. Such sites are often to be found in the late 5th and early 4th millennium cal BC, in the Michelsberg environment in the west and in the latest Ertebølle and early Funnel Beaker orbits in the east, in the northern lowlands.

The Funnel Beaker groups evolved out of coastal fishing communities at the time when the various regional post-LBK groups declined. We can rather speak about taking over specific elements of the Neolithic within still foraging economies. In the genetic mixture there are no leading rules, and the patterns show extremely strong regional variations (Bramanti *et al.* 2009).

At several sites between the end of the LBK period and the intensive phases of the later full Neolithic, exchange relations between farmers and foragers become detectable, and also, the regional continuity of hunter-gatherer subsistence as far as the advent of the Bronze Age. It remains still open, to what extent 'encapsulated' hunter-gatherer groups or central and western Neolithic groups with already mixed Anatolian and hunter-gatherer ancestry are most typical (Allentoft *et al.* 2022; Cummings *et al.* 2022, 5). However, the northern coastland of Germany is marked by long-lasting settlements of late Mesolithic peoples. The long-lasting exchange between Mesolithic processes and approaches by their southern neighbours, the farming groups, seems to involve tools and food, and probably also innovation, new technologies and information, resulting in a high-level amalgamation. An example for the long separation of groups living next to each other is the cemetery at Ostorf, on a small lake island near the Baltic Sea, with some excellently preserved burials. Many of the graves include hunter-gatherer-fisher grave goods, such as arrow points, fishing hooks and animal tooth pendants, reflecting a hunter-gatherer-fisher population during the Funnel Beaker (TRB) period. Their diet was determined by freshwater food (Lübke *et al.* 2009).

The parallel existence of earliest TRB and Ertebølle becomes also apparent at the cemetery of Groß Fredenwalde on the north-eastern edge of Germany (Terberger *et al.* 2015). After a short-lived early LBK site nearby, there is a long standstill for almost a millennium, with a survival of the mosaic-like tradition of different dietary pathways (4300–4200 cal BC). After 4000 cal BC, along with exclusively agricultural life, the Baltic coastal groups still show an elevated fish consumption (Kotula *et al.* 2020).

In the north German plain, thus, the fading cultural and biological impact from the south combined with the strong and long-lasting fisher and forager lifestyle appear to determine the long-lasting turn to the Neolithic, until the 4th millennium (and even longer further north and east). These pivotal differences in time, tempo and participants between the Balkans and northern central Europe point to the region where the process possibly may have turned.

THE CARPATHIAN BASIN

The third region to zoom in on will be a closer look at late foragers and first farmers in the Carpathian basin: the last region with direct Balkan migrant groups (this connects it with south-east Europe), and the first region with a growing local contribution as well as genetic influx (which grows further towards the north).

The basin is divided into two major zones, both geological and climatic (the so-called central European Balkan agro-ecological barrier), with a warmer and drier southern, and a more Atlantic north-western climate. This 'barrier' is, meanwhile, a contact zone, creating a longer-term permeable frontier between groups in both regions (Bánffy and Sümegi 2012). So, what we see in the early 6th millennium cal BC is a far from simple scenario (Fig. 8.2); the closer one looks, the more patchy the 'wave of advance' increasingly becomes.

The map for the first half of the 6th millennium cal BC (Fig. 8.3) shows why the south-west part of the Carpathian basin is a key area. The newcomers' spread splits into two main branches in the frontier zone: in the east and central basin called Körös culture (or, in Romanian, Criș), and in the west, in Transdanubia, the periphery of the Starčevo culture. While the Körös branch developed locally in the following centuries, the zone in mid-Transdanubia played a crucial role in the formation of the LBK and thus for the first farmers of extended areas across Europe.

In the next phase (Fig. 8.4), a new cultural unit, the LBK, was born in the northern Starčevo margins. Archaeologically, the Starčevo input is clear, but the presence of the Mesolithic groups long remained an open question, only recently starting to be filled with data. Thus, there is still scanty but increasing evidence for Mesolithic habitation (Duffy *et al.* 2022). In the eastern lowland, the Alföld or Great Hungarian Plain, a Mesolithic niche with many sites has been found. A systematic survey near old oxbow channels detected several sites yielding characteristic geometric microlithic scatters. Four of these sites have been excavated (Kertész 1996; Bánffy *et al.* 2007). At Jásztelek, a round hut was found with an entrance at the southern side. Based on lithics, the site must be late Mesolithic, so the

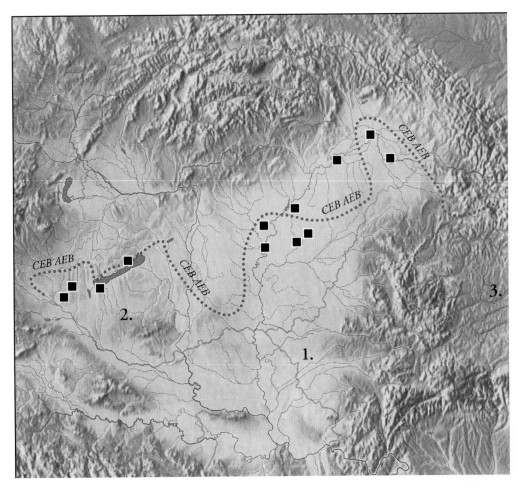

Figure 8.2. The central European Balkan agro-ecological barrier that is a contact zone (source: Bánffy and Sümegi 2012).

foragers here might have lived during the onset of the 6th millennium. This was the time when the first farmers were spreading northwards in the Great Hungarian Plain. Previously, it would have hardly occurred to researchers that these migrants may have had any contact with (rather invisible) late foragers. But the settlement deposit from Váncsod in the northern Körös region, found quite recently, sheds light on two things (Szeverényi and Priskin 2020). First, the inhabitants must have received the information about Tokaj obsidian, far away north from their outreach area, probably from those who had access and control over the obsidian sources in the wooded mountains. Secondly, the Körös groups were used to the Banat flint and other local flint sources in their area of origin. Their interest now turned to the north, towards new possibilities. This eagerness for novel knowledge and networks can be seen as a triggering effect for the Neolithisation process.

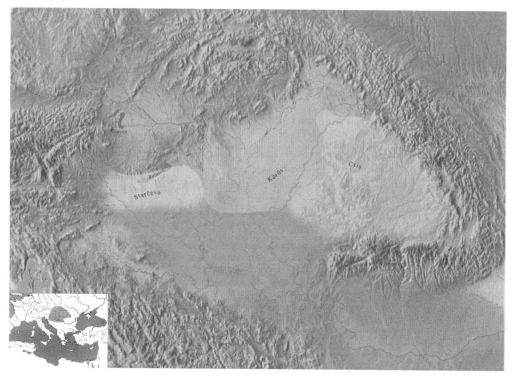

Figure 8.3. Early Neolithic cultural formations in the Carpathian basin: first half of the 6th millennium cal BC (source: author).

The ambition of reaching out further northwards continues after the Körös period. While in its early phase, with settlements exclusively on flat loess landscapes, the early LBK was rather unified in all its habits and materiality, later on many local groups formed, like Tiszadob, Bükk and Szilmeg. These groups occupy the mountains that the LBK people had earlier avoided (Csengeri 2014). The known sites increase and material culture including pottery starts to show foreign features. These are facts long known, but now the question becomes timely, whether it was local forager interactions that could make such an imprint on their place in the landscape and their material finds.

Some years ago, our dataset was significantly extended by the results of a large German-Hungarian project (led by Kurt Alt and the author), with more than 700 skeletons sampled, from the 6th to the 5th millennia cal BC. Thus, the archaeological data could be amplified with the results of both mitochondrial aDNA analyses (Szécsényi-Nagy *et al.* 2015; forthcoming) and autosomal results (Lipson *et al.* 2017). The results show a gradual increase in hunter-gatherer ancestry over time, although these never reach the levels seen, for example, in Middle Neolithic populations in Germany or Iberia. Further, in all three regions we can detect that incidental admixture between farmers and foragers began shortly after initial contact; the sparse Mesolithic population may have a role in the low rate. More intensive hunter-gatherer presence – along the main Balkan route – can only be detected

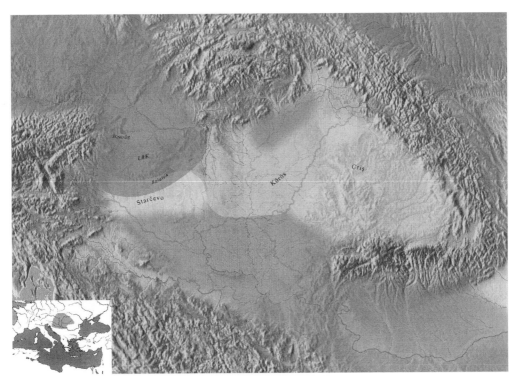

Figure 8.4. Cultural transformations at the transition to the middle Neolithic in the mid-6th millennium cal BC in the Carpathian basin (source: author).

in the Danube Gorges area (Fig. 8.5), and it is also clear that hunter-gatherer ancestry in Neolithic populations increased for at least a thousand years.

The Alföld Körös and LBK groups of the 6th millennium cal BC never expanded beyond the Great Hungarian Plain, differentiating into regional groups instead. Regarding the western part of the Carpathian basin, combined data from sites and off-site coring as well as re-evaluations of old finds preceded the first thorough and planned excavation of a Transdanubian Mesolithic settlement. After having identified a one-time lake that eventually dried but with fishing tools including bone harpoons proving a Mesolithic presence, a large project began in an intensive niche. At one of the settlements, Regöly, a round hut, similar to the one in Jásztelek, was brought to light (Eichmann *et al.* 2010). Postholes were cut into its edge; in the case of the deeper ones, even the inclination angle could be measured. This feature can most certainly be identified as a domestic building.

Similarly to the access to obsidian in the Alföld, here the red radiolarite from Szentgál in the Balaton upland proved to be the main target of exchange. Mesolithic and early Neolithic Starčevo, and subsequently LBK communities, used flints from this source almost exclusively. No matter the lower quality of radiolarite as compared to obsidian, this raw material, as well as completed forms, signalled late Mesolithic contacts between the Carpathian basin and southern Czechia (Mateiciucová 2008), and accompanied the entire

Eszter Bánffy

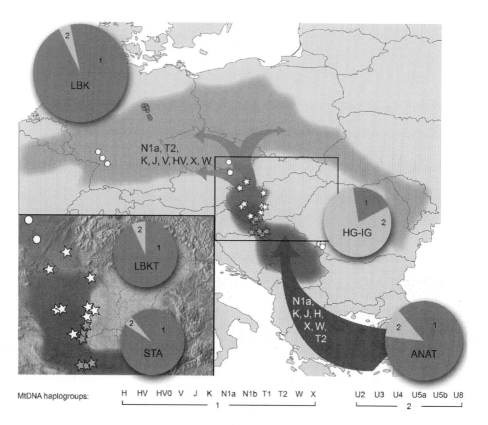

Figure 8.5. Comparison between the main Balkan route and the Danube Gorges, including data from Mathieson et al. *2018 (source: Szécsényi-Nagy* et al. *forthcoming, fig. 19).*

distribution of the LBK groups along the Danube basin and further to the north and west. In western Germany, such Szentgál radiolarite flints have been found with the first farming groups arriving there (Zimmermann 1995).

According to our current data, there must have been an overlapping period between the end of the late Mesolithic and the start of early farming settlement in Transdanubia. This must have been the case in between the many sites found near each other in between the Regöly Mesolithic settlement and the large, first phase of the Alsónyék mega-site. The time of the Starčevo occupation there was precisely dated (Oross *et al.* 2016) but late datable forager skeletons are still lacking. Yet strong indications for coexistence and exchange are provided by the presence of Szentgál flints (controlled by foragers) in Starčevo contexts. The Starčevo genetic ancestry shows the so-called mitochondrial Neolithic package, with minimal local signals (Lipson *et al.* 2017; Szécsényi-Nagy *et al.* forthcoming).

The missing link between Starčevo farmers and locals, who both contributed to the birth of the first central European farming communities, the LBK in the Balaton region and westwards, has been found and excavated in a region that is mostly suitable for fishing and to a limited extent for agriculture. A sudden rise in the water level in the early

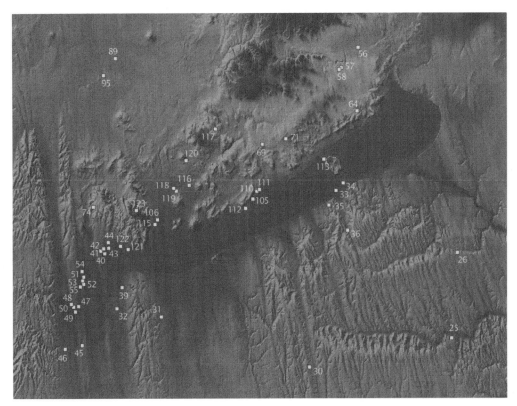

Figure 8.6. Formative LBK sites along one-time lakeshore areas in the Balaton region (source: author).

6th millennium cal BC may have inundated Mesolithic lakeshore settlements (Fig. 8.6), but the Formative LBK sites are located exactly at the edges of the one-time lacustrine areas. The earliest LBK sites thus reflect a clear Mesolithic settlement pattern.

The only fully excavated Formative site to date is Szentgyörgyvölgy-Pityerdomb (Bánffy 2004). The two timber and wattle-and-daub longhouses – as shown elsewhere – may have been invented by late Starčevo communities and were thus brought with the first farmers to the Balaton region (Bánffy and Höhler-Brockmann 2020). The rich assemblages of chipped stone come exclusively from Szentgál, some 200 km away from Pityerdomb and controlled by local foragers. The pottery, constituted by some 14,000 sherds, are of real Starčevo character, yet with many signs speaking for LBK features, including incised linear decorations (Bánffy and Whittle 2022). The new identity shows traces of an amalgamation and joint innovation. The Formative LBK (that is, perhaps the first four to five generations) must have been piecemeal sedentary and based on farming adapted to the wetland. Thus, the input of the local foragers in the settlement pattern, and the subsistence strategies in a non-loess soil context, become visible and traceable.

Intensive contacts including sharing goods and knowledge are often traceable in the material record (Benz 2010, 10), as is the case in Transdanubia. Yet the barely existing local Mesolithic DNA lineages raise the question about the nature of such contacts. Did foragers and farmers network without interbreeding – either by rule or on a voluntary basis? There are examples for separation between neighbouring farming and forager communities, either by mutual disdain of the other lifeways, or through concerns (Nicolaisen 1976). We can also presume that the idea of kinship worked in a special way, such as a combination of primarily social and then increasing biological relatedness. In later generations and in northerly regions the higher scale of local ancestry is apparent; in the LBK populations of the 54th–52nd centuries the Mesolithic U2 and U5a haplotypes reach 15% in north-east Hungary and in northern Transdanubia (Szécsényi-Nagy *et al.* forthcoming, fig. 22).

The higher ratio of mobility in the western, Transdanubian part of the Carpathian basin is also traceable on the basis on Sr isotope analyses (Depaermentier *et al.* 2020; forthcoming). Whilst the first farmers were clearly mobile in the entire Carpathian basin, the early LBK groups only moved from Transdanubia towards modern Austria, southern Czechia and Germany.

To summarise the genetic picture of the Neolithisation process and subsequent centuries, the contrast between locals and the newly arrived farming groups is sharp. Yet, from the beginnings, the small signs of admixture of immigrants with local groups were detectable in the mtDNA haplogroup diversity, which shortly started to rise. There seems to be a delay of some 120 years to reach more than 10% of the local forager proportion in the genetic data. In the Carpathian basin, thus, it seems that the exchange and social contact network preceded interbreeding, but only for a few generations. This growing local signal fits well with the archaeological diversity of later LBK groups.

OUTLOOK

My last focus will follow the first farming groups along the Danube valley. The early phase of the settlement Brunn 2 in eastern Austria, defined by longhouses and Formative LBK pottery, closely resembles Pityerdomb in Transdanubia. Recently, some aspects of the site have been processed and published (Stadler and Kotova 2019), along with a genetic investigation of the earliest skeletons (Nikitin *et al.* 2019). This latter result can also be called an eye-opener, to understand the increasing local genetic input north and westwards of the 'central European Balkan agro-ecological barrier', a phenomenon of growing U haplogroups in the ancestry similar to the situation in neighbouring northern Transdanubia, mentioned above. In Brunn 2, the mixed ancestry between West European hunter-gatherers becomes apparent. Two of the individuals had a mixture of forager-related and Balkan farming-related ancestry, one of them with approximately 50% of each, while the third individual had Neolithic migrant ancestry. Strontium isotope analysis revealed that the individual of roughly half and half forager and farmer descent was non-local to the area. Overall, our data indicate interbreeding between farmers whose ancestors ultimately came from western Anatolia and local foragers. These contacts started within the first few generations after the farmers' arrival, and highlight the integrative nature and mixed composition of the early LBK communities.

Lastly, the settlement of Vedrovice (in the south of the Czech Republic) was founded by a small community of incomers who probably originated in western Hungary towards the end of the Formative phase of the LBK in the 55th century cal BC. Most settlement burials were of immigrant people. Links with western Hungary are evident in the material culture, notably among the ceramic elements, and in the presence of Transdanubian Szentgál radiolarite. Apparently, soon after the settlement was founded, it attracted people from hunting-gathering communities within the region and outside it (Zvelebil and Pettitt 2013). The two groups mingled. The later establishment of the cemetery makes locally born individuals rise to dominance, which resulted in new practices, such as establishing a burial place outside of the settlement.

CONCLUSION

Among many stories, this chapter has shed light on three different ways to the Neolithic transition in continental Europe. I have tried to involve both archaeological and bioarchaeological data; their comparison resulted both in cases of some contradiction and cases where the two kinds of results chime together. Following the time of the transition and the later Neolithic centuries, cultural, economic and genetic contacts happened first probably among locals, then between locals and newcomers. This is a many-coloured garland of unfolding stories, encounters, adaptations and human choices; each of the niches seems different. All reflect on a somewhat hidden aspect of the beginnings of sedentary life that involves one-time living people with personal decisions, contacts and perhaps even networking with neighbouring groups, all played out at the local level.

Finally, I would like to stress that only successful transition processes are detectable for archaeologists and bioarchaeologists, while probably countless experiments that ended in cul-de-sacs were undertaken. Failed attempts, however, are also meaningful, because they are part of the Neolithic transition, and even more so, because we could learn so much from failures when thinking in sustainable lifeways in current times and for the future.

REFERENCES

Allentoft, M.E., Sikora, M., Refoyo-Martinez, A., Irving-Pease, E.K., Fischer, A., Barrie, W. *et al.* 2022. Population genomics of Stone Age Eurasia. *bioRxiv* preprint, 1–71. https://doi.org/10.1101/2022.05.04.490594.

Ammerman, A.J. and Cavalli-Sforza, L.L. 1984. *The Neolithic transition and the genetics of populations in Europe*. Princeton: Princeton University Press.

Bánffy, E. 2004. *The 6th millennium BC boundary in western Transdanubia and its role in the central European transition (The Szentgyörgyvölgy-Pityerdomb settlement)*. Budapest: Institute of Archaeology, Hungarian Academy of Sciences.

Bánffy, E., Eichmann, W.J. and Marton, T. 2007. Mesolithic foragers and the spread of agriculture in western Hungary. In J. Kozłowski and M. Nowak (eds), *Mesolithic-Neolithic interactions in the Balkans and in the Middle Danube basin*, 53–82. Oxford: Archaeopress.

Bánffy, E. and Höhler-Brockmann, H. 2020. Burnt daub talking: the formation of the LBK longhouse (a working hypothesis). *Quaternary International* 560–561, 179–96.

Bánffy, E. and Sümegi, P. 2012. The early neolithic agro-ecological barrier in the Carpathian Basin: a zone for interaction. In P. Anreiter, E. Bánffy, L. Bartosiewicz, W. Meid and C. Metzner-Nebelsick (eds), *Archaeological, cultural and linguistic heritage: Festschrift for Erzsébet Jerem in honour of her 70th birthday*, 57–69. Budapest: Archaeolingua.

Banffy, E. and Whittle, A. 2022. Szentgyörgyvölgy-Pityerdomb and the formative phase of the LBK revisited. In E. Kaiser, M. Meyer, S. Scharl und S. Suhrbier (eds), *Wissensschichten: Festschrift für Wolfram Schier zu seinem 65. Geburtstag*, 145–61. Rahden: Marie Leidorf.

Benz, M. 2010. The principle of sharing – an introduction. In M. Benz (ed.), *The principle of sharing: segregation and construction of social identities at the transition from foraging to farming*, 1–18. Berlin: ex oriente.

Bocquet-Appel, J.-P., Naji, S., Vander Linden, M. and Kozłowski, J. 2012. Understanding the rates of expansion of the farming system in Europe. *Journal of Archaeological Science* 39, 531–46.

Borić, D., Cristiani, E., Duričić, L., Filipović, D., Allué, E., Vušović-Lučić, Z. and Borovinić, N. 2021. Holocene foraging in the Dinaric Alps: current research on the Mesolithic of Montenegro. In D. Borić, D. Antonović and B. Mihailović (eds), *Foraging assemblages Volume 1*, 264–73. Belgrade and New York: Serbian Archaeological Society and The Italian Academy for Advanced Studies in America, Columbia University.

Borić, D. and Price, T.D. 2013. Strontium isotopes document greater human mobility at the start of the Balkan Neolithic. *Proceedings of the National Academy of Sciences of the United States of America* 110(9), 3298–303.

Bramanti, B., Thomas, M.G., Haak, W., Unterländer, M., Jores, P., Tambets, K. *et al.* 2009. Genetic discontinuity between local hunter-gatherers and central Europe's first farmers. *Science* 326, 137–40.

Brami, M.N., Winkelbach, L., Schulz, I., Schreiber, M., Blöcher, J., Diekmann, Y. and Burger, J. 2022. Was the fishing village of Lepenski Vir built by Europe's first farmers? *bioRxiv* preprint, doi. org/10.1101/2022.06.28.498048.

Csengeri, P. 2014. Újabb középső neolitikus arcos edények Borsod-Abaúj-Zemplén megyéből. *A Miskolci Herman Ottó Múzeum Közleményei* 53, 41–66.

Cummings, V. Hofmann, D., Bjørnevad-Ahlqvist, M. and Iversen, R. 2022. Muddying the waters: reconsidering migration in the Neolithic of Britain, Ireland and Denmark. *Danish Journal of Archaeology* 11, 1–25, https://doi.org/10.7146/dja.v11i.129698.

Depaermentier, M., Kempf, M., Bánffy, E. and Alt, K.W. 2020. Mobility patterns through the 6th-5th millennia BC in the Carpathian Basin with strontium and oxygen stable isotope analyses. *PLoS One*, 2020 15(12): e0242745, doi.org/10.1371/journal.pone.0242745.

Depaermentier, M.L.C., Kempf, M., Mörseburg, A. Knipper, C. Szécsényi-Nagy, A., Regenye, J. *et al.* forthcoming. Multiproxy isotope analyses reveal scale-based mobility and social patterns in Neolithic Hungary. In E. Bánffy and A. Gramsch (eds), *The Neolithic of the Sárköz and adjacent regions in Hungary: bioarchaeological studies*. Confinia et Horizontes 2. Langenweißbach: Beier and Beran.

Duffy, P., Marton, T. and Borić, D. 2022. Locating Mesolithic hunter-gatherer camps in the Carpathian Basin. *Journal of Archaeological Method and Theory*, doi.org/10.1007/s10816-022-09570-w.

Eichmann, W.J., Kertész, R. and Marton, T. 2010. Mesolithic in the LBK heartland of Transdaubia, Hungary. In D. Gronenborn and J. Petrasch (eds), *Die Neolithisierung Mitteleuropas – The spread of the Neolithic to central Europe*, 211–33. Mainz: Römisch-Germanisches Zentralmuseum.

Frieman, C.J. and Hofmann, D. 2019. Present pasts in the archaeology of genetics, identity, and migration in Europe: a critical essay. *World Archaeology* 51, 528–45.

Furholt, M. 2017. Massive migrations? The impact of recent aDNA studies on our view of third millennium Europe. *European Journal of Archaeology* 21, 159–91.

Horejs, B., Bulatović, A., Bulatović, J., Brandl, M., Burke, C., Filipović, D. and Milić, B. 2019. New insights into the later stage of the Neolithisation process of the central Balkans: first excavations at Svinjarička Čuka 2018. *Archaeologia Austriaca* 103, 175–226.

Kertész, R. 1996. The Mesolithic in the Great Hungarian Plain: a survey of evidence. In L. Tálas (ed.), *At the fringes of three worlds: hunters-gatherers in the Middle Tisza valley*, 5–39. Szolnok: Damjanich Museum.

Kotula, A., Piezonka H. and Terberger, T. 2020. The Mesolithic cemetery of Groß Fredenwalde (NE Germany) and its cultural affiliations. *Lietuvos Archeologija* 46, 65–84.

Krauß, R., De Cupere, B. and Marinova, E. 2018. Foraging and food production strategies during the Early Neolithic in the Balkans-Carpathian area: the site of Bucova Pusta in Romanian Banat. In M. Ivanova, B. Athanassov, V. Petrova, D. Takorova and P.W. Stockhammer (eds), *Social dimensions of food in the prehistoric Balkans*, 157–72. Oxford: Oxbow Books.

Lipson, M., Szécsényi-Nagy, A., Mallick, S., Pósa, A.M., Stégmár, B., Keerl, V. *et al.* 2017. Parallel ancient genomic transects reveal complex population history of early European farmers. *Nature* 551, 368–72.

Lübke, H., Lüth, F. and Terberger, T. 2009. Fishers or farmers? The archaeology of the Ostorf cemetery and related Neolithic finds in the light of new data. *Bericht der Römisch-Germanischen Kommission* 88, 307–38.

Marinova, E.M., Filipović, D., Obradović, D. and Allué E.A. 2013. Wild plant resources and land use in Mesolithic and early Neolithic south-east Europe: archaeobotanical evidence from the Danube catchment of Bulgaria and Serbia. *Offa* 69, 467–78.

Mateiciucová, I. 2008. *Talking stones: the chipped stone industry in Lower Austria and Moravia and the beginnings of the Neolithic in Central Europe (LBK), 5700–4900 BC*. Brno: Masarykova univerzita.

Mathieson, I., Alpaslan-Roodenberg, S., Posth, C., Szécsényi-Nagy, A., Rohland, N., Mallick, S. *et al.* 2018. The genomic history of southeastern Europe. *Nature* 555, 197–203.

Nicolaisen, J. 1976. The Penan of the seventh division of Sarawak: past, present, and future. *Sarawak Museum Journal* 24, 35–61.

Nikitin, E.G., Stadler, P., Kotova, N., Teschler-Nicola, M., Price, D.T., Hoovern, J., Kennett, D.J., Lazaridis, J., Rohland, N., Lipson, M. and Reich, D. 2019. Interactions between earliest Linearbandkeramik farmers and central European hunter gatherers at the dawn of European Neolithization. *Scientific Reports*, 9:19544, doi.org/10.1038/s41598-019-56029-2.

Oross, K., Bánffy, E., Osztás, A., Marton, T., Nyerges, É.Á., Köhler, K., Szécsényi-Nagy, A., Alt, K.W., Bronk Ramsey, C., Goslar, T., Kromer, K. and Hamilton, D. 2016. The early days of Neolithic Alsónyék: the Starčevo occupation. *Bericht der Römisch-Germanischen Kommission* 94, 93–121.

Ottoni, C., Cheronet, O., Sparacello, O., Dori, I., Coppa, A., Antonović, D., Vujević, D., Price, T.D., Pinhasi, R. and Cristiani, E. 2021. Tracking the transition to agriculture in Southern Europe through ancient DNA analysis of dental calculus. *Proceedings of the National Academy of Sciences of the United States of America* 118 (32) e2102116118, doi.org/10.1073/pnas.2102116118.

Price, T.D. 2021. Transitions – endings: introduction. In D. Borić, D. Antonović and B. Mihailović (eds), *Foraging assemblages Volume 2*, 695–97. Belgrade and New York: Serbian Archaeological Society and The Italian Academy for Advanced Studies in America, Columbia University.

Price, T.D., Larsson, L., Magnell, O. and Borić, D. 2021. Sedentary hunters, mobile farmers: the spread of agriculture into prehistoric Europe. In D. Borić, D. Antonović and B. Mihailović (eds), *Foraging assemblages Volume 2*, 579–83. Belgrade and New York: Serbian Archaeological Society and The Italian Academy for Advanced Studies in America, Columbia University.

Robb. J. 2013. Material culture, landscapes of action, and emergent causation: a new model for the origins of the European Neolithic. *Current Anthropology* 54, 657–83.

Stadler, P. and Kotova, N. 2019. *Early Neolithic settlement Brunn am Gebirge, Wolfholz, Site 2 in Lower Austria and the origin of the Western Linear Pottery culture (LPC)*. Langenweißbach and Wien: Beier and Beran.

Szeverényi, V. and Priskin, A. 2021. Váncsod, Szénás-dűlő (62490). In B. Kolozsi, Nagy, E. Gy. and Priskin, A. (eds), *Sztrádaörökség. Válogatás az M35-ös és M4-es autópálya régészeti feltárásaiból*, 167–76. Debrecen: Déri Múzeum.

Szécsényi-Nagy, A., Brandt, G., Haak, W., Keerl, V., Jakucs, J., Möller-Rieker, S. *et al.* 2015. Tracing the genetic origin of Europe's first farmers reveals insights into their social organization. *Proceedings of The Royal Society B* 282: 20150339, doi.org/10.1098/rspb.2015.0339.

Szécsényi-Nagy, A., Keerl, V., Jakucs, J., Köhler, K., Oross, K., Osztás, A., Marton, T., Mende, B.G., Alt, K.W. and Bánffy, E. forthcoming. Ancient population genetics of the 6000–4000 cal BC period of the Carpathian basin. In E. Bánffy and A. Gramsch (eds), *The Neolithic of the Sárköz and adjacent regions in Hungary: bioarchaeological studies*. Confinia et Horizontes 2. Langenweißbach: Beier and Beran.

Terberger, T., Kotula, A., Sebastian, L., Schult, M., Burger, J. and Jungklaus, B. 2015. Standing upright to all eternity: the Mesolithic burial site at Groß Fredenwalde, Brandenburg (NE Germany). *Quartär* 6, 133–53.

Watkins, T. 2018. The Epipalaeolithic-Neolithic as the pivotal transformation of human history. *Documenta Praehistorica* 45, 14–28.

Zimmermann, A. 1995. *Austauschsysteme von Silexartefakten in der Bandkeramik Europas*. Bonn: Habelt.

Živaljević, I., Dimitrijević, V., Jovanović, J., Blagojević, T., Pendić, J., Putica, A. *et al.* 2021. Revealing the 'hidden' Pannonian and Central Balkan Mesolithic: new radiocarbon evidence from Serbia. *Quaternary International* 574, 52–64.

Živaljević, I., Dimitrijević, V. and Stefanović, S. 2017. Faunal remains from Kula, a Mesolithic-Neolithic site at the exit of the Danube Gorges (Serbia). In M. Mărgărit and A. Boroneanţ (eds), *From hunter-gatherers to farmers. Human adaptations at the end of the Pleistocene and the first part of the Holocene. Papers in honour of Clive Bonsall*, 113–34. Târgovişte: Editura Cetatea de Scaun.

Zvelebil, M. and Pettitt, P. 2013. Biosocial archaeology of the Early Neolithic: synthetic analyses of a human skeletal population from the LBK cemetery of Vedrovice, Czech Republic. *Journal of Anthropological Archaeology* 32, 313–29.

Chapter 9

Ancestry and identity in the Balkans and the Carpathian basin between the 5th and 3rd millennia cal BC

Bianca Preda-Bălănică and Yoan Diekmann

Thousands of kurgans (burial mounds) were built on the plains landscapes of the Balkans and the Carpathian basin during the first half of the 3rd millennium cal BC. For a long time, they have been interpreted as belonging to 'newcomers', that is, steppe migrants who already started to arrive in the 5th millennium cal BC, in contrast to flat burial grounds traditionally assigned to 'local' communities. By bringing together information about the genetic ancestry of individuals and the mortuary archaeology of burial practices, we investigate the relationship between descent and identity in the kurgans and flat cemeteries of the region. While many individuals with no steppe-related ancestry are buried according to Balkan-Carpathian basin burial practices, we find a significant number of them were also buried following Pontic-Caspian steppe practices. Our results show that operating with the prevalent dichotomy only obscures the complexity of processes taking place in the region in the second half of the 4th millennium and first half of the 3rd millennium cal BC, suggesting ancestry is at most one factor amongst others contributing to social identity.

INTRODUCTION

In the past decade, palaeogenetics have not only reshaped our understanding of European prehistory, but also deeply influenced archaeological research practice. Since 2015, the well-known 20th-century archaeological theory of a massive migration from the eastern steppes into central Europe in the 3rd millennium cal BC has been the research focus of multiple teams of geneticists, resulting in high-profile publications (Allentoft *et al.* 2015; Haak *et al.* 2015). Reactions from the archaeological side were not long in coming, either of support and engagement or rejection and caution towards the shortcomings of the approach (Kristiansen *et al.* 2017; Furholt 2018). Given the enormous potential to further the understanding of past societies, researchers are currently seeking to build a fruitful dialogue and collaboration between archaeology and genetics.

With this paper, we aim to explore ways in which the two disciplines can pose questions and interpret the archaeological record collaboratively. The focus is on the arrival of steppe-related genetic ancestry from the Pontic-Caspian steppe into the Balkans and the Carpathian basin, starting from the 5th, but especially during the 3rd millennium cal BC, and its impact on the transformation of burial practices in the region. Thousands of kurgans were built in the plain landscapes that were traditionally interpreted as belonging to 'newcomers', steppe migrants, as opposed to flat burial grounds assigned to 'locals'. However, how dichotomous is this scenario really? Here, the relationship between descent and identity in kurgans and flat cemeteries is investigated by bringing together information about the genetic ancestry of individuals and burial practices.

Mortuary archaeology has long been concerned with the interrelation between funerary practices and the expression of individuals' identity. In the 1960s and 1970s, researchers examined the display of social identity in mortuary contexts and established the key concept of the *social persona* of the deceased, a 'composite of the social identities maintained in life and recognized as appropriate for consideration at death' (Goodenough 1965, 7; Binford 1971, 17). This paradigm was overturned in the 1980s, with studies arguing that identities expressed in mortuary rituals are not mere reflections of social identity, but rather idealised and manipulated for the purpose of status aggrandisement and social advertisement (Parker Pearson 1982, 112). The way 'identities' are understood today is not as static and fixed anymore, but negotiated relationally and contextually (Fowler 2013, 511).

BURIAL PRACTICES IN THE BALKANS-CARPATHIAN BASIN AND THE PONTIC-CASPIAN STEPPE

In the Balkans and the Carpathian basin, in the second half of the 5th millennium cal BC, the custom of burying the dead in flat cemeteries separate from settlements was common in the Kodjadermen-Gumelniţa-Karanovo VI, Tiszapolgár-Bodrogkeresztúr, and – to a smaller extent – in the Bubanj-Salcuţa-Krivodol societies, while documented burials assigned to the Cucuteni-Tripolye culture are almost non-existent (Bognár-Kutzián 1963; Bailey 2000; 2005). Individuals were most often buried crouched on either the right or left side, their position and grave goods, including ceramic vessels, tools and ornaments made of various materials, sometimes being gender-differentiated (Sofaer Derevenski 1997; Bailey 2000). In the coastal region of Bulgaria, cemeteries contained wealthy graves of individuals laid on their backs or crouched on their sides, some accompanied by thousands of exquisite grave goods, for example made of gold, copper, or shells (Krauß *et al.* 2014).

A dramatic change occurred in the 4th millennium cal BC, as only very scarce indications of habitation and a handful of graves are documented in the Balkan lowlands in the first half of the millennium, and a similar decline is recorded in the Carpathian basin as well (Horváth and Virág 2003; Georgieva 2018, 103). The region markedly resettled only in the second half of the 4th millennium cal BC, with the trans-regional phenomenon of Baden, Coţofeni-Kostolac in central Europe and the central Balkans, and Ezero in Bulgaria (Demoule 2017, 57–8). Funerary customs were heterogeneous, with both inhumation and cremation in flat graves and under small mounds being attested in the Baden-Coţofeni area, and flat inhumations and cremations in the Ezero area (Leshtakov 2011; Sachsse 2011; Diaconescu 2020). The first half of the 3rd millennium cal BC is marked by the preservation of these burial traditions, but also the emergence of new ones. Flat isolated graves or cemeteries continue to exist north and south of the lower Danube, sometimes in connection with settlement sites, while burial mounds with stone covering and stone cist burials are documented in the intra-Carpathian region (Ciugudean 2011; Frînculeasa *et al.* 2022). Inhumations of individuals crouched on their sides accompanied by local grave goods, especially pottery, are most common, although cremations are also found.

In the Pontic-Caspian steppe, the mid-5th millennium cal BC was the start of a deep transformation of burial practices. This is the period when monumental funerary architecture in the steppe emerges, with simple, small, stone or earth constructions marking the graves (Rassamakin 2011, table 1). Prestigious grave goods were placed in graves, including stone sceptres/maceheads, ornaments, tools and weapons made of shell, gold, copper and flint (Govedarica 2004). Monumental architecture developed during the 4th millennium cal BC into elaborate funerary structures with ditches, cromlechs, stone circles and rings made with black and yellow clay, covered by mounds (Rassamakin 2011, table 1). In this period, innovations including arsenic bronzes, new weapon types such as shaft-hole axes and daggers, and wooden wagons circulated across the steppe, and were incorporated in the burial practices of different societies, such as Usatovo and Maykop (Anthony 2007). In the first half of the 3rd millennium cal BC, simpler, larger earthen kurgans were built over Yamnaya burials (Rassamakin 2011, table 1). Even though grave goods were rather scarce in these burials, regionally variable preferences for pottery, tanged daggers or other metal items, bone pins, anthropomorphic stone stelae, hair rings or necklaces made of animal teeth are noted (Preda-Bălănică 2021, 152). Various traditions of placing the deceased in graves existed, either extended, supine, or crouched on the side, each with their own timeline. Of these, the supine position with raised knees is the earliest and most lasting one, and became a trademark of steppe funerary rituals along with red ochre staining (Rassamakin 2013, 116, fig. 11).

In this study, we examine the relationship between the genetic ancestry of individuals and the funerary rituals performed at their death to explore aspects of individual and group identity. Two non-trivial conceptual links have to be made explicit: genetic ancestry and the identity of individuals throughout their life, on the one hand; and the identity of individuals throughout their life and funerary rituals performed at their death, on the other. First, biological relatedness has previously been argued to not necessarily be the only or even the strongest articulation of identity for the living, as concepts of kin are culturally and contextually specific (Büster 2022). Secondly, the identity of the deceased undergoes a transformation during the mortuary process that leaves behind the record which archaeologists are studying (Fowler 2013, 511).

ANCESTRY IN THE BALKAN-CARPATHIAN BASIN AND PONTIC-CASPIAN STEPPE

Soon after technological, molecular and computational advances made it possible to sequence ancient individuals at genomic scale, palaeogenetic studies confirmed earlier results based on mitochondrial DNA that European early farmers (EFs) were genetically distinct from contemporary Holocene hunter-gatherers (HGs) (Bramanti *et al.* 2009; Skoglund *et al.* 2012), thereby strongly supporting the demic diffusion model of the Neolithic revolution. Fuelled by rapid increase in the number of genomes that could be sequenced, a second long-standing archaeological migration hypothesis was supported shortly afterwards, by finding steppe-related genetic ancestry from the Pontic-Caspian region across late Neolithic Europe (Allentoft *et al.* 2015; Haak *et al.* 2015). (The term 'steppe-related ancestry' accounts for the fact that the ancestry profile of the steppe is currently insufficiently sampled. Despite this, we refer to it simply as 'steppe ancestry' for the sake of brevity in the remainder of this chapter.) The success of genetic ancestry in the context of major prehistoric migrations firmly established it in the palaeogenetic community as a way to describe population structure, in Europe most commonly as a three-way admixture model with HG, EF and a steppe component (Lazaridis *et al.* 2014; Haak *et al.* 2015). Within such a model, the geographic location of the eastern Balkans and Carpathian basin destines these regions to act as a contact zone between central European – dominated by Aegean farmers admixed with limited spatio-temporally varying amounts of HG ancestry – and Pontic-Caspian steppe populations, as indeed attested by occasional findings of individuals with steppe ancestry starting from the 5th millennium cal BC (Mathieson *et al.* 2018). The origin of steppe ancestry itself has been modelled as a mixture of older ancestries of geographically adjacent HG populations in eastern Europe and the Caucasus (Jones *et al.* 2015).

Despite its pervasive use and often being the basis for the more consequential archaeological interpretations of the genetic data in palaeogenetic papers, the concept of ancestry has been criticised on multiple grounds. While archaeologists have for example picked up on the knee-jerk interpretations of changes in ancestry as 'massive migrations' without considering the finer impact on social realities (Furholt 2018), population geneticists have pointed out conceptual problems. Ancestry in palaeogenetics is loosely defined and routinely derived from genetic similarity measures, often in relation to reference populations composed and labelled *a priori* (Coop 2022). These ultimately arbitrary choices implicitly determine the time periods in which the resulting categories are archaeologically meaningful, that is, they represent conceivably interacting populations, but do not preclude their use in other contexts (Mathieson and Scally 2020). Moreover, while ancestral populations corresponding to Holocene HG, EF and steppe ancestries are separated by sufficient amounts of genetic drift to be discernible based on allele frequency differentiation, once all major ancestry components are present and admixed, demographic events tend to leave more subtle shifts not sufficiently pronounced to reconstruct them from summary statistics of allele frequency differences.

In the following, we set out to illustrate how some of these criticisms may be addressed. We ask what the relationship is between ancestry and burial practices, thereby considering the migrational impact beyond mere genetic makeup. In particular, we avoid the troublesome interpretation of migration as replacement of the local population, by explicitly incorporating a cultural layer, here focusing on social identity. As discussed in the previous section, the link between funerary practices and social identity is complex; the same is true for ancestry. When shared ancestry is due to biological relatedness, direct remembrance of origin is a realistic option, but finding and inferring relatedness or timing admixture to a few generations in the past is challenging. Instead, we use ancestry here as a proxy for differences in appearance, the (at least partially) genetically determined aspect relevant for identity that is directly 'accessible' to the individual and their social group. We stress that correlation between ancestry and phenotype is limited, and the relation of the latter to identity is again complex. Some phenotypic traits could in theory be predicted directly from genetic data, but most ancient genomes are sequenced shallowly mostly at ascertained neutral markers that by definition do not influence any phenotype, as these are the only ones reflecting demography. We note that powerful recent phasing and imputation approaches may partially alleviate this problem.

MATERIALS AND METHODS

We gathered archaeological information from publications on 97 individuals for which genome data were available that were discovered in mortuary contexts in the study region, dated roughly between 5000/4900 and 2500/2400 cal BC by means of either radiocarbon dates or relative chronology (Fig. 9.1). We partitioned the individuals into two distinct phases by splitting them at *c.* 3500 cal BC, as steppe ancestry is rare (a single individual) and burials of Pontic-Caspian steppe character are absent in our dataset before 3500 cal BC. We note that the samples are not evenly distributed spatio-temporally; the Carpathian basin and eastern Bulgaria are better represented than the area north of the lower Danube, and there are about twice as many samples dated between 5000–3500 cal BC (n=61) than 3500–2500 cal BC (n=36). The burial ritual of the selected contexts was evaluated and labelled as being of 'Balkan/Carpathian basin' (BCB) or 'Pontic-Caspian steppe' (PCS) character. To this end, a combination of diagnostic criteria was considered, for example the absence or presence of a burial mound, the funerary structure, ochre staining, and the position and orientation of the deceased, as well as the accepted assignments in the archaeological literature.

We retrieved the genomes for the 97 individuals from the Allen Ancient DNA Resource version 50.0 (https://reich.hms.harvard.edu/allen-ancient-dna-resource-aadr-downloadable-genotypes-present-day-and-ancient-dna-data, accessed March 2022).

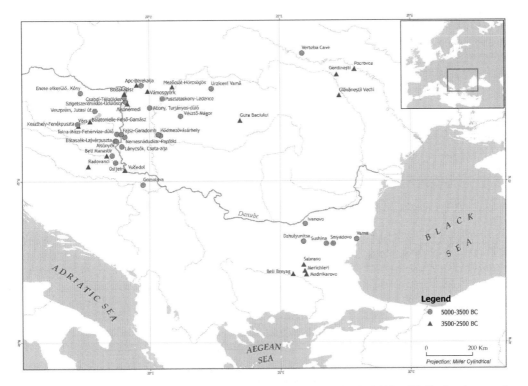

Figure 9.1. Map of the study region. Circles: samples dated between c. *5000–3500 cal BC; triangles: samples dated between* c. *3500–2500 cal BC (Map by Bogdan Olariu).*

The proportion of steppe ancestry was estimated with *qpAdm* from the Admixtools package (Patterson *et al.* 2012) based on a reference set of individuals labelled as Yamnaya. The logistic regression shown in Figure 9.3 was computed in R (R Core Team 2022) with *glm* and *logit* link function. Our entire annotated dataset and the script used to generate Figure 9.3 can be accessed at https://github.com/ydiekmann/Preda-Balanica_Oxbow_2022, along with further method details.

RESULTS AND DISCUSSION

Before 3500 cal BC, we find only a single individual with steppe ancestry in our dataset and no burials of Pontic-Caspian steppe character, in line with long-range migration between the Balkan/Carpathian basin and the Pontic-Caspian steppe being rare in that period. The individual with steppe ancestry was dated to *c.* 4606-4447 cal BC and found in Grave 29 from Smyadovo (I2181) (Mathieson *et al.* 2018, 200). Here, an adult man was laid in the grave pit in a crouched position on his left side, east–west oriented, along with two vessels, a flint and a string of beads of serpentinite, bone and *Spondylus* (Fig. 9.2, 3) (Chohadzieh and Mihaylova 2014, 45). The burial ritual shows similarities to the other graves on the site and to contemporary cemeteries in the eastern Balkans (Fig. 9.2, 4). The individual is inferred to have *c.* 40% steppe ancestry, but the low genome coverage precludes any attempt to date any actual admixture event, which could in theory be as recent as one generation in the past. Thus, in this particular case, genetic ancestry was not acknowledged in any way in the burial ritual. We do not know if the steppe origin was remembered, part of the identity of the individual during his life, or if it was obscured during funerary rituals (Frieman and Hofmann 2019, 537). David Anthony (2019, 42) suggested a possible interpretation, occasional marriage between higher-status families in the area and steppe people from the Volga as a means to secure peaceful interactions and exchanges under the umbrella of kinship, this individual remaining in the Varna region and identifying as a member of the native family.

Yet, although not available to be included into our dataset, graves displaying typical steppe burial practices also exist in the region. The grave from Csongrád-Kettőshalom, dated to *c.* 4442–4243 cal BC, is described as showing DNA similar to individuals from the Khvalynsk cemetery (Russia), which exemplifies the presence of individuals presumably originating from the steppe region in the Carpathian basin in the 5th millennium cal BC (Preda-Bălănică 2021, tab. 3; Anthony *et al.* 2022, 38). However, unlike in Smyadovo, here the presumed origin of the individual was acknowledged and symbolised in the burial ritual (Fig. 9.2, 1). The mourners were familiar with the burial practices from the steppe and the rules were strictly followed; ochre was procured and sprinkled in large quantities over the pit bottom and the deceased individual, who was laid with the head towards the west, on his back, with raised knees, and an ochre lump was placed next to him, along with a 13.2 cm long obsidian blade, limestone and *Spondylus* shell beads, and beads made of curved copper plate (Ecsedy 1971, 9).

Currently, there are no autosomal genomic data available for other sites displaying a typical steppe burial ritual and considered indicative of the arrival of the steppe ancestry into the region in the 5th millennium cal BC, such as Giurgiuleşti, or Decea Mureşului, to

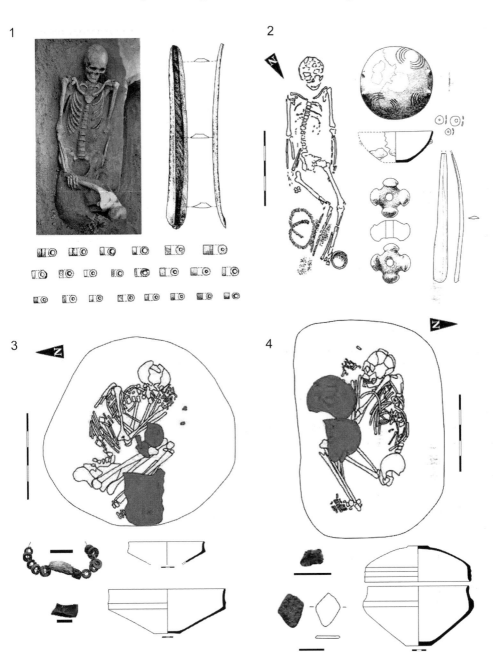

Figure 9.2. Balkan/Carpathian basin and Pontic-Caspian burial practices in the 5th millennium cal BC. 1. Csongrád-Kettőshalom, Grave 1 (after Ecsedy 1971, fig. 3, 1–4; Dani et al. 2022); 2. Decea Mureşului, Grave 12 (after Govedarica 2004, Abb. 8, 2, Taf. 3, 1–5); 3. Smyadovo, Grave 29 (after Chohadzhiev and Mihaylova 2014, fig. 35, 2–6); 4. Smyadovo, Grave 28 (after Chohadzhiev and Mihaylova 2014, fig. 33, 2–4, 6–7).

mention only two (Fig. 9.2, 2). Mitochondrial genomes were sequenced for Decea Mureșului (Hervella *et al.* 2015), but these do not allow steppe ancestry to be quantified.

Although relatively few samples (n=36) dated between the second half of the 4th until the middle of the 3rd millennium cal BC, our dataset contains variation both in steppe ancestry and burial practices, allowing for a statistical approach. We test the relationship between steppe ancestry and burial practices via logistic regression (Fig. 9.3), with the continuous proportion of steppe ancestry as predictor and the binary burial practice as response variable. The better ancestry allows to predict burial practice, the stronger we would infer its impact on identity to be. Interestingly, while many individuals with no steppe ancestry are buried according to BCB practices, many examples for PCS burials exist as well, suggesting ancestry is at most one factor amongst others contributing to social identity. In the following, we discuss some striking cases in more detail.

Several graves north and south of the lower Danube are particularly interesting, such are Individual no. 6 from a burial mound in Merichleri (I2165), Feature 3 containing two individuals in Mound 5/Beli Breyag (Bul6 and Bul8) (Fig. 9.4, 1), and Grave 1 from Glăvăneștii Vechi, Mound 1/1949 (I11912) (Comșa 1987; Alexandrov *et al.* 2016, 154,

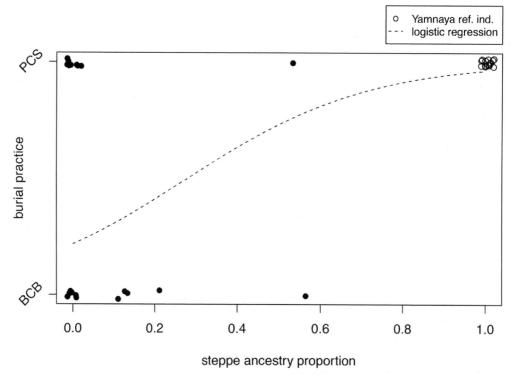

Figure 9.3. Proportion of steppe ancestry as a predictor for burial practice. Logistic regression on individuals in our dataset dated after 3500 cal BC. Positions on the axes are jittered to show overlapping points. Yamnaya reference individuals were added solely to allow for a meaningful regression. Abbreviations: Pontic-Caspian steppe (PCS), Balkan-Carpathian basin (BCB), reference individuals (ref. ind.).

fig. 3; Iliev 2018). None of the individuals found in these graves are confidently inferred to have steppe ancestry, as even though a model with steppe ancestry fits individual I2165 reasonably well, it lacks Eastern HG ancestry and is better modelled as a mixture of Balkan and Caucasus HGs. These are secondary graves dug into already existing mounds, with the specification that in Merichleri the oldest burial was a cremation accompanied by a small mound covered with limestones. The way of disposing of the dead illustrates steppe burial practices, as seen for instance in Mednikarovo, mound 2, grave 1 (Bul4), which is inferred to have *c.* 50% steppe ancestry (Fig. 9.4, 2) (Panayotov and Alexandrov 1995, 88, fig. 6). Individuals were laid in supine position with raised knees or slightly crouched on their sides, with arms bent at the elbows, oriented towards west or east; in some cases the bones of the deceased, especially the skull, and the pit bottom were stained with ochre. No grave goods were found with the exception of Individual no. 6 from Merichleri, who was accompanied by a stone ball and a small askos pot.

Steppe mortuary practices are clearly present in the Mezőcsát-Hörcsögös site, a mound built on top of a former bi-ritual Baden burial ground (Kalicz 1999). The graves of interest here are nos 1, 3, 4 and 10. In Grave 1 (I5116) a child was buried in a rectangular pit with rounded corners, west–east oriented, lying supine with knees initially raised and subsequently fallen to the right side and with the arms along the body. Close to the chest, a cup typical of local Copper Age pottery types was placed (Kalicz 1999, 59, figs 9, 1, 17, 4). Grave 3 (I5117) (Fig. 9.4, 3) contained an adult individual buried in an oval pit, lying supine with raised knees, with one arm on the chest and the other along the body, oriented south-west–north-east (Kalicz 1999, 59, figs 6, 3, 9, 3). Similarly, in Grave 10 (I5119), a child was laid supine with the knees initially raised and fallen to the right side and arms along the body, north–south oriented (Fig. 9.4, 4) (Kalicz 1999, 67, fig. 8, 1). Notably, the individual in Grave 4 (I5118) is buried in an unusual manner, initially laid in sitting position and subsequently falling forwards (Kalicz 1999, 63, fig. 6, 4). None of the above individuals are inferred to have steppe ancestry, although we caution that Grave 1 (I5116) has not enough coverage for confident estimation.

Researchers interpreted this discovery as a burial mound of Yamnaya migrants built on top of a former local burial ground in the late 4th or early 3rd millennium cal BC (Schasse 2011, 132; Heyd 2011, 538; Dani 2020, 4). While such a hypothesis is supported by numerous other examples of graves displaying attributes of the Yamnaya burial ritual dug into previous settlement sites or burial grounds and then covered by mounds (Heyd 2011, 542), in this case the burial did not include people of steppe origin, but contained people of local origin. Those who built the funerary monument placed the dead according to steppe burial practices.

Our analysis also brought to light that in the first half of the 3rd millennium cal BC, individuals with steppe genetic ancestry were found in funerary contexts that do not bear any signs of steppe burial practices, here in Vučedol contexts. This is exemplified by Grave 17 at the site of Beli Manastir (I3499), where an individual was buried who derived *c.* 20% of their ancestry from the steppe. The 25–30-year-old male was laid on the bottom of a circular pit in crouched position on the left side, with legs flexed and arms bent and brought towards the face, south–north oriented (Miloglav 2019, 133). Another example comes from Vučedol, where in the youngest construction horizon (III) two contracted skeletons were found in a double burial (pit 9/1985) (Forenbaher 1994, fig. 5).

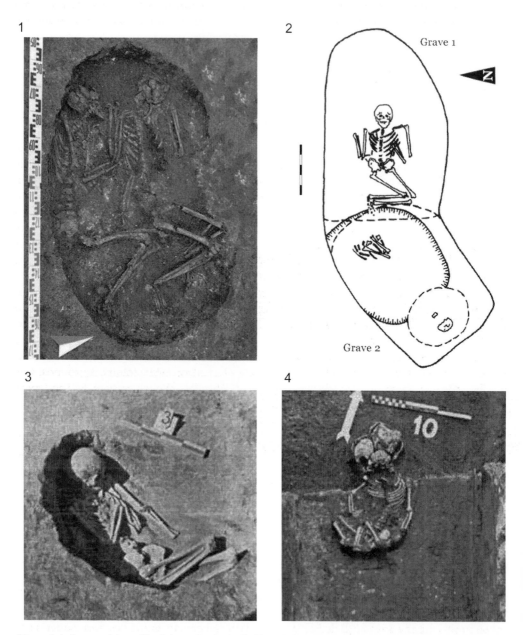

Figure 9.4. Steppe-originated burial practices in the Balkans/Carpathian basin between c. *5000–3500 cal BC. 1. Beli Breyag, mound 5, feature 3 (after Alexandrov et al. 2016, 154, fig. 3); 2. Mednikarovo mound 2, grave 1 (after Panayotov and Alexandrov 1995, 88, fig. 6); 3. Mezöcsát-Hörcsögös, Grave 3 (after Kalicz 1999, fig. 6, 3); 4. Mezöcsát-Hörcsögös, Grave 10 (after Kalicz 1999, fig. 8, 1).*

Individual 1 (I4175) was a 9–10-year-old male inferred to have *c.* 55% steppe ancestry buried together with a 17–19-year-old female, for whom there are unfortunately no autosomal genomic data available (Hincak *et al.* 2007, table 1).

To summarise, our dataset is currently underpowered to evaluate the period between 5000–3500 cal BC systematically. Yet we highlight examples of individuals where genetic ancestry either was or was not acknowledged in the burial ritual, suggesting social complexity with respect to identity already before the later migration. Continued research efforts will shed more light on the impact of the arrival of steppe-related ancestry and steppe burial practices in the region.

For the period between 3500–2500 cal BC, the cases discussed above clearly demonstrate that communities living in the Balkans and the Carpathian basin were building and using mounds as burial places, as well as practising burial rituals originating in the Pontic-Caspian steppe. The fact that not all people buried in kurgans had steppe origins is by no means a novel idea. In the last centuries of the 4th millennium cal BC burial mounds displaying a combination of steppe and local burial practices emerged in the plains north of the lower Danube, the eastern Balkans and the Carpathian basin, before the Yamnaya migration (Frînculeasa 2020). Building burial mounds peaked during the first half of the 3rd millennium cal BC, concurrent with a significant influx of steppe ancestry into the region, presumably as a direct consequence of the above-mentioned migration (Haak *et al.* 2015). However, isotopic studies have found that during this period a kurgan located in the Hungarian Plain, for example, was used as a burial place by individuals likely originating from the Apuseni Mountains (Gerling *et al.* 2012). For the moment, the small number of available genomes along with the absence of absolute dates makes it impossible to further distinguish between the two phases that were identified on archaeological grounds, that is, the last centuries of the 4th millennium cal BC, before the emergence of the typical Yamnaya graves in the region around 3100 cal BC, and after this moment until around 2500 cal BC, in order to investigate how the relation between genetic ancestry and burial practices was impacted. However, the results indicate that the spread of ancestry and the spread of ideas are not congruent, and are both relevant when considering such complex phenomena as identity.

CONCLUSIONS AND OUTLOOK

The arrival of steppe ancestry into south-eastern and then central and western Europe was concurrent amongst others with significant changes in economy and lifestyle, but the most obvious and unambiguous are transformations in mortuary rituals. Steppe ancestry has generally been associated with a specific set of burial practices, for which Martin Furholt (2019) coined the term 'Single Grave Burial Ritual'. The bottom-up approach taken in this study shows that correlation between the genetic ancestry of individuals and their identity expressed in mortuary practices should not be assumed, but investigated on a case-by-case basis.

In several instances, individuals without steppe ancestry were put to rest in ways typical of steppe burial practices. Alin Frînculeasa (2020, 55) considers that certain aspects of steppe burial practices were adopted by local groups wishing to display their status and wealth, while Marja Ahola (2020) talks about the spread of a 'steppe originated religion'. However, the mechanisms of this process are largely unknown and further insights could be provided by the detailed analysis of funerary contexts. Communities use the mortuary arena to make socio-political statements (Fowler 2013, 513); building a burial mound or not, the arrangement of funerary structures, the position and orientation in which the deceased are laid, and the selection of grave goods are therefore not accidental, but convey messages about individual and group identity. Likewise, individuals with steppe genetic ancestry were buried without any acknowledgement in burial practices of their origin, although we caution that this is currently illustrated by two examples only. As can be seen from our dataset, these coexist in the same space and time with graves of individuals with genetic steppe ancestry buried according to steppe burial practices and graves of individuals with Aegean farmer and Balkan hunter-gatherer ancestry, typically found in central Europe at the time, buried according to funerary practices in the different areas of the Balkans and the Carpathian basin. These results show that operating with the dichotomy between 'local' and 'newcomer' only obscures the complexity of processes taking place in the region in the second half of the 4th and first half of the 3rd millennium cal BC.

Although based only on a limited sample, we provide intriguing observations prompting further research. Strategic sampling of all graves in a burial mound could shed light on the different phases of its construction, and on the group(s) participating in the process. The interdisciplinary study of burials with methods from aDNA, stable isotope, bioarchaeology and funerary archaeology enables researchers to piece together complex narratives about individuals in the past, including their genetic ancestry, their mobility, activity patterns and diet, their group membership and social identity during their lifetime, as well as their identity as expressed in mortuary rituals. Only then can we hope to fully understand mobility and migration, interaction and admixture, transmission and transformation in a landscape shared by the living and the dead.

ACKNOWLEDGEMENTS

This paper was written with the support of the ERC Advanced project 788616: The Yamnaya Impact on Prehistoric Europe (YMPACT).

REFERENCES

Ahola, M. 2020. Creating a sense of belonging: religion and migration in the context of the 3rd millennium BC Corded Ware complex in the eastern and northern Baltic Sea region. *Norwegian Archaeological Review* 53(2), 114–34.

Alexandrov, S., Galabova, B. and Atanassova-Timeva, N. 2016. Spasitelni archeologicheski prouchvaniya na nadgrobna mogila № 5, zemlishte na s. Beli Bryag, obshtina Radnevo. In A. Aladzhov, (ed.), *Arheologicheski otkritiya i razkopki prez 2015*, 153–4. Sofia: National Institute of Archaeology with Museum.

Allentoft, M.E., Sikora, M., Sjögren, K.-G., Rasmussen, S., Rasmussen, M., Stenderup, J. *et al.* 2015. Population genomics of Bronze Age Eurasia. *Nature* 522, 167–72.

Anthony, D.W. 2007. *The horse, the wheel and language: how Bronze-Age riders from the Eurasian steppes shaped the modern world.* Princeton: Princeton University Press.

Anthony, D.W. 2019. Ancient DNA, mating networks, and the Anatolian split. In M. Serangeli and T. Olander (eds), *Dispersals and diversification: linguistic and archaeological perspectives on the early stages of-Indo-European*, 21–53. Leiden and Boston: Brill.

Anthony, D.W., Khokhlov, A.A., Agapov, S.A., Agapov, D.S., Schulting, R., Olalde, I. and Reich, D. 2022. The Eneolithic cemetery at Khvalynsk on the Volga River. *Praehistorische Zeitschrift* 97/1. https://doi.org/10.1515/pz-2022-2034

Bailey, D. 2000. *Balkan prehistory: exclusion, incorporation and identity.* London: Routledge.

Bailey, D.W. 2005. On the absence of burial ritual in Cucuteni-Tripolie communities. In V. Spinei, C.-M. Lazarovici, and D. Monah (eds), *Scripta praehistorica. Miscellanea in honorem nonagenarii magistri Mircea Petrescu-Dîmboviţa oblata*, 319–40. Iaşi: Trinitas.

Binford, L.R. 1971. Mortuary practices: their study and their potential. In J.-A. Brown (ed.), *Approaches to the social dimensions of mortuary practices*, 6–29. Society for American Archaeology, Memoir 25.

Bognár-Kutzián, I. 1963. *The Copper Age cemetery of Tiszapolgár-Basatanya.* Budapest: Akadémiai Kiadó.

Bramanti, B., Thomas, M. G., Haak, W., Unterlaender, M., Jores, P., Tambets, K., Antanaitis-Jacobs, I. *et al.* 2009. Genetic discontinuity between local hunter-gatherers and central Europe's first farmers. *Science* 326(5949), 137–40.

Büster, L. 2022. From human remains to powerful objects: ancestor research from a deep-time perspective. *Genealogy* 6, 23. https://doi.org/10.3390/genealogy6010023.

Chohadziev, S. and Mihaylova, N. 2014. *Smyadovo: prehistoric cemetery 2005–2008.* Sofia: Direct Services.

Ciugudean, H. 2011. Mounds and mountains: burial rituals in Early Bronze Age Transylvania. In S. Berecki, R.E. Németh and B. Rezi (eds), *Bronze Age rites and rituals in the Carpathian Basin. Proceedings of the International Colloquium from Târgu Mureş*, 21–57. Târgu Mureş: Bibliotheca Musei Marisiensis.

Comşa, E. 1987. Mormintele cu ocru din Movila I de la Glăvăneştii Vechi. *Studii şi Cercetări de Istorie Veche şi Arheologie* 4, 367–87.

Coop, G. 2022. Genetic similarity and genetic ancestry groups. *arXiv* http://arxiv.org/abs/2207.11595

Dani, J. 2020. Kurgans and their builders. The Great Hungarian Plain at the dawn of the Bronze Age. *Hungarian Archaeology* 9(2), 1–20.

Dani, J., Preda-Bălănică, B. and Angi, J. 2022. The emergence of a new elite in southeast Europe: people and ideas from the steppe region at the turn of the Copper and Bronze Ages. In A. Gyucha and W. Parkinson (eds), *From farmers to kings: wealth, power, and hierarchy in prehistoric southeast Europe,* in press. Los Angeles: Cotsen Institute of Archaeology Press.

Demoule, J.P. 2017. The transition between Neolithic and Early Bronze Age in Greece, and the 'Indo-European problem'. In M. Gori and M. Ivanova (eds), *Balkan dialogues: negotiating identity between prehistory and the present*, 52–63. Abingdon: Routledge.

Diaconescu, D. 2020. Step by steppe: Yamnaya culture in Transylvania. *Praehistorische Zeitschrift* 91, 17–44.

Ecsedy, I. 1971. A new item relating the connections with the east in the Hungarian Copper Age (a Marosdécse-type grave in Csongrád). *A Móra Ferenc Múzeum Évkönyve* 2, 9–17.

Forenbaher, S. 1994. The Late Copper Age architecture at Vučedol, Croatia. *Journal of Field Archaeology* 21, 307–23.

Fowler, C. 2013. Identities in transformation: identities, funerary rites, and the mortuary process. In L. Nilsson Stutz and S. Tarlow (eds), *The Oxford handbook of the archaeology of death and burial*, 511–26. Oxford: Oxford University Press.

Frieman, C.J. and Hofmann, D. 2019. Present pasts in the archaeology of genetics, identity, and migration in Europe: a critical essay. *World Archaeology* 51, 528–45.

Frînculeasa, A. 2020, Earthen burial mounds and the Coțofeni culture south of the Carpathians. The archaeological research in Aricestii-Rahtivani – Movila pe Răzoare, Ziridava. *Studia Archaeologica* 34, 35–90.

Frînculeasa, A., Garvăn, D., Simalcsik, A., Negrea, O., Munteanu, R., Dinu, C. *et al.* 2022. Ritualul Iamnaia și persistențe locale în prima jumătate a mileniului al III-lea (Complexe funerare cercetate în anul 2021 în nordul Munteniei). *Revista de Arheologie, Antropologie și Studii Interdisciplinare* 4, in press.

Furholt, M. 2018. Massive migrations? The impact of recent aDNA studies on our view of third millennium Europe. *European Journal of Archaeology* 21, 159–91.

Furholt, M. 2019. Re-integrating archaeology: a contribution to aDNA studies and the migration discourse on the 3rd millennium BC in Europe. *Proceedings of the Prehistoric Society* 85, 115–29.

Georgieva, P. 2018. Possible approaches to tracing the fate of the population of the Varna, Kodjadermen-Gumelnița-Karanovo VI and Krivodol-Sălcuța cultures. In S. Dietz, F. Mavridis, Ž. Tankosić and T. Takaoğlu (eds), *Communities in transition: the circum-Aegean area during the 5th and 4th millennia BC*, 95–106. Oxford: Oxbow Books.

Gerling, C., Bánffy, E., Dani, J., Köhler, K., Kulcsár, G., Szeverényi, V. and Heyd, V. 2012. Immigration and transhumance in the Early Bronze Age Carpathian basin: the occupants of a kurgan. *Antiquity* 86, 1097–111.

Goodenough, W.H. 1965. Rethinking "status" and "role": toward a general model of the cultural organization of social relationships. In M. Banton (ed.), *The relevance of models for social anthropology*, 1–24. New York: Praeger.

Govedarica, B. 2004. *Zepterträger: Herrscher der Steppen. Die frühen Ockergräber des älteren Äneolithikums im karpatenbalkanischen Gebiet und im Steppenraum Südost- und Osteuropas.* Mainz: Philipp von Zabern.

Haak, W., Lazaridis, I., Patterson, N., Rohland, N., Mallick, S., Llamas, B. *et al.* 2015. Massive migration from the steppe was a source for Indo-European languages in Europe. *Nature* 522, 207–11.

Hervella, M., Rotea, M., Izagirre, N., Constantinescu, M., Alonso, S., Ioana, M. *et al.* 2015. Ancient DNA from south-east Europe reveals different events during Early and Middle Neolithic influencing the European genetic heritage. *PLoS ONE* 10 (6), doi:10.1371/journal. pone.0128810.

Heyd, V. 2011. Yamnaya groups and tumuli west of the Black Sea, ancestral landscapes. In E. Borgna and S. Müller-Celka (eds), *Ancestral landscapes: burial mounds in the Copper and Bronze Ages (central and eastern Europe, Balkans, Adriatic, Aegean, 4th–2nd millennium BC). International Conference, Udine/Italy, May 15th–18th 2008*, 535–55. Lyon: Maison de l'Orient et de la Méditerranée.

Hincak, Z., Drmić-Hofman, I. and Mihelić, D. 2007. Anthropological analysis of neolithic and Early Bronze Age skeletons - a classical and molecular approach (East Slavonia, Croatia). *Collegium Antropologicum,* 31(4), 1135–41.

Horváth, L.A. and Virág, Zs.M. 2003. History of the Copper Age. In Zs. Visy, M. Nagy and L. Bartosiewicz (eds), *Hungarian archaeology at the turn of the millennium*, 125–27. Budapest: Ministry of National Cutlural Heritage.

Iliev, S. 2018. A tumulus from the Early Bronze Age near the town of Merichleri, southeast Bulgaria. In S. Alexandrov, Y. Dimitrova, H. Popov, B. Horejs and K. Chukalev (eds), *Gold & bronze: metals, technologies and interregional contacts in the eastern Balkans during the Bronze Age,* 288–92. Sofia: National Archaeological Institute with Museum, Bulgarian Academy of Sciences.

Jones, E.R., Gonzalez-Fortes, G., Connell, S., Siska, V., Eriksson, A., Martiniano, R. *et al.* 2015. Upper Palaeolithic genomes reveal deep roots of modern Eurasians. *Nature Communications* 6, 8912.

Kalicz, N. 1999. A késő rézkori Báden kultúra temetője Mezőcsát-Hörcsögösön és Tiszavasvári-Gyepároson. *A Herman Ottó Múzeum Évkönyve* 37, 57–101.

Krauß, R., Zäuner, S. and Pernicka, E. 2014. Statistical and anthropological analysis of the Varna necropolis. In H. Meller, R. Risch and E. Pernicka (eds), *Metalle der Macht – Frühes Gold und Silber. 6. Mitteldeutscher Archäologentag vom 17. bis 19. Oktober 2013 in Halle (Saale)*, 371–87. Halle: Landesmuseum für Vorgeschichte.

Kristiansen, K., Allentoft, M., Frei, K., Iversen, R., Johannsen, N., Kroonen, G. *et al.* 2017. Retheorising mobility and the formation of culture and language among the Corded Ware culture in Europe. *Antiquity* 91, 334–47.

Lazaridis, I., Patterson, N., Mittnik, A., Renaud, G., Mallick, S., Kirsanow, K., Sudmant, P.H. *et al.* 2014. Ancient human genomes suggest three ancestral populations for present-day Europeans. *Nature* 513 (7518), 409–13.

Leshtakov, K. 2011. Bronze Age mortuary practices in Thrace: a prelude to studying the long-term tradition. In E. Borgna and S. Müller-Celka (eds), *Ancestral landscapes: burial mounds in the Copper and Bronze Ages (central and eastern Europe, Balkans, Adriatic, Aegean, 4th–2nd millennium BC). International Conference, Udine/Italy, May 15th–18th 2008*, 567–77. Lyon: Maison de l'Orient et de la Méditerranée.

Mathieson, I., Alpaslan-Roodenberg, S., Posth, C., Szécsényi-Nagy, A., Rohland, N., Mallick, S. *et al.* 2018. The genomic history of southeastern Europe. *Nature* 555 (7695), 197–203.

Mathieson, I. and Scally, A. 2020. What Is ancestry? *PLoS Genetics* 16 (3), e1008624.

Miloglav, I. 2019. Vučedolska kultura. Vučedol culture. In J. Balen, I. Miloglav and D. Rajković (eds), *Povratak u prošlost. Bakreno doba u sjevernoj Hrvatskoj/Back to the past. Copper Age in northern Croatia*, 113–45. Zagreb: Archaeological Museum, Faculty of Humanities and Social Sciences of the University of Zagreb, and Archaeological Museum, Osijek.

Panayotov, I. and Alexandrov, A. 1995. Maritsa-Iztok. *Arheologičeski proučvaniya* 3, 87–113.

Parker Pearson, M. 1982. Mortuary practices, society and ideology: an ethnoarchaeological study. In I. Hodder (ed.), *Symbolic and structural archaeology*, 99–113. Cambridge: Cambridge University Press.

Patterson, N., Moorjani, P., Luo, Y., Mallick, S., Rohland, N., Zhan, Y., Genschoreck, T., Webster, T. and Reich, D. 2012. Ancient admixture in human history. *Genetics* 192 (3), 1065–93.

Preda-Bălănică, B. 2021. Still making waves. Marija Gimbutas in current archaeological debates. In V. Heyd, G. Kulcsár and B. Preda-Bălănică (eds), *Yamnaya interactions. Proceedings of the International Workshop held in Helsinki, 25–26 April 2019*, 137–70. Budapest: Archaeolingua.

R Core Team 2022. R: a language and environment for statistical computing. *R Foundation for Statistical Computing, Vienna, Austria*, https://www.R-project.org/.

Rassamakin, Y. 2011. Eneolithic burial mounds in the Black Sea Steppe from the first burial symbols to monumental ritual architecture. In E. Borgna and S. Müller-Celka (eds), *Ancestral landscapes: burial mounds in the Copper and Bronze Ages (central and eastern Europe, Balkans, Adriatic, Aegean, 4th–2nd millennium BC). International Conference, Udine/Italy, May 15th–18th 2008*, 293–305. Lyon: Maison de l'Orient et de la Méditerranée.

Rassamakin, Y. 2013. From the late Eneolithic period to the Early Bronze Age in the Black Sea steppe: what is the Pit Grave culture (late fourth to mid-third millennium BC)? In V. Heyd, G. Kulcsár and V. Szeverényi (eds), *Transitions to the Bronze Age: interregional interaction and socio-cultural change in the third millennium BC Carpathian basin and neighbouring regions*, 113–38. Budapest: Archaeolingua.

Sachsse, C. 2011. Burial mounds in the Baden culture: aspects of local developments and outer impacts. In E. Borgna and S. Müller-Celka (eds), *Ancestral landscapes: burial mounds in the Copper and Bronze Ages (central and eastern Europe, Balkans, Adriatic, Aegean, 4th–2nd millennium BC). International Conference, Udine/Italy, May 15th–18th 2008*, 127–34. Lyon: Maison de l'Orient et de la Méditerranée.

Skoglund, P., Malmström, H., Raghavan, M., Storå, J., Hall, P., Willerslev, E., Thomas, M., Gilbert, P., Götherström, A. and Jakobsson, M. 2012. Origins and genetic legacy of Neolithic farmers and hunter-gatherers in Europe. *Science* 336(6080), 466–9.

Sofaer Derevenski, J. 1997. Age and gender at the site of Tiszapolgár-Basatanya, Hungary. *Antiquity* 71, 875–89.

Chapter 10

The genetics of the inhabitants of Neolithic Britain: a review

Selina Brace and Tom Booth

This chapter aims to review studies of the genetics of the inhabitants of Mesolithic and Neolithic Britain from the late 5th to the end of the 3rd millennium cal BC. We lay out the current thinking on the genetic ancestries and population history of Mesolithic and Neolithic continental Europe, then home in on Britain. We discuss the likely origins of Neolithic migrations into Britain and outline the difficulties in determining likely source populations. We also address the issue of admixture, focusing on interactions amongst incoming groups, their descendants and the local Mesolithic-derived populations of Britain. We discuss the different proxies for population size and genetic insularity, namely runs of homozygosity/heterozygosity and identity-by-descent, and suggest that the large genetic shift observed in Britain at the beginning of the 4th millennium cal BC may be associated with low population size in Late Mesolithic Britain. We also provide a summary of close genetic relatives that have thus far been identified at Neolithic funerary sites and what these relatives suggest about funerary behaviour and social organisation. Our concluding section assesses the genetic data from the 3rd millennium cal BC, which whilst limited, indicate substantial population continuity from the preceding millennium. We conclude that while the genetic shifts that bookend the Neolithic period in Britain are similarly large-scale, closer analysis reveals differences that illustrate different dynamics of genetic change.

INTRODUCTION

The published main text of archaeogenetics papers is often limited in terms of both words and citations, and therefore there is rarely space to explore the full interpretative potential of the results. In addition, new results from relevant ancient populations and new analyses will often throw a different light on previously published results. Archaeogeneticists do not typically revisit their publications, even in light of relevant new studies, probably due to the volume and speed at which they are published. Therefore, attempts to review publications, with a fuller discursive account of explanations and taking into consideration new data and analyses, will increasingly be necessary to keep models of ancient archaeogenetics up to date. In this paper, we will attempt to review studies of the genetics of Mesolithic and Neolithic Britain in the late 5th into the 4th millennium cal BC, and what we have learned since the first study reporting data from Neolithic Britain (Olalde *et al.* 2018).

POPULATION HISTORY OF MESOLITHIC AND NEOLITHIC CONTINENTAL EUROPE

Mesolithic populations from across Europe carry a variety of diverse genetic ancestries. Genetic ancestries reflect the extent to which individuals or groups of people share recent ancestors, and while labelling of genetic ancestry groups is useful for discussion, variation across groups is continuous, and these do not represent simple bounded categories. The main type of ancestries, predominant in western, central and southern Europe, are often referred to as 'Western European Hunter-Gatherer' ancestries (WHG), although they have sometimes been referred to as 'Villabruna' ancestries, after the earliest site where these ancestries have been found (Skoglund *et al.* 2012; Olalde *et al.* 2014; Fu *et al.* 2016; Yang and Fu 2018). Some Mesolithic groups in Europe also carry ancestries deriving from Palaeolithic hunter-gatherer groups who resettled Europe after the Last Glacial Maximum, from *c.* 16,000 cal BC and were associated with Magdalenian artefacts (Jones *et al.* 2015; Fu *et al.* 2016; Olalde *et al.* 2019; Villalba-Mouco *et al.* 2019). This category of ancestries is referred to as 'GoyetQ2' (previously 'El Miron'), again named after the oldest burial where this ancestry has been found, at the cave site of Goyet in present-day Belgium. 'GoyetQ2' ancestries have only ever been observed as a minority ancestry component of Mesolithic groups in Europe. The strongest signal of this ancestry is in south-west Europe, particularly parts of Iberia, although it has also been identified as a component of ancestries in Mesolithic populations of western and northern continental Europe (Olalde *et al.* 2019; Villalba-Mouco *et al.* 2019; Brunel *et al.* 2020; Rivollat *et al.* 2020).

A third category of genetic ancestries is found in Mesolithic populations of eastern Europe, which are referred to as Eastern European Hunter-Gatherer ancestries (EHG). Unlike GoyetQ2 ancestries, EHG ancestries can form a majority or even exclusive component of Mesolithic groups in eastern Europe, particularly around areas in present-day Ukraine and the eastern Baltic (Yang and Fu 2018). Later Mesolithic populations of northern Scandinavia comprise a characteristic mix of WHG and EHG ancestries that is sometimes referred to as 'Scandinavian hunter-gatherer' (SHG) ancestries (Günther *et al.* 2018). Different concentrations of these ancestries across Europe during the Mesolithic mean there is a general south-west–north-east cline in these three ancestries across Europe through the Mesolithic. Some individuals and groups in south-east Europe carry partial ancestries that predominate in Anatolia, the same ancestries that become dominant across Europe through the Neolithic (Mathieson *et al.* 2018; Lazaridis *et al.* 2022). This is presumably because of interactions between hunter-gatherers from south-east Europe and adjacent regions of Anatolia. These general clines of Mesolithic ancestries fluctuate through time (Allentoft *et al.* 2022).

It is also possible to discriminate between WHG-related ancestries from different parts of Europe, particularly where there are individuals from which we have high quality (high coverage) data. The genetics of the Mesolithic skeleton from La Brana, Iberia, are distinguishable from those of Loschbour, from present-day Luxembourg, because of the skeleton from La Brana harbouring a minority proportion of GoyetQ2-related ancestries (Villalba-Mouco *et al.* 2019). But Loschbour is also somewhat distinguishable from KO1, an early Neolithic individual from south-east Europe who exclusively carries WHG-related ancestry (Rivollat *et al.* 2020). The KO1 and Loschbour genomes are often taken as proxies for Mesolithic-derived ancestries from south-east and western Europe respectively, but such a view is potentially naive to the complexities of population fluctuations in Mesolithic Europe, as well as anachronistic in using genomes dispersed over thousands of years.

Between 7000 cal BC and 4000 cal BC, groups carrying Early European Farmer (EEF)-related ancestries from Neolithic Anatolia slowly dispersed across Europe via two routes: along the Mediterranean coast into the western Mediterranean region and along the Danube into central Europe (Haak *et al.* 2015; Olalde *et al.* 2015). This dichotomous model of human dispersal is a simplified model and almost certainly does not capture the complexity of what actually happened, which probably involved complex patterns of dispersals in several directions. These groups interacted and mixed with populations carrying ancestries derived from local Mesolithic groups, although in most cases the Mesolithic-associated ancestry component comprised a variable minority of whole ancestry over the long term (Skoglund and Mathieson 2018). Different histories of regional interactions between incoming and local populations and their descendants across Europe meant that these broad 'Mediterranean' and 'Danubian' dispersal routes produced two genetically discernible populations, largely distinguished by the amount and type of ancestries they carried from the various Mesolithic populations (Haak *et al.* 2015; Olalde *et al.* 2015; 2019; Mathieson *et al.* 2018; Allentoft *et al.* 2022). These two groups can be separated by the Rhine (Rivollat *et al.* 2020). Generally (although not universally), particularly up until the 5th millennium cal BC, Neolithic groups from west of the Rhine are descended from the Mediterranean dispersals and are defined by higher levels of Mesolithic-derived ancestry more generally and a greater genetic affinity to the Loschbour genome than the KO1 genome. Certain Neolithic groups from Iberia can be further distinguished from other aspects of the Mediterranean dispersals by excess Mesolithic-derived ancestry as well as specific ancestries related to GoyetQ2. The Mediterranean dispersals are characterised by successive episodes of local admixture with Mesolithic-descended groups producing complex patterns of variation in genetic ancestry.

By contrast, Neolithic groups east of the Rhine associated with the Danubian expansions show lower levels of admixture with Mesolithic-derived groups and share greater genetic affinities with KO1 than with the Loschbour genome. The Danubian dispersal has subsequently been characterised as involving some admixture between populations carrying EEF-related ancestry and local Mesolithic-descended populations in south-east Europe in the 7th millennium cal BC, followed by relatively rapid expansion across the loess soils into parts of central and western Europe during the 6th millennium cal BC, with little subsequent admixture with populations derived from local Mesolithic groups (Rivollat *et al.* 2020; Allentoft *et al.* 2022).

The trend for a 'Middle Neolithic hunter-gatherer resurgence' involving a sudden uptick in levels of Mesolithic-derived genetic ancestries in the late 5th and early 4th millennia cal BC has been noted in disparate parts of continental Europe (Haak *et al.* 2015; Lipson *et al.* 2017; Mathieson *et al.* 2018; Olalde *et al.* 2018; 2019). This phenomenon is more common amongst populations in western Europe, usually descended from Mediterranean dispersals, but is also apparent in populations who inhabited parts of Europe east of the Rhine (Bollongino *et al.* 2013; Haak *et al.* 2015; Lipson *et al.* 2017; Allentoft *et al.* 2022). There are two broad explanations for this resurgence of Mesolithic-derived ancestry, namely 1) local Mesolithic populations and early farmers carrying EEF-related ancestries co-existed in parallel, sometimes for thousands of years, before merging more completely; and 2) a new group of people carrying EEF ancestry moved into the area and admixed with local groups. This new population would have to have harboured higher levels of Mesolithic-derived ancestries.

Methods that estimate the number of generations since there was admixture with groups wholly carrying certain kinds of genetic ancestries, such as DATES or ALDER, can be used to try to distinguish between these two scenarios (Loh *et al.* 2013; Narasimhan *et al.* 2019; Furtwängler *et al.* 2020; Rivollat *et al.* 2020). DNA is inherited in segments, but recombination that occurs every generation means that these segments are split apart and become shorter. DATES and ALDER can estimate whether Mesolithic-derived ancestry was a result of recent admixture, indicated by long segments of DNA associated with these ancestries across the genome, or distant admixture, in which case the Mesolithic-derived admixture will consist of shorter, broken-up segments. If Middle Neolithic resurgence of Mesolithic-derived ancestries is as a result of recent mergers between groups carrying EEF ancestry and groups wholly carrying Mesolithic-derived ancestries, then the signal of admixture should be recent. If the upsurge in WHG ancestry is due to admixture with a group with EEF ancestry that simply harboured higher levels of Mesolithic-derived ancestries, the signal of admixture will be many generations ago. One weakness of these methods is that they give a single date estimate with a confidence interval and do not accommodate multiple episodes of ancestral admixture. If there had been several episodes of admixture with individuals carrying wholly Mesolithic-derived ancestry in an individual's or group's ancestral history, then this method would provide an average of the timing of admixture. Application of this method to various Neolithic populations from Europe has found evidence for both processes (Bollongino *et al.* 2013; Lipson *et al.* 2017; Brunel *et al.* 2020; Rivollat *et al.* 2020). In some places, such as Blatterhöhle Cave in Westphalia, in north-west Germany, the WHG ancestry resurgence is related to recent admixture between populations carrying EEF-related ancestry and Mesolithic-derived groups, while in other regions, such as northern France, there seems to have been admixture between two groups carrying EEF-related ancestry but disparate levels of Mesolithic-derived ancestry (Bollongino *et al.* 2013; Lipson *et al.* 2017; Brunel *et al.* 2020; Rivollat *et al.* 2020).

EARLY GENETIC STUDIES OF NEOLITHIC BRITAIN

The first studies that reported specifically on the genetics of people in Neolithic Britain were those of Olalde *et al.* (2018), Brace *et al.* (2019) and Sánchez-Quinto *et al.* (2019). All three studies reached similar conclusions: that from *c.* 4000 cal BC people in Britain predominantly carried EEF-related genetic ancestries. A substantial minority component of their ancestry, usually around 25%, but with a range of between 20 and 40%, was derived from WHG genetic ancestries, which predominated in much of western, central and southern Mesolithic Europe. They all found that the Neolithic populations from Britain were predominantly descended from Neolithic groups who had dispersed along the Mediterranean. However, a minority component of the ancestries derived from groups who had dispersed along the Danube into central Europe, and who were ultimately descended from people associated with *Linearbandkeramik* (LBK) societies.

Sánchez-Quinto *et al.* (2019) highlighted that all burials they investigated from societies who built megalithic tombs from Britain, Ireland and Scandinavia showed some level of ancestry derived from these Mediterranean dispersals. The 5th millennium cal BC also saw the expansion of populations derived from Neolithic groups from the western Mediterranean into areas that had been previously inhabited by Neolithic populations descended from the Danubian migrations (Rivollat *et al.* 2016; 2020; Beau *et al.* 2017). These expansions and interactions probably led to the mixed Mediterranean/Danubian ancestral signatures in Neolithic populations of Britain. They concluded that this may indicate that the 5th millennium cal BC was a time when expansions of Neolithic populations carrying Mediterranean-derived ancestry out of western Europe, perhaps via maritime routes, may have influenced the development of megalith-building societies across north-west Europe (Sánchez-Quinto *et al.* 2019).

Brace *et al.* (2019), Olalde *et al.* (2018) and Sanchez-Quinto *et al.* (2019) all discuss the affinities of Neolithic populations of Britain to Mediterranean dispersals of people through comparisons to Neolithic populations from Iberia. Unfortunately, this was read by some researchers as arguing that groups had migrated directly to Britain from the Iberian peninsula into Britain (Thomas 2022). Iberian Neolithic genomes were chosen for comparison in all of these studies because they were (at the time) the highest quality and most abundant genomes associated with the Mediterranean Neolithic dispersals. The comparison of British and Iberian Neolithic genomes was useful in determining whether Neolithic populations of Britain shared greater affinities with the Mediterranean or Danubian dispersals of groups. In fact, both Olalde *et al.* (2018) and Brace *et al.* (2019) found that the Neolithic population of Britain shared greater genetic affinities with Neolithic individuals from southern France than Iberia, but as the genomes available from southern France were fewer in number and of lower quality, they were sub-optimal to use as a source population for the British Neolithic. The more probable scenario was that Neolithic groups from Britain and Iberia were both distantly descended from groups of people who had dispersed into the western Mediterranean and split, with one group moving into northern parts of France and another moving south-west into Iberia. This point is made by Brace *et al.* (2019) but it is easy to see how it could have been obscured by the repeated references to Neolithic Iberia. (See also Sheridan and Whittle, this volume, for a discussion of the 'Iberian' question.)

Brace *et al.* (2019) estimated the excess levels of Mesolithic-derived admixture in Neolithic Britain in part by comparing Neolithic populations of Britain against Neolithic groups from Iberia dating to the 5th and 4th millennia cal BC. When earlier populations from the Iberian peninsula who existed before the Middle Neolithic 'resurgence' of Mesolithic-derived ancestries were used, they detected no additional admixture in the small number of Neolithic samples from Wales, around 10% additional admixture in samples from England and around 20% in Scotland. This fitted one of their other observations: that there was a significant south-west–north-east cline in Mesolithic-derived ancestries, with north-east Britain (particularly Orkney), and to a lesser extent south-east Britain, showing slightly higher levels of Mesolithic-derived ancestries. When they used samples from Iberia in the 4th millennium cal BC, there was no additional Mesolithic-derived admixture in any region of Britain. They reasoned that the 5th millennium cal BC Neolithic samples from Iberia probably provided the most appropriate estimates, as samples dating to

4th millennium cal BC were too late to have been plausible sources for Neolithic Britain and the samples dating to the 5th millennium cal BC both predated the Neolithic in Britain and were more likely to have been closer to the Mediterranean dispersals of people that were ancestral to both groups.

Using DATES software (Narasimhan *et al.* 2019), Brace *et al.* (2019) attempted to determine whether this additional Mesolithic-derived admixture was due to groups of Neolithic migrants and their descendants having children with local groups derived from the Mesolithic population in Britain, or was a result of additional admixture in continental Europe. This analysis found evidence for early and more recent Mesolithic admixture in Britain. However, the only samples with evidence for recent admixture all came from western Scotland. All the other Mesolithic-derived admixture detected was estimated to have occurred dozens of generations previously, before populations carrying the EEF-related ancestries had arrived in Britain. This result will represent an average of Mesolithic-derived ancestry admixture over the preceding few generations, but suggested that any excess Mesolithic-derived ancestries were largely already present in migrating populations. Brace *et al.* (2019) therefore concluded that the differences in levels of Mesolithic-derived admixture across Neolithic Britain were more likely to be down to different source populations with slightly different levels of Mesolithic-derived admixture having entered different parts of Britain.

ORIGINS OF NEOLITHIC MIGRATIONS INTO BRITAIN

It is clear from the aDNA data that Neolithic populations of Britain were probably the descendants of people who had migrated from north-west continental Europe, most probably proximal regions of France (Olalde *et al.* 2018; Brace *et al.* 2019; Sánchez-Quinto *et al.* 2019; Scheib *et al.* 2019). However, narrowing down the precise areas from where the Neolithic migrants to Britain had come, and determining whether this involved single or multiple sources, has been difficult to determine genetically, even with new data from Neolithic north-west continental Europe (Brunel *et al.* 2020; Rivollat *et al.* 2020). This is in part because of an increasingly complex picture of the genetics of north-west Europe, involving repeated population migrations, expansions and admixtures (Rivollat *et al.* 2020). Available samples for comparison also limit our ability to narrow down likely sources. Some sampled populations are from pertinent regions of north-west Europe but belong to the wrong sort of time period to represent plausibly the source of migrations to Britain. Some groups are from the right sort of time period, but not the correct place. As is often the case with ancient DNA, we have to triangulate a likely origin by investigating levels of genetic similarity to available samples, using them as proxies for other unsampled populations, even if they are inappropriately situated or anachronistic, and using the results to act as a guide in developing one or a series of plausible scenarios.

There are a few ways in which we can investigate different aspects of genetic similarity between populations of Neolithic Britain and continental Europe to try to get a sense of where migrations into Britain originated. The most reliable involves simply looking at which Neolithic populations are most genetically similar to one another, which translates into those groups being more likely to share recent ancestry. This seems straightforward, but can be affected by technical issues related to methods of data generation and analysis. For instance, the relatively distinctive ancestries deriving from Mesolithic populations of Europe and Early European Farmers mean that they can overwhelm any direct relationship between populations.

Rivollat *et al.* (2020) studied the genetics of Neolithic populations from variable regions of France and found that Neolithic individuals from Britain showed some affinities with Neolithic groups of the 5th millennium cal BC from southern France, the Atlantic Coast, Normandy and the Paris basin. As in Brace *et al.* (2019), they detected possible regional variation across Britain and Ireland, suggesting migrations from at least two sources, with Ireland and western Britain showing more influence from Atlantic sources whereas eastern Britain was probably more influenced by migrations from Normandy, the Paris basin and the western Mediterranean. However, these conclusions have been challenged by Ariano *et al.* (2022) who found that Neolithic populations of both Britain and Ireland were genetically close to one another, and probably had similar sources. The extent to which this challenges suggestions of regional variation by Brace *et al.* (2019) and Rivollat *et al.* (2020) will depend on how differentiated Neolithic populations of north-west Europe were.

Another way of assessing likely source populations for migrations into Britain is through the consideration of paternal (Y-chromosome haplogroup) and maternal lineages (mitochondrial (Mt) haplogroup). Consideration of these loci with respect to connections between populations has to be done with care for a number of reasons. Firstly, these loci represent only a small proportion of each individual's genetic ancestry: a restricted overall proportion of an individual's ancestors. Genome-wide data are considered more robust, particularly for problems of sample size, as they allow for an individual to be treated as representative of a sample of their genetic ancestors, representing possibly hundreds of people whose remains have not survived into the archaeological record. These arguments do not apply to uniparental loci, and sample size issues are highly relevant.

Secondly, Y and Mt haplogroups are prone to founder effects and drift, whereby an offshoot of a particular population may by chance carry different proportions of particular lineages. If these two populations become relatively isolated from one another, these differences can become exacerbated through genetic drift, where lineages that were at low frequency in the source population become more common in the derived group over time. Finally, given there is some evidence that certain types of highly visible Neolithic funerary monuments across Europe were primarily used for the burial of people belonging to specific lineages, particularly paternal lineages (Sánchez-Quinto *et al.* 2019; Cassidy *et al.* 2020; Fowler *et al.* 2022), there is a danger that there will be a bias towards these groups and the true diversity of paternal lineages of Neolithic people who lived in the area will be hidden.

There is less diversity in paternal than maternal lineages amongst Neolithic populations of Europe and so it is easier to look at paternal lineages when assessing connections between populations. As it happens, Neolithic paternal lineages in Britain are particularly non-diverse, exclusively comprising derivatives of haplogroup I, usually I2a (Olalde *et al.* 2018; Brace *et al.* 2019; Sánchez-Quinto *et al.* 2019; Patterson *et al.* 2022). Temporally and geographically proximal populations that broadly match this distribution of paternal lineages include groups who inhabited western Iberia, Atlantic and Mediterranean France and western Germany in the 5th millennium cal BC (Rivollat *et al.* 2020). Geographically proximate Neolithic populations examined by Brunel *et al.* (2021) include sites in the Grand-Est region of eastern France and a range of sites in southern France (although it should be noted that paternal lineages could not be obtained in a high proportion of samples used in this study). Interestingly, populations sampled from two sites in northern France, Gurgy 'les Noisats' in the Paris basin and Fleury-sur-Orne in Normandy show none of the paternal lineages that have been found so far in Neolithic Britain and Ireland, although any inferences taken from these observations regarding the origins of the Neolithic population of Britain have to be heavily caveated by the factors we have discussed above.

ADMIXTURE WITH LOCAL MESOLITHIC POPULATIONS OF BRITAIN

Determining the source of migrations into Britain near the beginning of the 4th millennium cal BC is not just important for understanding inward migration but also the level of admixture with Mesolithic-derived populations living in Britain. The volatility of levels of Mesolithic-derived ancestry amongst Neolithic populations of north-west continental Europe in the 4th millennium cal BC means that whichever population we choose as the likely source of migrations to Britain can change the estimate of additional admixture with Mesolithic-derived populations in Britain (Rivollat *et al.* 2020; Thomas 2022).

Thomas (2022) notes that no population dating to the 5th millennium cal BC from areas of northern France proximal to Britain studied by Rivollat *et al.* (2020) consistently retains levels of Mesolithic-derived ancestry as high as what is seen in Neolithic Britain. He puts forward an alternative narrative of the Neolithic transition from Britain whereby a 'minimal Neolithic' is established in south-east Britain as a result of interactions between Mesolithic groups in Britain and small groups of pioneer migrants from continental Europe at the end of the 5th millennium cal BC. This minimal Neolithic sets the groundwork for subsequent substantial migrations through the first half of the 4th millennium cal BC. In this model, the small amount of excess Mesolithic-derived admixture in Neolithic Britain compared to populations from northern France studied by Rivollat *et al.* (2020) may have been related to interactions that took place between incoming and local populations and their descendants at the end of the 5th millennium cal BC (Thomas 2022). The failure of this admixture to show up in the DATES analysis may be down to either methodological issues or the fact that most samples from Neolithic Britain post-date 3800 cal BC and are too distant from the admixture event for it to show up. An alternative position proposed by Thomas (2022) is that local and incoming populations did not have children with one another in this minimal Neolithic period, or at least those that did were marginal in the broader population history of Neolithic Britain.

The figure of Mesolithic-derived admixture which Thomas (2022) cites (around 26%) for Neolithic Britain includes samples from western Scotland that show evidence for recent admixture with Mesolithic-derived groups who lived in Britain. If we take similar figures from Patterson *et al.* (2022, online table 5), the mean estimates for levels of Mesolithic-derived admixture in Britain, excluding outlier samples from western Scotland, are 22% for southern Britain (England and Wales) and 23% for northern Britain (Scotland). Even using these figures, there is certainly still a step change in levels of Mesolithic-derived ancestry from regions of Neolithic France sampled by Rivollat *et al.* (2020) compared to Britain, but this is in the range of 7–9%.

A different study that investigated ancient human genomes from different regions of Neolithic France (Brunel *et al.* 2020) suggests that levels of Mesolithic-derived admixture in other populations dating to the 5th and early 4th millennia cal BC did carry levels of Mesolithic-derived admixture comparable to what we see in Neolithic populations of Britain. Specifically, around 22% of the ancestry of populations from the eastern Grand-Est region of France was derived from Mesolithic populations of Europe, while these ancestries account for around 30% of the ancestry of people from the Hauts-de-France region of northern France. It may well be that none of these studied populations represent the precise source of migrations into Britain, but variable levels of Mesolithic-derived ancestries found in populations from different parts of 5th millennium cal BC France by Brunel *et al.* (2020) and Rivollat *et al.* (2020) show the volatility of levels of these ancestries in these regions. Therefore, it is reasonable to suggest that there could have been several populations in varied regions of north-west continental Europe that account for the levels of Mesolithic-derived ancestry observed in Neolithic Britain.

The DATES results presented in Brace *et al.* (2019) have been replicated and refined through a different method (ALDER) based on similar principles by Rivollat *et al.* (2020; see also Loh *et al.* 2013). This analysis identified that the average date of admixture with Mesolithic-derived populations in the ancestral histories of people from Neolithic England and Scotland (outside the outlier individuals from western Scotland) was the late 6th millennium cal BC. In genomes from Wales, this estimate was later in the mid-5th millennium cal BC, although the reliability of this estimate may be questionable given that Neolithic genomes available from Wales show, if anything, lower levels of Mesolithic-derived ancestry than Neolithic genomes from other parts of Britain (Brace *et al.* 2019). The genomes from Wales are of lower quality and are later, dating to *c.* 3000 cal BC, and it is possible that this estimate represents a methodological ceiling.

Thomas (2022) argues that the fact that the results of these methods could represent a palimpsest of different admixture events means that they cannot be used to dismiss the possibility that there were early minor admixture events between incoming and local populations in Britain in the late 5th millennium cal BC. While this may be true it is difficult to see why this would result in an ALDER estimate of admixture as far back as 5000 cal BC. The late 5th millennium cal BC is so much closer in time to the individuals from which we have genetic data than 5000 cal BC is distant, that if admixture had taken place just before 4000 cal BC we would expect there to be clear tell-tale longer segments of DNA associated with Mesolithic-derived populations that would drag the ALDER estimate younger than 5000 cal BC.

It is not possible to test properly the minimal Neolithic narrative proposed by Thomas (2022) using the genetic data available, as the model is predicated on explaining why signatures of recent admixture with Mesolithic-derived populations in Britain may be absent from the samples available from Neolithic Britain. This is especially true if early interactions that took place as part of the minimal Neolithic did not involve incoming and local groups having children with one another. Therefore Thomas' (2022) model does present a reasonable explanation of the genetic evidence. Crellin and Harris (2020) criticise archaeogeneticists for favouring simple models to explain their data, but this is not based on an arbitrary preference; it is related to a probabilistic epistemology that is central to genetics methods. Geneticists tend to favour simple models because from a probabilistic perspective, complex models are more likely to be incorrect, as they involve more degrees of freedom, which means there are more ways in which they might be wrong. Therefore, given that there is no firm evidence for much recent admixture with Mesolithic-derived populations in Neolithic Britain and that plausible source populations in continental north-west Europe could account completely for levels of Mesolithic-derived ancestries, the minimal Neolithic phase proposed by Thomas (2022) is unnecessary to explain genetic change in Britain in the 4th millennium cal BC. Whether the archaeological evidence favours Thomas' (2022) model over others is something that will continue to be discussed.

A small or negligible genetic contribution from local Mesolithic-derived groups to Neolithic populations of Britain does not necessarily translate into those groups having been marginalised or forcefully displaced by a migration 'event' involving sudden cross-Channel movements of absolutely large numbers of people. The conclusions presented by Brace *et al.* (2019) leave room for this process having involved small-scale movements of people over centuries. If populations carrying EEF-related ancestry and those descended from local Mesolithic populations lived largely in parallel with communities of migrants and their descendants for long periods, disparities in population size, fertility, infant mortality and survival to adulthood could all have contributed to Mesolithic-descended groups having a small or even negligible genetic legacy in the long term (Booth *et al.* 2021). Such a scenario is consistent with findings from sites such as the Coneybury Anomaly, where faunal remains suggest a meeting between a group of farmers presumably descended from continental migrants and a group of hunter-gatherers presumably descended from local Mesolithic populations (Gron *et al.* 2018).

ADMIXTURE IN WESTERN SCOTLAND

Data published in Patterson *et al.* (2022) further highlight the exceptional levels of excess Mesolithic-derived ancestries in burials from western Scotland, indicative of recent admixture with Mesolithic-descended populations in Britain (Brace *et al.* 2019). There are now eight Neolithic individuals showing evidence for recent admixture with local Mesolithic groups and all come from cave sites (and one shell midden) in western Scotland: Distillery Cave, Raschoille Cave, Carding Mill Bay and Ulva Cave (Olalde *et al.* 2018; Brace *et al.* 2019; Patterson *et al.* 2022). Moreover, the dates of these individuals extend well into the first half of the 4th millennium cal BC, providing indirect evidence for communities wholly descended from Mesolithic groups persisting in western Scotland for hundreds of years after groups carrying EEF-related ancestries first arrived.

Other individuals buried in some of the same caves in western Scotland show levels of Mesolithic-derived ancestries that are similar to those of the Neolithic population of Britain more generally. However, so far no analysed individual from these sites shows a genetic ancestry entirely derived from local Mesolithic groups. This situation is reminiscent of signatures of genetic ancestry across Britain between *c*. 2450 cal BC and *c*. 2000 cal BC when genetic ancestries of sampled burials were mostly derived from a new wave of migrants from continental Europe, but where there were sporadic occurrences of people with substantial levels of ancestry derived from local Neolithic groups (Olalde *et al*. 2018; Booth *et al*. 2021; Patterson *et al*. 2022). The communities burying their dead in the caves of western Scotland (and depositing bodies on a shell midden there) must have lived adjacent to people descended from local Mesolithic groups for hundreds of years, but only had children with them some of the time. It is of interest that the archaeological context of two individuals showing higher Mesolithic-derived admixture from Carding Mill Bay II was a shell midden in a crevice at the foot of a cliff (Connock 1990); laying out the dead on a shell midden to allow natural decomposition through exposure is the funerary practice of Late Mesolithic groups on the Inner Hebridean island of Oronsay, a day's sail to the south-west of Oban. This situation could chime with Mithen's (2022) account of the beginnings of a 'mesoneolithic' biocultural merger in and around the islands of western Scotland, although the genetic evidence would be more consistent with his alternative 'dual population' model.

These patterns of Mesolithic-derived admixture in western Scotland have no effect on the levels of these ancestries in the rest of Neolithic Britain over the long term (Brace *et al*. 2019; Patterson *et al*. 2022). This means that groups in western Scotland who were admixing more extensively with local Mesolithic-derived populations must have been fairly marginal to the broader population of Neolithic Britain and either did not survive or were so small relative to the total population that they had very little impact on general genetic ancestries over the long term. This is evidence, as Thomas (2022) suggests, that similar regional persistence of Mesolithic-descended populations alongside groups carrying EEF-related ancestries could have occurred in other unsampled or under-sampled regions of Britain, but would not show up in the national-level data. However, this would mean that regional communities involved in these processes were unusual, small and marginal to other groups. The one Mesolithic genome from the 5th millennium cal BC is also from western Scotland, from a bone buried in the Cnoc Coig shell midden on the island of Oronsay. The female burial carried no EEF-related ancestry (Brace *et al*. 2019). The radiocarbon date suggests she probably died before the arrival of groups carrying EEF-related ancestries, but some overlap is possible.

NEOLITHIC INHABITANTS OF GUERNSEY

The study by Patterson *et al*. (2022) also included the first Neolithic ancient genomes from the Channel Islands, specifically the island of Guernsey. These genomes provide an interesting opportunity to investigate demographic processes on a small island, as well as potentially providing some insight into the Neolithic populations of Brittany, the most likely source of any population movements into Guernsey, which in turn adds to discussion of likely proximate source population for migrations to Britain. The character of the genetics of Neolithic Brittany are unknown and may remain so to some degree due to the paucity of relevant human remains.

Eight individuals have been sequenced from two megalithic tombs on Guernsey: Le Déhus and The Common (Herm). The two burials from The Common are radiocarbon dated to 3646–3527 cal BC (95% confidence; 4817±28 BP; MAMS-14945) and 3954–3773 cal BC (95% confidence; 5050±29 BP; MAMS-14949; Patterson *et al.* 2022). Radiocarbon dating of the human bone from Le Déhus indicates that two, and potentially three, phases of deposition are represented. Three individuals date to between 4300 cal BC and 3900 cal BC. Two others are much later, dating to between 3100 cal BC and 2900 cal BC. The last sample dates to 2567–2301 cal BC (95% confidence; 3987±23 BP; SUERC-96208; marine calibrated).

Around 16–17% of the ancestry of samples from Le Déhus dating to the end of the 5th or beginning of the 4th millennium cal BC can be attributed to Mesolithic populations of Europe. This is also true of the samples from The Common where Mesolithic-derived ancestries are also between 16–17%. This is very similar to levels of Mesolithic-derived ancestries observed in other populations from northern France reported by Rivollat *et al.* (2020) and therefore below levels seen in Neolithic Britain. However, by the end of the 4th and beginning of the 3rd millennium cal BC Mesolithic-derived ancestries in burials at Le Déhus had risen substantially to 32–36%. The latest individual potentially dating to the second half of the 3rd millennium cal BC maintains this high level of Mesolithic-derived ancestries at 30%. It is notable that this person does not carry any ancestry derived from the migrations from the Pontic-Caspian steppe that began transforming genetic ancestries of populations in northern Europe between 3000 cal BC and 2400 cal BC (Allentoft *et al.* 2015; Haak *et al.* 2015). The radiocarbon date from this individual potentially overlaps with dates of others from Britain and continental western Europe who did carry steppe-related ancestry (Olalde *et al.* 2018; Brunel *et al.* 2020; Patterson *et al.* 2022).

The contrast in levels of Mesolithic-derived ancestries amongst the Neolithic samples from Guernsey suggests that there was some resurgence of these ancestries sometime between 3500 cal BC and 3000 cal BC. As in other parts of Europe, this resurgence could be because of more extensive admixture with local Mesolithic-descended groups, or the arrival of a new population carrying EEF-related ancestries with elevated levels of Mesolithic-derived ancestries (or a mixture of both; Bollongino *et al.* 2013; Haak *et al.* 2015; Lipson *et al.* 2017; Rivollat *et al.* 2020). These Guernsey individuals have not been subject to ALDER or DATES analysis and so it is difficult to distinguish between these two scenarios. It seems unlikely that two populations could have lived in parallel and sustained themselves on a small island like Guernsey without reproducing with one another for several centuries. On the other hand, such a scenario could be plausible if these Mesolithic-descended groups had persisted across the Channel Islands and the admixture we see in the samples from Le Déhus was as a result of mixing with populations drawn from across the islands. This situation could have been facilitated if there had been a decline in populations carrying EEF-related ancestries on Guernsey in the late 4th millennium cal BC, something to which Neolithic populations living on small islands may have been particularly susceptible (Ariano *et al.* 2022).

Two males sampled from Le Déhus dating to the 4300–3900 cal BC phase of deposition are 2nd–3rd-degree relatives and shared a paternal but not a maternal lineage. These two people could have been paternal first cousins, half siblings, uncle/nephew, grandfather/grandson, great-uncle/great-nephew or great-grandfather/grandson. The emphasis on a paternal relationship is consistent with finds from other Neolithic megalithic tombs (Sánchez-Quinto *et al.* 2019; Cassidy *et al.* 2020; Fowler *et al.* 2022).

POPULATION SIZE AND INSULARITY IN NEOLITHIC BRITAIN

Disparities in population size between incoming groups carrying EEF-related ancestries and their descendants, and local Mesolithic-derived groups, provide an irresistible way of helping to explain why EEF-related ancestries came to predominate amongst the inhabitants of so many areas of Neolithic Europe (Haak *et al.* 2015). Methods which utilise observations such as runs of homozygosity/heterozygosity assess the extent to which long stretches of the genome carry the same two genetic variants on each chromosome and provide a measure of the diversity of an individual's gene pool (Kirin *et al.* 2010). Genetic diversity is affected by population size, with large populations maintaining higher diversity, although homozygosity/heterozygosity can also be affected by processes such as admixture, which increase genetic diversity of a population. Runs of homozygosity can be caused by processes which decrease population diversity, such as bottlenecks or inbreeding.

Analyses of runs of homozygosity/heterozygosity have been performed several times for Mesolithic and Neolithic populations of Europe, and generally all have indicated that levels of homozygosity were lower in Neolithic populations descended from EEF-related groups than in Mesolithic populations from similar regions (Haak *et al.* 2015; Kılınç *et al.* 2017; Lipson *et al.* 2017; Mathieson *et al.* 2018; Olalde *et al.* 2019). This includes Britain, where levels of heterozygosity in the Mesolithic Cheddar Man, who dates to the late 9th millennium cal BC, were notably lower than for populations carrying EEF-related ancestries who inhabited Britain from around 4000 cal BC (Brace *et al.* 2019). The Cheddar Man genome was the only Mesolithic genome from Britain that was of a high enough quality to be able to run this type of analysis, and it may be questionable how appropriate it is to compare this Early Mesolithic individual to Neolithic genomes, which are so temporally distant. However, the suggestion that the population that inhabited Britain after 4000 cal BC was substantially larger than the one that lived before 4000 cal BC is supported by other proxies of population size (Collard *et al.* 2010; Timpson *et al.* 2014; Woodbridge *et al.* 2014).

When we are discussing disparities in population size, this is not just covering movements of large numbers of people, but also potentially the production of descendants over the long term. As we have discussed, there is evidence from several regions of Europe that groups carrying EEF-related ancestries often admixed in only a limited way with local Mesolithic-derived people initially, before admixing more substantially hundreds, sometimes thousands of years later (Bollongino *et al.* 2013; Lipson *et al.* 2017; Mathieson *et al.* 2018). This pattern is to some extent necessary to explain the smaller legacy of Mesolithic-derived inhabitants over the long term. If Mesolithic-descended populations were not small and there had been substantial admixture between these groups as soon as communities carrying EEF-related ancestries arrived in the area, then when the population grew, there would already have been a substantial Mesolithic-derived component to their ancestry.

Moreover, in a situation where groups carrying EEF-related ancestries and Mesolithic-descended populations lived in parallel and had children infrequently, the minority long-term genetic legacy of Mesolithic-descended groups necessitates that groups carrying EEF-related ancestries grew more quickly over the same period.

'Population replacement' as used in relation to migration in archaeogenetics papers is often misunderstood as being something total and involving aggressive displacement of previous inhabitants by large numbers of migrants (Booth 2019). Population replacement is a technical term in biology which refers to a shift in genetic ancestry at a population level, of any size, with no mechanism inferred. As we have discussed above, the processes responsible for a population replacement could have involved small groups of people arriving over several hundred years. If their diet, lifestyle or culture meant that they tended to have even slightly more children who lived to adulthood than neighbouring communities, then over hundreds of years this would translate into a substantial shift (or 'replacement') of genetic ancestries.

In Neolithic Britain, the challenge is to explain why the genetic shift we see was so large compared to other regions of Europe which involved interactions between similar populations (Brace *et al.* 2019). One possibility helping to explain this pattern would be that the Late Mesolithic population of Britain was especially small or scarce in many regions of Britain. Otherwise, factors affecting fertility, infant mortality and likelihood of living to adulthood would come into play, which may suggest that Mesolithic lifestyles in Britain differed from other Mesolithic populations in regions of continental Europe. The alternative or complementary perspective is that populations carrying EEF-related ancestries had lifestyles and practices that differed from those of similar populations in continental Europe, which meant that rates of child survival to reproductive age were higher. The biological relationships found in the Hazleton North long cairn may provide one potential example of this (Fowler *et al.* 2022). At Hazleton there was evidence that both men and women had children with multiple partners. If this was as a result of polyamory rather than serial monogamy then this practice would have increased the fertility of men particularly, as it would have reduced the times between the birth of their children. If future analyses indicate that these sorts of practices were less common in Continental Europe, then this could be one factor explaining why levels of local Mesolithic-derived ancestry were so low amongst Neolithic groups. In addition, low population sizes, or densities, in parts of Late Mesolithic Britain and Europe more generally would mean, intentionally or not, that migrant and local groups would have found it easier to avoid each other, making it easier to explain the persistence of parallel societies of groups variably carrying EEF-related ancestries (Bollongino *et al.* 2013; Lipson *et al.* 2017; Mathieson *et al.* 2018; Brace *et al.* 2019).

The only Mesolithic genome available from Britain dating to the 5th millennium cal BC, from Cnoc Coig on Oronsay, is too low quality to be analysed for metrics that might give an indication of population sizes in Late Mesolithic Britain (Brace *et al.* 2019). All other Mesolithic genomes date to the period of the Mesolithic before Britain became an island. Mesolithic hunter-gatherers of Ireland show high levels of homozygosity suggesting a relatively small endogamous population, albeit one that was able to avoid inbreeding (Cassidy *et al.* 2020). It is currently not possible to assess whether a similar process could have occurred in Late Mesolithic Britain after it was separated from continental Europe.

Another way of looking at population size and genetic insularity is through the extent to which individuals share 'identity-by-descent (IBD)' segments of DNA (Speidel *et al.* 2019; Ringbauer *et al.* 2021). Rather than relying on the extent to which samples share similar individual genetic variants (alleles), this method is more powerful in examining the extent to which individuals and population share long segments of DNA that are inherited together (Speidel *et al.* 2019; Ringbauer *et al.* 2021). Ariano *et al.* (2022) used IBD-sharing amongst other analyses to investigate the population history of Neolithic Malta, but also Neolithic Europe more broadly. They found a contrast between groups descended from the Mediterranean and Danubian Neolithic dispersals, with higher IBD-sharing between populations along the Danubian route. This means that populations associated with the Danubian dispersals were much more connected genetically, suggesting there was a lot of interaction and back-migration between these groups. This seems to be less true for groups associated with Mediterranean dispersals where levels of IBD-sharing were lower. This was especially true for populations that had moved on to islands, suggesting that once Neolithic groups had moved on to an island, the sea then became a barrier to further gene flow. (See also Ariano and Bradley, this volume.)

The analysis of IBD-sharing amongst Neolithic populations of Britain and Ireland found that IBD-sharing was higher within groups from the western Mediterranean and northern France, as expected, but that Britain and Ireland were also substantially separated from these Continental groups (Ariano *et al.* 2022). This suggested that once populations carrying EEF-related ancestries moved to Britain and Ireland from Continental Europe, there was continued intermarriage across the Irish Sea, but comparatively little across the Channel. Ariano *et al.* (2022) also found that IBD-sharing amongst the Neolithic population of Orkney was higher again than that observed between Neolithic populations of Britain and Ireland, suggesting that the Neolithic populations of Orkney were highly endogamous. Most published ancient genomes from Orkney date to the second half of the 4th millennium cal BC or the first half of the 3rd millennium cal BC, in the Middle–Late Neolithic, and may be quite specific to Orkney in this time period.

Patterson *et al.* (2022) applied an analysis that used runs of homozygosity to look at changes in effective population size in Britain through later prehistory. Runs of homozygosity provide a sense of the background relatedness of a particular population, which can be translated into an effective population size, with large runs of homozygosity indicating higher interrelatedness and lower effective population size. Effective population size is not census population size (although there is a relationship between the two). Effective population size can be thought of as how many people were reproducing with one another at any one time. Examining changes in effective population size through time can provide some indication of relative changes in population size, periods of population growth or shrinkage even if it does not provide a direct idea of actual population size.

Patterson *et al.* (2022) found that estimates of effective population size in Neolithic Britain in the 4th millennium cal BC were surprisingly low, around 4000, although with a confidence interval, which varied between around 2500 and 10,000. There is substantial uncertainty in relating effective population sizes to census size, but estimates suggest the census population should be between three and ten times the effective population size (Fernandes *et al.* 2021). This gives an estimate for the total population of Britain in the

4th millennium cal BC as between 12,000 and 40,000 people, although with a lower bound of 7500 and a higher bound of 100,000. These estimates are extremely broad, but generally suggest that the population of Britain in the 4th millennium cal BC was no more than 100,000 people and possibly substantially less than this.

There are caveats to this estimate. For instance, if our sample of Neolithic genomes was wholly or predominantly drawn from people who were closely related to each other rather than to the rest of the population, then this would give a false impression of background relatedness of the population as a whole and produce an underestimate of population size. In Ireland, close biological relatives were identified across different passage tombs, and patterns of IBD-sharing indicated that even those individuals that were not close relatives were still more related to each other than to the population of Britain and Ireland as a whole, suggesting the existence of a social stratum of closely related groups who more often were buried in passage tombs (Cassidy *et al.* 2020). Fowler *et al.* (2022) demonstrated that tombs could hold many close biological relatives.

We cannot reject the possibility that funerary treatment correlated with relatedness in Neolithic Britain to some degree and that we have so far sampled a biased sample of the population as a whole. However, Cassidy *et al.* (2020) did not observe similar patterns of relatedness in the data from Neolithic Britain as they found in the passage tombs or Ireland. While genomes sequenced from Neolithic Britain do primarily originate from tombs, the style of tomb varies considerably, and a high proportion of genomes come from cave burials, with a minority from a variety of different monumental and non-monumental contexts (Olalde *et al.* 2018; Brace *et al.* 2019; Sánchez-Quinto *et al.* 2019; Scheib *et al.* 2019; Patterson *et al.* 2022). To argue that these effective population size estimates may be down to higher relatedness between the people that have been sampled for DNA analysis is to infer these highly related individuals could be subject to a wide variety of funerary treatments. Perhaps, as has been suggested for the Chalcolithic–Early Bronze Age period, those individuals outside of these relative groups were subject to cremation, which destroys the DNA, or other funerary treatments that left no archaeological trace (Booth 2019).

RELATIVES IN NEOLITHIC BRITAIN

The use of DNA to identify relatives in Neolithic tombs of Britain and Ireland has been discussed at length by Cassidy *et al.* (2020) and Fowler *et al.* (2022). Few tombs from Britain and Ireland have had a high enough number of genomes sequenced from their occupants to be assessed for the presence of close relatives. Most tombs from which we have a decent number of genomes tend to show that a good proportion of the inhabitants were not close biological relatives (Olalde *et al.* 2018; Brace *et al.* 2019; Sánchez-Quinto *et al.* 2019; Cassidy *et al.* 2020; Patterson *et al.* 2022). When close relatives are found in tombs, they are more often males rather than females and tend to be related on their paternal side suggesting that patrilineage to some extent determined who was buried in these monuments (Sánchez-Quinto *et al.* 2019; Cassidy *et al.* 2020; Fowler *et al.* 2022). As we have discussed, people buried in passage tombs in Ireland were more related to each other than the Neolithic population of the rest of Britain and Ireland. Together, all these results have been used to argue that Neolithic societies in Britain were patrilocal and practised female exogamy, although these sorts of inferences rely on the (often unstated) assumption that occupants of tombs reflect cohabitants in life, which, while a reasonable argument, may not necessarily have been the case.

The spectacular results from Hazleton North chambered cairn, where 27 individuals out of 35 analysed from the tomb were close relatives from a five-generation genealogy provide an exception to the otherwise equivocal evidence for the role of biologically associated social ties in determining who was interred in Neolithic tombs (Fowler *et al.* 2022). All the men recovered from the tomb were related on their paternal sides, either biologically or through adoption and there was a distinct absence of adult female daughters, again potentially indicating a patrilocal system employing female exogamy, although other interpretations are possible. This result contrasts substantially with for instance the result from Isbister chambered tomb in Orkney where none of the seven individuals that have been sequenced so far were close biological relatives (Olalde *et al.* 2018). However, all of the genomes from Isbister date to the late 4th or first half of the 3rd millennium cal BC, and so the absence of relatives may relate to the different use of tombs in Middle–Late Neolithic Orkney and the extended periods of time over which they were used.

Two individuals from the Fussell's Lodge long barrow were 2nd–3rd-degree relatives and did not share a maternal lineage and so were more likely to have been paternally related (Cassidy *et al.* 2020). Unfortunately, the age-at-death of these two individuals is unknown, but if the female was an adult this could disrupt the trend with respect to the absence from Neolithic tombs of adult females who were paternally related to other inhabitants. Two individuals sequenced from the Trumpington Meadows Neolithic grave in Cambridgeshire were brothers. The impression so far from the limited evidence we have from Neolithic funerary monuments in Britain is that different types of tombs or even individual tombs may have been regarded in different ways when it came to the interment of people whose social ties mapped on to biological relationships (Fowler *et al.* 2022).

The genetic ancestry profiles of the relatives identified at Hazleton North also give us an insight into the nature of population movements in the early 4th millennium cal BC. All the relatives from the tomb had very similar genetic ancestry profiles with no significant variability in genetic ancestries derived from the Mesolithic populations of Britain. This means that individuals who are missing from the five-generation tree, but who would have contributed substantial genetic ancestry to the members whose genomes we have sequenced, would also not have had variable Mesolithic-derived ancestries. The consistency in genetic ancestries across dozens of individuals over several generations could only have occurred if migrations into Britain involved movements of groups of people who largely had children amongst themselves (Booth *et al.* 2021).

Genetic relatives are also notable by their paucity from Neolithic cave sites (Olalde *et al.* 2018; Brace *et al.* 2019; Patterson *et al.* 2022). The available data suffer in the same ways as the data from tombs; there are usually only one or two genomes available from individual sites, making assessments of overall patterns of relatedness difficult. The highest number of genomes we have from a single cave is 10 from Raschoille Cave in Oban, western Scotland. None of the individuals sampled were close biological relatives and they carried a variety of maternal and paternal lineages. Genetic relatives have, however, been identified from a cave and a shell midden in western Scotland, MacArthur Cave and Carding Mill Bay II, both also in Oban (Patterson *et al.* 2022). A pair of brothers or possibly a father and son were identified from MacArthur Cave, while two adult females from Carding Mill Bay II were 1st-degree relatives, either sisters or a mother-daughter pair. The Carding Mill Bay II relatives shared similar elevated levels of admixture from Mesolithic-derived groups, suggesting that they were more likely to have been sisters. If these individuals were adults when they died, this would contrast with relationships observed so far in tombs where paternally related female relatives were usually absent (Cassidy *et al.* 2020; Fowler *et al.* 2022). Unfortunately, the samples we have so far are too few to assess whether the frequency of relatives identified from these caves in western Scotland is significant.

A perhaps overlooked result from Brace *et al.* (2019) was the identification of three 1st-degree relatives recovered from the Whitehawk causewayed enclosure in Brighton comprising a mother and her two sons or two brothers and their sister. The bones had come from disarticulated deposits that had been scattered across the three enclosure ditches. Skeletal representation suggested that bodies had decomposed or been defleshed elsewhere before selected bones were collected and deposited in the ditches. This finding is interesting because, unlike what has been observed in many Neolithic tombs, this deposit seems to be referencing a maternal relationship. Does this mean that different types of relationship were considered important at different monuments and matrilineal descent was emphasised at causewayed enclosures? This result may also be a strong point against theories that processes of bodily disarticulation in Neolithic chambered tombs were intended to anonymise the dead, allowing them to become part of a faceless mass of ancestors (Barber 1989). The fact that these bones were redeposited at the same site may suggest their identities in life were known to the communities handling them. Alternatively, if the disarticulated bones deposited at Whitehawk had been collected from a tomb set out in a similar way to Hazleton North, then there would have been a high chance that simply collecting a random set of bones from a single chamber would have produced bones from a series of maternal relatives (Fowler *et al.* 2022). Further work on assemblages of human remains from different types of monuments, but especially causewayed enclosures, is required to assess how human remains were chosen for deposition at different types of monument.

The sensational finding that one of the burials from the Newgrange passage tomb in Ireland, an adult male, was the product of an incestuous relationship between 1st-degree relatives has not been repeated in any sampled burials from Neolithic Britain (Cassidy *et al.* 2020). In fact, patterns of homozygosity amongst all other Neolithic burials from Britain and Ireland suggest that instances of acute inbreeding such as found at Newgrange must have been rare (Brace *et al.* 2019; Cassidy *et al.* 2021; Ariano *et al.* 2022). Instead, observed levels of homozygosity suggest that Neolithic populations of Britain more often tried to avoid inbreeding. However, runs of homozygosity in one of the burials from the Hazleton North tomb suggested that they were the child of second or third cousins (Fowler *et al.* 2022).

BRITAIN IN THE 3RD MILLENNIUM CAL BC

Compared to the increasingly complex information that we have for the genetics of Neolithic Britain in the 4th millennium cal BC, our understanding of the first half of the 3rd millennium cal BC is lacking. This is partly because we only have five genomes from outside

Orkney that date to this period, from Orchid Cave and Rhos Ddigre in Denbighshire, Wales; Totty Pot in Cheddar, Somerset; Bryn Yr Hen Bobl on Anglesey and Thornholme in Yorkshire (Brace *et al.* 2019; Olalde *et al.* 2019; Patterson *et al.* 2022). Of these only two are of reasonable quality (Thornholme and Rhos Ddigre) and all but two (Totty Pot and Bryn yr Hen Bobl) date to the first quarter of the 3rd millennium cal BC. This is no surprise given the paucity of unburnt human skeletal remains available from this period.

All individuals show levels of EEF-related and Mesolithic-derived ancestries consistent with one another and populations who inhabited Britain from the beginning of the 4th millennium cal BC. The low number of samples means that it could be argued that these genomes may not be representative of all regions of Britain, although they do come from fairly dispersed places. Taken at face value the results suggest that there was no resurgence of Mesolithic-derived ancestries after 3000 cal BC and that there were also no substantial genetic interactions with populations outside Britain and Ireland, consistent with the conclusions of Ariano *et al.* (2022) that the populations of Britain and Ireland were genetically quite insular through the Neolithic.

The paucity and low quality of the genomes we have from Late Neolithic Britain mean it is difficult to use the genetic evidence to address outstanding questions of whether there was a population decline in this period (Collard *et al.* 2010; Timpson *et al.* 2014; Woodbridge *et al.* 2014; Downey *et al.* 2016; Colledge *et al.* 2019). Figure 2b from Patterson *et al.* (2021), charting changes in effective population size in later prehistory, leaves blank the period 3000–2500 cal BC, as the data and number of genomes we have from this period are insufficient to make any strong assertions about population size. This may be something that can be addressed in future with sequencing of further Late Neolithic genomes, but also through compensating for the poor quality of existing genomes through processes such as imputation, which uses reference panels of ancient and modern human genetic variation to fill in the gaps of ancient genomes.

Further Chalcolithic and Early Bronze Age genomes from Britain dating to 2500–2000 cal BC sequenced as part of the Patterson *et al.* (2022) study continue to suggest that for large parts of this period, a population largely genetically continuous with the Neolithic population of Britain persisted alongside migrants from continental Europe and their descendants who carried steppe-related ancestries (Booth *et al.* 2021). This is apparent in the trend for individuals of this period having either no or insubstantial ancestry derived from the Neolithic population of Britain, indicating an archaeologically invisible population descended from Neolithic populations who had children with people from the visible population only infrequently. The evidence for the persistence of populations descended from the Neolithic population of Britain into the late 3rd millennium cal BC in multiple regions of Britain and their detectable, albeit small, influence on the broader genetics of Britain by the beginning of the 2nd millennium cal BC represent a point of departure of the two 'transitions' at the beginning and the end of the Neolithic in Britain (Olalde *et al.* 2018; Brace *et al.* 2019; Booth *et al.* 2021; Patterson *et al.* 2022). Beyond headlines of 'population replacement', the demographic processes responsible for major changes in genetic ancestries in these periods were probably quite different.

Analysis by Patterson *et al.* (2022) suggests that effective population size between 2500 cal BC and 2000 cal BC was not so much larger than in the period of the Neolithic between 4000 cal BC and 3000 cal BC. With the caveats discussed above regarding potential bias influencing estimates of effective population size, this suggests that population sizes in Britain from 2500–2000 cal BC were also surprisingly low. This would also mean that, like in the early 4th millennium cal BC, migrations to Britain in the second half of the 3rd millennium cal BC could have comprised small-scale movements of people who were able to expand relatively rapidly rather than rapid movements of absolutely large numbers of people. Low population sizes and densities in certain regions of Britain during prehistory may help to explain the large-scale changes in genetic ancestry that we see, in that it is easier to see how migrations and proliferation of small communities of people could have had a substantial transformative effect on genetic ancestries over the long term.

There are five genomes available from Neolithic Orkney dating to between 3000 cal BC and 2500 cal BC, mainly from the Isbister tomb. Their genetic ancestries are very similar to those of Neolithic populations from the rest of Britain, but as we have discussed above, they show a high degree of genetic insularity suggesting that once groups carrying EEF-related ancestries arrived, they largely had children amongst themselves and did not intermarry much with communities on the mainland. Another way besides endogamy in which the genetic homozygosity of the population of Orkney could be explained is through population decline, and perhaps this pattern in Orkney is indicative of a wider trend of population contraction across Britain as a whole. However, given that we see similar patterns of homozygosity and genetic insularity in other Neolithic societies on small islands, the most plausible explanation for now is that the high homozygosity observed in populations of the Orcadian Neolithic reflects patterns of interaction within an insular context.

The latest genome from Isbister dates to 2572–2348 cal BC (95% confidence; 3962±29 BP; SUERC-68721), overlapping considerably with the first appearance of populations carrying steppe-related ancestries in Britain including mainland Scotland (Olalde *et al.* 2018). Recent genetic analysis of human remains dating to *c.* 1700–1300 cal BC, in the Middle Bronze Age, from the Links of Noltland settlement in Orkney suggests that while there was a major turnover in genetic ancestry as a result of the arrival of individuals carrying steppe-related ancestries, there was a major retention of paternal lineages from the Neolithic (Dulias *et al.* 2022). Short of Orkney having been flooded by women from mainland Scotland, this result suggests that genetic ancestry change in Orkney through the Bronze Age was more likely to have been mediated by marriage alliances between Beaker-using groups descended from Continental migrants on the mainland and local populations descended from Neolithic groups on Orkney. The observation that this kind of large-scale whole ancestry change could be mediated by socio-political manoeuvring means that similar processes could have been responsible for large-scale ancestry changes across mainland Britain, although producing slightly different results, and counters the urge to necessarily see this sort of change in terms of invasion and conquest (Booth *et al.* 2021).

CONCLUSION

Publication of new data and repeated analysis of published genomes have meant that our understanding of the genetics of Britain from the beginning of the 4th millennium cal BC has been refined considerably since the first data were published in 2018, although many questions still remain. It is clear that groups carrying EEF-related ancestry began moving into Britain around the beginning of the 4th millennium cal BC. These migrants were themselves descended from long-term dispersals of people into the western Mediterranean from Anatolia. Movements into Britain occurred around the same time as a secondary expansion of people carrying this ancestry derived from western Mediterranean, extending as far as Scandinavia. It is likely that these migrations into Britain took place over several hundred years, but once these new groups and their descendants became established there was little, if any, further intermarriage with groups from continental Europe, although marriage networks were maintained across the Irish Sea. There is little evidence from most parts of Britain for admixture between these incomers and their descendants and populations derived from the local Mesolithic inhabitants outside western Scotland, where there is indirect evidence for Mesolithic-descended populations having persisted for several generations after the first continental migrants arrived. This does not mean that local Mesolithic populations were overwhelmed by a sudden large-scale wave of migrants from continental Europe; it could mean small populations inhabited many regions of Britain in the late 5th millennium cal BC and that migrant-descended communities may have grown comparatively rapidly. Patterns of relatives in tombs indicate that burial in these contexts was often based on patrilineality, but matrilineality also played a part and rules of deposition may have varied across different tombs and in different monumental and non-monumental contexts (Fowler *et al.* 2021). Lack of quality genomes means our view of the first half of the 3rd millennium cal BC is hazy, although what we do have indicates substantial population continuity from the 4th millennium cal BC. Populations of Orkney in the late 4th and early 3rd millennia cal BC were particularly endogamous, which might provide important context for Middle–Late Neolithic cultural developments on these islands. There is indirect evidence that Neolithic-descended populations persisted in several regions of Britain alongside new continental migrants carrying steppe-related ancestries through the second half of the 3rd millennium cal BC and had a detectable, albeit small, influence on overall genetic ancestries over the long term. While genetic ancestry changes at the beginning and the end of the Neolithic in Britain were large and may have involved small local populations, the dynamics of the transformation of genetic ancestries are different, indicating distinct processes. Future data and analyses will undoubtedly continue to refine our view of the Neolithic inhabitants of Britain.

REFERENCES

Allentoft, M.E., Sikora, M., Refoyo-Martinez, A., Irving-Pease, E.K., Fischer, A., Barrie, W. *et al.* 2022. Population genomics of Stone Age Eurasia. *bioRxiv* preprint, 1–71. https://doi.org/10.1101/2022.05.04.490594.

Allentoft, M.E., Sikora, M., Sjögren, K.-G., Rasmussen, S., Rasmussen, M., Stenderup, J. *et al.* 2015. Population genomics of Bronze Age Eurasia'. *Nature* 522(7555), 167–72.

Ariano, B., Mattiangeli, V., Breslin, E.M., Parkinson, E.W., McLaughlin, T.R., Thompson, J.E. *et al.* 2022. Ancient Maltese genomes and the genetic geography of Neolithic Europe. *Current Biology: CB*, http://dx.doi.org/10.1016/j.cub.2022.04.069.

Barber, J. 1989. Isbister, Quanterness and the Point of Cott: the formulation and testing of some middle range theories. In J. Barrett and I. Kinnes (eds), *The archaeology of context in the Neolithic and Bronze Age: recent trends*, 57–62. Sheffield: J.R. Collis Publications.

Beau, A., Rivollat, M., Réveillas, H., Pemonge, M.-H., Mendisco, F., Thomas, Y., Lefranc, P. and Deguilloux, M.-F. 2017. Multi-scale Ancient DNA analyses confirm the western origin of Michelsberg farmers and document probable practices of human sacrifice. *PloS One* 12(7), e0179742

Bollongino, R., Nehlich, O., Richards, M.P., Orschiedt, J., Thomas, M.G., Sell, C., Fajkosová, Z., Powell, A. and Burger, J. 2013. 2000 years of parallel societies in Stone Age central Europe. *Science* 342(6157), 479–81.

Booth, T.J. 2019. A stranger in a strange land: a perspective on archaeological responses to the palaeogenetic revolution from an archaeologist working amongst palaeogeneticists. *World Archaeology* 51, 586–601.

Booth, T.J., Brück, J., Brace, S., and Barnes, I. 2021. Tales from the Supplementary Information: ancestry change in Chalcolithic–Early Bronze Age Britain was gradual with varied kinship organization. *Cambridge Archaeological Journal* 31(3), 379–400.

Brace, S., Diekmann, Y., Booth, T.J., van Dorp, L., Faltyskova, Z., Rohland, N. *et al.* 2019. Ancient genomes indicate population replacement in early Neolithic Britain. *Nature Ecology & Evolution* 3(5), 765–71.

Brunel, S., Bennett, E.A., Cardin, L., Garraud, D., Barrand Emam, H., Beylier, A. *et al.* 2020. Ancient genomes from present-day France unveil 7,000 years of its demographic history. *Proceedings of the National Academy of Sciences of the United States of America* 117(23), 12791–8.

Cassidy, L.M., Maoldúin, R.Ó., Kador, T., Lynch, A., Jones, C., Woodman, P.C. *et al.* 2020. A dynastic elite in monumental Neolithic society. *Nature* 582(7812), 384–8.

Collard, M., Edinborough, K., Shennan, S., and Thomas, M.G. 2010. Radiocarbon evidence indicates that migrants introduced farming to Britain. *Journal of Archaeological Science* 37(4), 866–70.

Colledge, S., Conolly, J., Crema, E., and Shennan, S. 2019. Neolithic population crash in northwest Europe associated with agricultural crisis. *Quaternary Research* 92(3), 686–707.

Connock, K.D. 1990. A *Shell Midden* at Carding Mill Bay, Oban. *Scottish Archaeological Review* 7, 74–6.

Crellin, R.J. and Harris, O.J.T. 2020. Beyond binaries. Interrogating ancient DNA. *Archaeological Dialogues* 27, 37–56.

Downey, S.S., Haas, W.R., Jr, and Shennan, S.J. 2016. European Neolithic societies showed early warning signals of population collapse. *Proceedings of the National Academy of Sciences of the United States of America* 113(35), 9751–6.

Dulias, K., Foody, M.G.B., Justeau, P., Silva, M., Martiniano, R., Oteo-García, G. *et al.* 2022. Ancient DNA at the edge of the world: continental immigration and the persistence of Neolithic male lineages in Bronze Age Orkney'. *Proceedings of the National Academy of Sciences of the United States of America* 119(8). http://dx.doi.org/10.1073/pnas.2108001119.

Fernandes, D.M., Sirak, K.A., Ringbauer, H., Sedig, J., Rohland, N., Cheronet, O. *et al.* 2021. A genetic history of the Pre-Contact Caribbean. *Nature* 590(7844), 103–10.

Fowler, C., Olalde, I., Cummings, V., Armit, I., Büster, L., Cuthbert, S., Rohland, N., Cheronet, O., Pinhasi, R. and Reich, D. 2022. A high-resolution picture of kinship practices in an early Neolithic tomb. *Nature* 601(7894), 584–7.

Fu, Q., Posth, C., Hajdinjak, M., Petr, M., Mallick, S., Fernandes, D. *et al.* 2016. The genetic history of Ice Age Europe. *Nature* 534(7606), 200–205.

Furtwängler, A., Rohrlach, A.B., Lamnidis, T.C., Papac, L., Neumann, G.U., Siebke, I. *et al.* 2020. Ancient genomes reveal social and genetic structure of Late Neolithic Switzerland. *Nature Communications* 11(1), 1915.

Gron, K.J., Fernandez-Dominiguez, E., Gröcke, D.R., Montgomery, J., Nowell, G.M., Patterson, W.P. and Rowley-Conwy, P. 2018. A meeting in the forest: hunters and farmers at the Coneybury 'Anomaly', Wiltshire. *Proceedings of the Prehistoric Society* 84, 111–44.

Günther, T., Malmström, H., Svensson, E.M., Omrak, A., Sánchez-Quinto, F., Kılınç, G.M. *et al.* 2018. Population genomics of Mesolithic Scandinavia: investigating early postglacial migration routes and high-latitude adaptation. *PLoS Biology* 16(1), e2003703.

Haak, W., Lazaridis, I., Patterson, N., Rohland, N., Mallick, S., Llamas, B. *et al.* 2015. Massive migration from the steppe was a source for Indo-European languages in Europe. *Nature* 522(7555), 207–11.

Jones, E.R., Gonzalez-Fortes, G., Connell, S., Siska, V., Eriksson, A., Martiniano, R. *et al.* 2015. Upper Palaeolithic genomes reveal deep roots of modern Eurasians. *Nature Communications* 6, 8912.

Kirin, M., McQuillan, R., Franklin, C.S., Campbell, H., McKeigue, P.M., and Wilson, J.F. 2010. Genomic runs of homozygosity record population history and consanguinity. *PloS One* 5(11), e13996.

Kılınç, G.M., Koptekin, D., Atakuman, Ç., Sümer, A.P., Dönertaş, H.M., Yaka, R. *et al.* 2017. Archaeogenomic analysis of the first steps of Neolithization in Anatolia and the Aegean. *Proceedings of The Royal Society, Biological Sciences* http://dx.doi.org/10.1098/rspb.2017.2064.

Lazaridis, I., Alpaslan-Roodenberg, S., Acar, A., Açıkkol, A., Agelarakis, A., Aghikyan, L. *et al.* 2022) The genetic history of the Southern Arc: a bridge between west Asia and Europe'. *Science* 377(6609), eabm4247.

Lipson, M., Szécsényi-Nagy, A., Mallick, S., Pósa, A., Stégmár, B., Keerl, V. *et al.* 2017. Parallel palaeogenomic transects reveal complex genetic history of early European farmers. *Nature* 551(7680), 368–72.

Loh, P.-R., Lipson, M., Patterson, N., Moorjani, P., Pickrell, J.K., Reich, D., and Berger, B. 2013. Inferring admixture histories of human populations using linkage disequilibrium. *Genetics* 193(4), 1233–54.

Mathieson, I., Alpaslan-Roodenberg, S., Posth, C., Szécsényi-Nagy, A., Rohland, N., Mallick, S. *et al.* 2018. The genomic history of southeastern Europe. *Nature* 555(7695), 197–203.

Mithen, S. 2022. How long was the mesolithic–neolithic overlap in western scotland? evidence from the 4th millennium BC on the Isle of Islay and the evaluation of three scenarios for Mesolithic–Neolithic interaction. *Proceedings of the Prehistoric Society*, First View, 1–25. https://doi.org/10.1017/ppr.2022.3.

Narasimhan, V.M., Patterson, N., Moorjani, P., Rohland, N., Bernardos, R., Mallick, S. *et al.* 2019. The formation of human populations in south and central Asia. *Science* 365(6457). http://dx.doi.org/10.1126/science.aat7487.

Olalde, I., Allentoft, M.E., Sánchez-Quinto, F., Santpere, G., Chiang, C.W.K., DeGiorgio, M. *et al.* 2014. Derived immune and ancestral pigmentation alleles in a 7,000-year-old Mesolithic European. *Nature* 507(7491), 225–8.

Olalde, I., Brace, S., Allentoft, M.E., Armit, I., Kristiansen, K., Booth, T. *et al.* 2018. The Beaker phenomenon and the genomic transformation of northwest Europe. *Nature* 555(7695), 190–6.

Olalde, I., Mallick, S., Patterson, N., Rohland, N., Villalba-Mouco, V., Silva, M. *et al.* 2019. The genomic history of the Iberian Peninsula over the past 8000 years. *Science* 363(6432), 1230–4.

Olalde, I., Schroeder, H., Sandoval-Velasco, M., Vinner, L., Lobón, I., Ramirez, O. *et al.* 2015. A common genetic origin for early farmers from Mediterranean Cardial and central European LBK cultures. *Molecular Biology and Evolution* msv181. http://dx.doi.org/10.1093/molbev/msv181.

Patterson, N., Isakov, M., Booth, T., Büster, L., Fischer, C.-E., Olalde, I. *et al.* 2022. Large-scale migration into Britain during the Middle to Late Bronze Age. *Nature* 601(7894), 588–94.

Ringbauer, H., Novembre, J., and Steinrücken, M. 2021. Parental relatedness through time revealed by runs of homozygosity in ancient DNA. *Nature Communications* 12(1), 5425.

Rivollat, M., Jeong, C., Schiffels, S., Küçükkalıpçı, İ., Pemonge, M.-H., Rohrlach, A.B. *et al.* 2020. Ancient genome-wide DNA from France highlights the complexity of interactions between Mesolithic hunter-gatherers and Neolithic farmers. *Science Advances* 6(22), eaaz5344.

Rivollat, M., Réveillas, H., Mendisco, F., Pemonge, M.-H., Justeau, P., Couture, C., Lefranc, P., Féliu, C. and Deguilloux, M.-F. 2016. Ancient mitochondrial DNA from the Middle Neolithic necropolis of Obernai extends the genetic influence of the LBK to west of the Rhine. *American Journal of Physical Anthropology* 161(3), 522–9.

Sánchez-Quinto, F., Malmström, H., Fraser, M., Girdland-Flink, L., Svensson, E.M., Simões, L.G. *et al.* 2019. Megalithic tombs in western and northern Neolithic Europe were linked to a kindred society. *Proceedings of the National Academy of Sciences of the United States of America* 116(19), 9469–74.

Scheib, C.L., Hui, R., D'Atanasio, E., Wohns, A.W., Inskip, S.A., Rose, A. *et al.* 2019. East Anglian early Neolithic monument burial linked to contemporary megaliths. *Annals of Human Biology* 46(2), 145–9.

Skoglund, P., Malmström, H., Raghavan, M., Storå, J., Hall, P., Willerslev, E., Gilbert, M.T.P., Götherström, A. and Jakobsson, M. 2012. Origins and genetic legacy of Neolithic farmers and hunter-gatherers in Europe. *Science* 336(6080), 466–9.

Skoglund, P. and Mathieson, I. 2018. Ancient genomics of modern humans: the first decade. *Annual Review of Genomics and Human Genetics* 19, 381–404.

Speidel, L., Cassidy, L., Davies, R.W., Hellenthal, G., Skoglund, P. and Myers, S.R. 2019. Inferring population histories for ancient genomes using genome-wide genealogies. *Molecular Biology and Evolution* 38(9), 3497–511.

Thomas, J. 2022. Neolithization and population replacement in Britain: an alternative view. *Cambridge Archaeological Journal* 32(3), 507–25.

Timpson, A., Colledge, S., Crema, E., Edinborough, K., Kerig, T., Manning, K., Thomas, M.G. and Shennan, S. 2014. Reconstructing regional population fluctuations in the European Neolithic using radiocarbon dates: a new case-study using an improved method. *Journal of Archaeological Science* 52, 549–57.

Villalba-Mouco, V., van de Loosdrecht, M.S., Posth, C., Mora, R., Martínez-Moreno, J., Rojo-Guerra, M. *et al.* 2019. Survival of Late Pleistocene hunter-gatherer ancestry in the Iberian peninsula. *Current Biology: CB* 29(7), 1169–1177.e7.

Woodbridge, J., Fyfe, R.M., Roberts, N., Downey, S., Edinborough, K. and Shennan, S. 2014. The impact of the neolithic agricultural transition in Britain: a comparison of pollen-based land-cover and archaeological 14C date-inferred population change. *Journal of Archaeological Science* 51, 216–24.

Yang, M.A. and Fu, Q. 2018. Insights into modern human prehistory using ancient genomes. *Trends in Genetics: TIG* 34(3), 184–96.

Chapter 11

Islands apart? Genomic perspectives on the Mesolithic–Neolithic transition in Ireland

Lara M. Cassidy

The Mesolithic and Neolithic cultures of Britain and Ireland were both intimately related and worlds apart. The islands also have distinct histories of archaeological thought surrounding the nature of Neolithisation. In this chapter, I consider the agricultural transition in Ireland through the lens of ancient genomics and compare it to that of Britain. The origins, isolation and legacy of Ireland's Late Mesolithic population are reflected upon in the light of new genetic data and archaeological discussion. I then turn my attention to the source and size of Ireland's Neolithic population. By combining recently published datasets from three genomic surveys of France, including a key sample from Escalles (a Neolithic causewayed enclosure near Calais), I find a potential shared origin for both British and Irish farming communities in the Chasséo-Michelsberg culture of the northern French coast. I estimate a large number of incoming migrants to the islands, perhaps in the tens of thousands, which could imply multiple and long-lasting streams of migration from the continent. Finally, the genomic evidence for patriliny and kinship-based hierarchy in Neolithic Ireland is discussed.

INTRODUCTION

A decade has passed since the publication of the first ancient human genome sequence from Europe, belonging to a Copper Age man from the Ötztal Alps (Keller *et al.* 2012). The authors found him most closely related to present-day Sardinians and noted that this may reflect a relatively recent diffusion of Neolithic people across Italy, followed by further demographic shifts on the mainland. However, with only a single genome they were cautious in their interpretations. At that time, human geneticists were conflicted as regards to the origins of Europe's gene pool, with some studies arguing for long-term population continuity since the Palaeolithic (Haak *et al.* 2005; Soares *et al.* 2010). These results were further used to support models of agricultural spread that centred on indigenous adoption, with only a minor role for migrants. But at the same time, improvements in excavation and dating schemes were sharpening up the chronologies of Europe's Neolithisation and the picture emerging in many regions was one of abrupt bursts of agricultural expansion, with little evidence of the transitional economies expected in adoptionist models (Rowley-Conwy 2011).

Models centred on the large-scale movements of people were later vindicated by a quick succession of ancient genomics papers that demonstrated that population turnovers accompanied Neolithic spread in central Europe (Gamba *et al.* 2014; Lazaridis *et al.* 2014), Scandinavia (Skoglund *et al.* 2014), Iberia (Günther *et al.* 2015; Haak *et al.* 2015) and Ireland

(Cassidy *et al.* 2016). Incoming farmers to these regions were shown to derive the majority of their ancestry from a population closely related to that of the Neolithic of western Anatolia (Broushaki *et al.* 2016). The first Neolithic genome from Britain and Ireland, belonging to a woman from a megalithic tomb at Ballynahatty, Co. Down (Cassidy *et al.* 2016), derived approximately 80% of her ancestry from this source. The remaining 20% stemmed from admixture events with European hunter-gatherers that occurred as her ancestors spread across the continent, many through the Mediterranean route of expansion (Cassidy *et al.* 2016; Olalde *et al.* 2018). France appears to have been a particular hotspot for such admixture (Rivollat *et al.* 2020; Seguin-Orlando *et al.* 2021). Today, genomic data from approximately 170 British and Irish Neolithic individuals exist (Olalde *et al.* 2018; Brace *et al.* 2019; Sánchez-Quinto *et al.* 2019; Scheib *et al.* 2019; Cassidy *et al.* 2020; Dulias *et al.* 2022; Patterson *et al.* 2022; Fowler *et al.* 2022), all showing similar profiles to Ballynahatty. Gene flow from hunter-gatherer populations on the islands into farming communities appears to have been minimal. The only current evidence that it took place comes from cave sites and a shell midden in the west of Scotland (Brace *et al.* 2019) and a court tomb in the west of Ireland (Cassidy *et al.* 2020).

From the genomic data, it is then clear that we are dealing with a colonisation model for the introduction of agriculture to Ireland and Britain. Bayesian analyses of radiocarbon datasets are also in harmony with this conclusion, implying that the Neolithisation of the islands was a relatively speedy affair (Whittle *et al.* 2011; Whitehouse *et al.* 2014; McLaughlin *et al.* 2016). However, in the past, archaeological opinion on the relative contributions of local and migrant groups has been decidedly mixed. One survey found that those who specialised in the Irish transition were more open to the possibility of a colonisation event, although the most popular answer was 'unsure', while British researchers were more likely to stress the complexity of the process and relate this to combination models involving both adoption and migration (Warren 2008). Indeed, models that fell close to one or other extreme have previously been branded as polarising and unhelpful (Cummings and Harris 2011). However, a polar position does not necessitate a less complex or accurate view of a process. A massive influx of new people over generations would still have resulted in a rich tapestry of local and migrant interactions across the islands. Here the questions of tempo and relative population sizes are key.

The potential intricacies of Neolithic migration to the islands have been much dissected (Sheridan 2007; 2010; Whittle *et al.* 2011; Thomas 2022). According to Whittle *et al.* (2011), farming communities appear to have arrived on the south-east edges of England around the 41st century cal BC and, after several centuries of consolidation in the south, spread abruptly into most other regions *c.* 3800 cal BC. The earliest evidence of cereals and rectangular houses in Ireland dates to 3720–3680 cal BC (Cooney *et al.* 2011; Whitehouse *et al.* 2014), with the initiation of court tomb construction (*c.* 3700–3570 cal BC) beginning soon afterwards (Schulting *et al.* 2012). There is also incontrovertible evidence for an earlier presence of Neolithic people at Poulnabrone portal tomb, where four individuals of the same ancestry as Ballynahatty were interred *c.* 3820–3745 cal BC (Schulting 2014; Cassidy *et al.* 2020). Notably, Alison Sheridan has suggested a distinct stream of migration from Brittany may have been responsible for the construction of closed megalithic chambers and simple passage tombs in Ireland around 4000 cal BC (Sheridan 2010; 2016), although relevant radiocarbon evidence remains scant (but see Schulting *et al.* 2017).

A multi-disciplinary approach is required to address some of the above complexities and tease apart any differences between the two islands over the course of the Mesolithic–Neolithic transition. Ancient genomic data are a new and useful tool with which to understand prehistoric demography and social organisation, although they are by no means an investigative Swiss army knife. In this spirit, the current chapter will provide an up-to-date genomic perspective on the Neolithisation of Ireland. The origins and demography of Ireland's Late Mesolithic and Early Neolithic populations will be considered in the context of those from Britain, as well as the potential forms of social organisation that existed among the island's megalithic communities.

THE IRISH LATE MESOLITHIC

Defining the demographic characteristics of Ireland's Mesolithic population on the eve of agriculture is vital to our understanding of the Neolithic colonisation event. The central question is one of population size. The larger the island's Late Mesolithic population, the harder it is to explain their minimal genetic contribution to farming communities without invoking some degree of violent conflict or social exclusion. A large effective population size would also suggest higher levels of connectedness and inward migration from societies across the sea. Analysis of the first two Irish hunter-gatherer genomes has, however, revealed signatures of isolation and historically small population sizes (Cassidy *et al.* 2020). These results are reflected upon here, in the light of new genetic datasets (Antonio *et al.* 2019; Jensen *et al.* 2019; Brunel *et al.* 2020) and archaeological discussion (Warren 2021; Chapple *et al.* 2022).

Despite the 4000-year duration of the island's Mesolithic, sites with human remains dated to the period number in the single digits (Meiklejohn and Woodman 2012). At present, genomic data have been successfully retrieved from two male individuals from cave sites in the west of the island. One genome from Killuragh (Woodman *et al.* 2017) dates to the Late Mesolithic (4793–4608 cal BC; 5725±55 BP; UBA-40235), while the other, from Sramore (Kador *et al.* 2014), falls close to the Mesolithic–Neolithic transition (4225–3961 cal BC; 5227±36 BP; UB-15772). Both can be considered part of the 'Western Hunter-Gatherer' (WHG) population (Fu *et al.* 2016), within which they form a distinct genetic grouping (Cassidy *et al.* 2020). For practical purposes, I designate this population 'Irish hunter-gatherers', although an individual in possession of this ancestry may not necessarily follow a hunting and gathering subsistence strategy, just as a modern individual of 'Irish' ancestry need never have set foot in Ireland. Indeed, given the late date of SRA62 it is possible this individual had contact with early agricultural communities arriving on the island.

Origins

The earliest observations of WHG ancestry come from Spain and Italy *c.* 17,000–15,000 cal BC (Fu *et al.* 2016; Bortolini *et al.* 2021), although the lineage's increased affinity to West Asian populations relative to earlier Europeans implies an ultimate origin further east. The spread of this ancestry northwards is associated with the expansion of temperate forests at the beginning of the Holocene, and with them diverse Mesolithic industries. In the west, WHG groups mixed with a divergent lineage associated with the cold-adapted

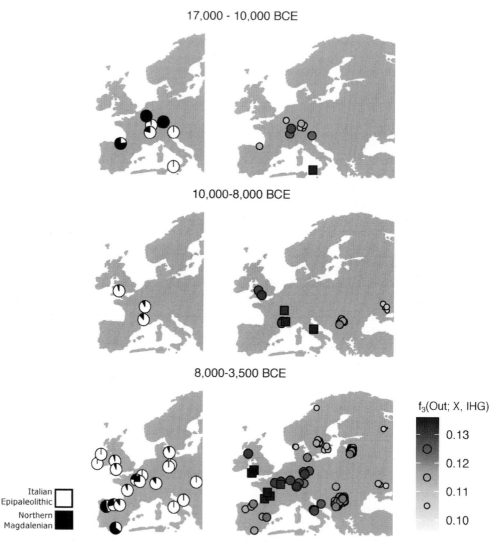

Figure 11.1. *The genetic affinities of Irish hunter-gatherers. The left-hand panels provide estimates of Magdalenian-related ancestry in European hunter-gatherer populations through time, estimated using qpAdm (Patterson et al. 2012). Population replacement can be observed in the north-west, with higher levels of Magdalenian ancestry seen in Spanish and French Mesolithic samples compared to Britain and Ireland. The right-hand panels show the results of outgroup F$_3$-statistics, with larger, darker values indicating stronger genetic affinity to the Irish hunter-gatherer population. The top 10 scores are shown as squares.*

Magdalenian culture (Fig. 11.1). The persistence of Magdalenian-related ancestry into the Mesolithic is most prominent in Iberia, where it existed in admixed form as early as 17,000 cal BC (Fu *et al.* 2016; Villalba-Mouco *et al.* 2019). In contrast, the Mesolithic populations in Britain and Ireland have little detectable ancestry from Magdalenian-related sources (Cassidy *et al.* 2020; Fig. 11.1). Britain and Ireland are believed to have been abandoned during the Younger Dryas with the exception of seasonal hunting groups (Dowd and Carden 2016), so this lack of continuity is not unexpected.

It is highly probable that Ireland's Mesolithic population derived from Britain, with the earliest evidence of permanent settlements on the island dating to approximately 7700 cal BC (Chapple *et al.* 2022). This aligns closely with the seemingly abrupt shift from Early to Late Mesolithic industries in Britain, traditionally marked by the appearance of small scalene triangles (Conneller *et al.* 2016). In outgroup F_3-statistics performed for this chapter (Fig. 11.1), Irish hunter-gatherers share highest levels of drift with two Late Mesolithic samples from south-western Britain dating to *c.* 7700–7100 cal BC (Brace *et al.* 2019). The next highest hits are three samples of a similar time depth from Les Perrats in western France (Brunel *et al.* 2020) and an Epigravettian genome from Sicily (Mathieson *et al.* 2018).

It is unclear whether the shift from Early to Late Mesolithic industries in Britain was accompanied by a substantial influx of new people, although it has been suggested that rising sea levels encouraged Doggerland populations to relocate (Waddington 2007). Here, using a D-statistic of the form D(Outgroup, X; SW_Brit_8800-8000, SW_Brit_7700-7100), I detect no significant gene flow into south-western Britain across this transition. However, the samples that show the highest excess allele sharing (Z=1.3-1.9) with the two Late Mesolithic genomes of this region are contemporaries from Les Perrats and Falkenstein in Baden-Württemberg (Fu *et al.* 2016; Mathieson *et al.* 2018), as well as Irish hunter-gatherers. Ongoing gene flow between Britain and the continent during this period would not be unexpected, given the presence of a land bridge and the high residential mobility that seems to have characterised this phase of the European Mesolithic (Crombé and Robinson 2014). However, resolving these relationships requires a larger number of north-western genomes and datasets that are amenable to haplotype-based analyses.

Isolation

The two Irish hunter-gatherers show the highest level of shared genetic drift seen for all tested pairwise comparisons of European genomes outside of close kin pairs (Cassidy *et al.* 2020) and similar to that seen for Jōmon hunter-gatherers from Japan (Cooke *et al.* 2021). Given the difference of approximately 23 human generations between their median radiocarbon values, we can rule out kinship as a cause for this inflation. Instead, as with the Jōmon, we can interpret this as the result of prolonged island isolation. In contrast, the two Late Mesolithic samples from south-western Britain exhibit a much lower level of shared drift and lack detectable differentiation from continental groups (Cassidy *et al.* 2020), which is likely to be a reflection of geography. Notably, Irish hunter-gatherers have no excess of long runs of homozygosity in their genome compared to other genomes of similar ancestry (Cassidy *et al.* 2020), implying that despite the island's impoverished array of flora and fauna, the human population was large enough to sustain outbreeding networks comparable to those found in Britain and the continent. Peter Woodman suggested that the island could sustain a Mesolithic population of 800 to 8000 people or 0.01 to 0.1 person per square kilometre (Woodman 1981). The current data support the larger estimate, or an even greater one.

While the Irish population appears genetically isolated prior to and during the 5th millennium cal BC, it has not yet been established how far back this isolation might have stretched. A relatively immediate founder effect upon colonisation of the island is one possible scenario, but the current data do not preclude a prolonged period of gene flow between the islands. Indeed, the possibly deliberate introduction of wild boar and felines to the island may imply a robust migratory stream (Montgomery *et al.* 2014) that was not stemmed until later periods. It is also worth reflecting on the transition from the Irish Early to Late Mesolithic during the 7th millennium cal BC and the potential drivers behind the changes in lithics, seemingly unique in Europe, with the exception of the Isle of Man. This transformation may reflect an increasingly insular population, perhaps one experiencing environmental stress (Riede 2009), although any association with the 8.2 kya cooling event remains highly debatable (Warren 2020). It is also possible that this new toolkit represents a secondary colonisation, although potential external sources are lacking. That said, genetic continuity across the transition should not be assumed. An Early Mesolithic genome from Ireland will be required to test this hypothesis.

Connections

Genomic data are only available from one Mesolithic individual in Britain post-dating the 8th millennium (Brace *et al.* 2019). This comes from the Cnoc Coig, Oronsay shell midden in the Inner Hebrides (5492±36 BP, calibrated to 4236–3769 cal BC, according to Bownes 2018: SUERC-69249). Intriguingly, a D-statistic of the form D (Outgroup, X; Southwest_British_LM, Irish_HG) produces the highest positive value when X is set as the Cnoc Coig genome. This implies an excess of allele sharing between Cnoc Coig and Irish hunter-gatherers relative to the Late Mesolithic samples from south-west Britain. However, given the very low coverage of the Cnoc Coig genome, the significance of this result is not certain (Z=1.88). It may hint at a connection between Ireland and Scotland at the beginning of the Irish Mesolithic and/or later points in time. The narrow sea crossing between the two regions is one of the more obvious avenues for gene flow between the islands. Unfortunately, the lack of Mesolithic human remains from elsewhere in Britain dating to the end of the period currently prevents further genomic investigation (Meiklejohn *et al.* 2011).

It is worth stressing that while the available data implicate the sea as a strong barrier to migration into Ireland, at least during the Late Mesolithic, it does not preclude all maritime contact. Parallels between Irish and European Mesolithic burial practices, ornaments and lithic technology have been drawn by Graeme Warren (2021), which could suggest low levels of movement, although the busy maritime networks as proposed by Garrow and Sturt (2011) are unlikely. Following a recent Bayesian analysis of radiocarbon dates, Chapple *et al.* (2022) have argued for an increase in the Irish population's size from 5300 cal BC onwards. While sea level rise may have amplified the levels of archaeologically visible activity through time, perceived changes in behaviour are also observed (*e.g.* the construction of lake edge platforms). This could suggest an 'edge effect', whereby agricultural expansion on the Continent influenced the island in some way (McLaughlin 2020), although even if the population existed in full isolation we would not expect it to remain culturally or technologically static. That said, a Mesolithic date on a cattle bone from Ferriter's Cove hints that some interactions were indeed occurring with continental farmers by the end of the period (Woodman *et al.* 1999); see Sheridan and Whittle (this volume) for a discussion of this. However, any new arrivals to the island in the approximately 700 years that separate the two men from Killuragh and Sramore made no detectable genetic impact, as they are symmetrically related to all other ancient populations thus far sampled.

THE IRISH NEOLITHIC

There are many outstanding questions regarding the nature of Neolithic migration to Ireland and Britain. One of the most pressing is perhaps the immediate origins of these farmers. How many came, where did they come from, and what subsequent episodes of population growth and restriction occurred as they dispersed over land and sea? Comparison with direct continental source population(s) can also aid in the interpretation of cultural and genetic phenomena within the islands, including interactions with local hunter-gatherers (Thomas 2022). Another set of questions relates to the social structures of these newcomers and their diversification through time. To address some of these issues, I will examine genomic data from the Irish Neolithic (Cassidy *et al.* 2016; 2020; Sánchez-Quinto *et al.* 2019) in the context of recently published studies from France and Britain (Brunel *et al.* 2020; Rivollat *et al.* 2020; Seguin-Orlando *et al.* 2021; Dulias *et al.* 2022; Fowler *et al.* 2022; Patterson *et al.* 2022). Notably, prior haplotypic analyses, which are sensitive to shallow levels of differentiation, have not been able to differentiate the Irish Neolithic from that of Britain, although clusters associated with Orkney and the developed passage tomb tradition in Ireland have been detected (Cassidy *et al.* 2020; Ariano *et al.* 2022). This implies that the islands' Neolithic populations stemmed from the same or highly similar sources.

Strands

Several candidate homelands for the Neolithic of Britain and Ireland have been identified along the French coast, from Brittany all the way into the Low Countries. In particular, strong parallels are seen between Chasséo-Michelsberg groups in northern France and the 'Carinated Bowl Neolithic' of the islands. Alison Sheridan has argued that the 'Carinated Bowl Neolithic' originated in the Nord-Pas de Calais region and is but one of several distinct strands of migration to the islands, albeit the seemingly most extensive one (*e.g.* Sheridan 2007; 2010; Sheridan and Whittle, this volume). She has also suggested a 'Breton' strand into western Britain and Ireland around 4000 cal BC, bringing the practice of constructing megalithic tombs, and a later 'Trans-Manche Ouest' strand linking Normandy and south-west England around 3800 cal BC. More recently, Julian Thomas has proposed that a 'minimal Neolithic' was initially co-created in the south-east of England by locals and small numbers of migrants, which went on to attract larger streams of migration to the islands from further down the French coast (Thomas 2022). He relates this later movement to the acceleration of Neolithisation after 3900 cal BC as proposed by Whittle *et al.* (2011) and to Sheridan's 'Trans-Manche Ouest' strand.

Previous aDNA work by Rivollat *et al.* (2020) reported a potential difference between Irish and British Neolithic populations. The authors suggested a greater affinity between Irish genomes and those from the western French site of Prissé-la-Charrière, relative to sites from northern France, which could support the Breton strand hypothesis. However, these tests did not account for potential batch effects. Unlike Ireland, the majority of British data have been produced using SNP capture, a molecular technique designed to enrich for informative sites in the genome (Haak *et al.* 2015; Mathieson *et al.* 2015). While cost-effective, the trade-off is that this targeting can introduce biases (Margaryan *et al.* 2020). When D-statistics are performed using only non-targeted British data, no difference is observed between the two islands with respect to the different French sites (Cassidy 2020; Table 11.1). This is in agreement with the aforementioned homogeneity of the British-Irish Neolithic population as seen in haplotypic analyses.

Table 11.1. *Select D-statistics for French, Scottish, English and Irish Neolithic populations. The results of the D-statistic D(Mbuti, Pop1; Pop2, Pop3) are shown. Shotgun sequence data (no target enrichment) are used for at least two populations in all tests. A positive value indicates increased allele sharing between Pop1 and Pop3, while negative values indicate increased sharing between Pop1 and Pop2. Values with a Z-score above 1.5 are highlighted in grey.*

Pop1	Pop2	Pop3	D-statistic	Z-score	Number of Sites
Michelsberg	Ireland	Scotland	-0.0007	-0.35	644738
Michelsberg	Ireland	England	0.0024	1.162	693033
Michelsberg	Scotland	England	0.0029	0.984	644715
Le Pirou	Ireland	Scotland	-0.0003	-0.061	77177
Le Pirou	Ireland	England	-0.0006	-0.114	82532
Le Pirou	Scotland	England	0.0002	0.031	77177
Fleury-sur-Orne	Ireland	Scotland	-0.0001	-0.064	909966
Fleury-sur-Orne	Ireland	England	0.0002	0.16	979294
Fleury-sur-Orne	Scotland	England	0	0.012	909948
Gurgy	Ireland	Scotland	-0.0012	-0.646	948026
Gurgy	Ireland	England	-0.0005	-0.369	1020355
Gurgy	Scotland	England	0.0004	0.207	948004
Prissé-la-Charrière	Ireland	Scotland	-0.0002	-0.074	627800
Prissé-la-Charrière	Ireland	England	-0.0008	-0.399	675230
Prissé-la-Charrière	Scotland	England	-0.0013	-0.409	627794
Escalles	Ireland	Scotland	0.0025	0.656	277819
Escalles	Ireland	England	0.0006	0.253	298367
Escalles	Scotland	England	-0.0017	-0.381	277813
Ireland	Scotland	Escalles	0.0022	0.636	277819
Ireland	England	Escalles	0.001	0.434	298367
Scotland	England	Escalles	0.004	0.971	277813

(Continued)

Table 11.1. (Continued)

Pop1	Pop2	Pop3	D-statistic	Z-score	Number of Sites
Ireland	Scotland	Prissé-la-Charrière	-0.0046	-2.422	627800
Ireland	England	Prissé-la-Charrière	-0.0066	-3.761	675230
Scotland	England	Prissé-la-Charrière	-0.0049	-1.947	627794
Ireland	Scotland	Fleury-sur-Orne	-0.0039	-1.95	909966
Ireland	England	Fleury-sur-Orne	-0.0052	-3.448	979294
Scotland	England	Fleury-sur-Orne	-0.0052	-2.21	909948
Ireland	Scotland	Gurgy	-0.0044	-2.201	948026
Ireland	England	Gurgy	-0.0054	-4.304	1020355
Scotland	England	Gurgy	-0.006	-3.57	948004
Ireland	Scotland	Michelsberg	0.0007	-0.35	644738
Ireland	England	Michelsberg	0.0024	1.162	693033
Scotland	England	Michelsberg	0.0029	0.984	644715
Ireland	Scotland	Le Pirou	0.0009	0.218	82532
Ireland	England	Le Pirou	-0.0046	-0.798	77177
Scotland	England	Le Pirou	-0.0016	-0.267	77177
Ireland	Escalles	Fleury-sur-Orne	-0.0062	-2.197	278541
Ireland	Escalles	Gurgy	-0.0048	-1.85	291815
Ireland	Escalles	Michelsberg	-0.0075	-2.389	197989
Scotland	Escalles	Fleury-sur-Orne	-0.0061	-1.195	259437
Scotland	Escalles	Gurgy	-0.0081	-2.032	271776
Scotland	Escalles	Michelsberg	-0.0092	-1.476	184514
England	Escalles	Fleury-sur-Orne	-0.0065	-1.798	278538
England	Escalles	Gurgy	-0.0045	-1.626	291811
England	Escalles	Michelsberg	-0.0035	-0.8	197987
Ireland	Le Pirou	Fleury-sur-Orne	-0.0071	-1.312	76226
Ireland	Le Pirou	Gurgy	-0.0055	-1.196	80334
Ireland	Le Pirou	Michelsberg	-0.0129	-1.66	54317
Scotland	Le Pirou	Fleury-sur-Orne	-0.0024	-0.25	71307
Scotland	Le Pirou	Gurgy	-0.0026	-0.395	75149
Scotland	Le Pirou	Michelsberg	-0.008	-0.811	50871
England	Le Pirou	Fleury-sur-Orne	-0.005	-0.92	76226
England	Le Pirou	Gurgy	-0.0044	-0.875	80334
England	Le Pirou	Michelsberg	-0.0178	-2.374	54317

Facilitating the co-analysis of datasets generated by different laboratories is of vital importance in future genomic studies of the Neolithic, especially when unpicking differences between closely related groups. Given that capture techniques only target a small fraction of the human genome and can create these confounding effects, future work on British and Irish samples may benefit from focusing on non-targeted approaches when endogenous content is sufficiently high.

Locals

There are no detectable differences in the level of European hunter-gatherer ancestry between Irish and British Neolithic populations. A rolling average of 18% is seen for both islands over the course of the Neolithic (Fig. 11.2). That said, admixture between indigenous hunter-gatherers and incoming farmers in Ireland did occur. A male interred at Parknabinnia court tomb is estimated to have had an Irish hunter-gatherer approximately five generations back in his family tree, the only current example of hunter-gatherer input into a megalithic community on the islands (Cassidy *et al.* 2020). This man died *c.* 3500 BC, approximately 300 years after the first interments at the neighbouring Poulnabrone portal tomb, suggesting perhaps centuries-long coexistence between locals and migrants in Ireland. Given the invisibility of Late Mesolithic burial practices (Meiklejohn and Woodman 2012),

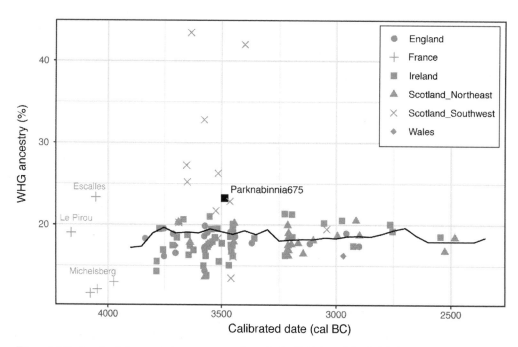

Figure 11.2. Levels of hunter-gatherer ancestry through the British and Irish Neolithic. Percentage hunter-gatherer ancestry was estimated with a two-way qpAdm model, using shotgun sequence data for reference and source populations. Source populations were Aegean early Neolithic samples and hunter-gatherer genomes from France, Luxembourg, Britain and Ireland. A rolling average is provided using a window size of 300 years and a step size of 50 years. Reference French values are also shown.

it is possible that these populations persisted on the island for further centuries, whether through voluntary or forced exclusion from farming societies. Notably, the genetic and cultural survival of European hunter-gatherers alongside farmers has been observed in Westphalia (Lipson *et al.* 2017) and Scandinavia (Skoglund *et al.* 2014).

Julian Thomas has suggested the initial Neolithic of south-east England involved substantial local input (Thomas 2022). Indeed, while the Neolithic appears to have arrived in most regions of the islands as a complete 'package' (Whittle *et al.* 2011), the south-east shows a more staggered uptake. Unfortunately, no ancient genomes from the very first English farmers are available and thus it is not possible to establish the level of admixture with local Mesolithic groups that occurred in these first generations, as later movements may have erased the signature. Moreover, the genetic profile of the continental source population is unknown. French populations appear heterogenous in hunter-gatherer ancestry (Seguin-Orlando *et al.* 2021), though many have estimates lower than those of Britain and Ireland (Rivollat *et al.* 2020). Here I estimate proportions between 13–16% for three Michelsberg samples from the Paris basin dating to *c.* 4000 cal BC. If the unknown source population(s) averaged 14%, a 1:20 ratio of local to migrant input could have produced the 18% average seen in Britain and Ireland, with variability through time and space, as captured in cave sites and a shell midden on the west coast of Scotland (Brace *et al.* 2019). Notably, only the earlier stages of the British and Irish Neolithic produce individuals with an estimated hunter-gatherer ancestry below 16% (Fig. 11.2)

Size

While it is clear that the end result of Neolithisation was a swamping of the Mesolithic gene pool, can we put estimates on the number of migrants involved? I attempt this here using IBDNe (Browning and Browning 2015), which considers the length distribution of genomic segments shared between individuals. To reduce temporal differences between samples, I consider two Neolithic populations, one earlier and one later (Fig. 11.3). Both trajectories suggest some level of a bottleneck *c.* 4500 cal BC followed by a rapid expansion, in keeping with expectations. The lowest point estimates of effective population size (Ne) during

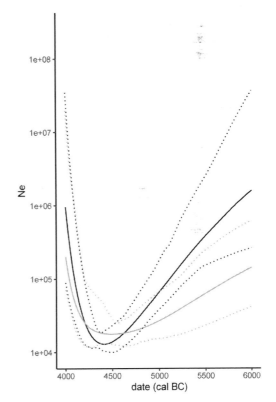

Figure 11.3. Estimation of the historical effective size of the Irish and British Early Neolithic Population. Dotted lines show the 95% confidence interval. Estimates for two different time transects are shown. Samples with median radiocarbon dates between 3600–3450 cal BC (n=27) are shown in black and one between 3850–3600 cal BC in grey (n=13).

this bottleneck are between 13,000 and 18,000, which, following the formula from Pankratov *et al.* (2020), may imply a census size of up to 60,000–90,000 people. This suggests a large number of migrants making their way across the Channel. After the bottleneck, Ne then rapidly approaches 1 million and beyond, implying high rates of fertility on the islands. However, these numbers are very preliminary and should be regarded with caution, especially those in the most recent generations, which are most certainly over-estimates. Denser genomic sampling and the application of methods that can take sample age into account are required for confirmation.

Notably, even the earliest Neolithic individuals from Ireland appear outbred, implying large community sizes (Cassidy *et al.* 2020). Recently, Ariano *et al.* (2022) estimated an Ne between approximately 2000 and 4000 for the Poulnabrone and Parknabinnia populations, which could indicate a census size of 10,000–20,000 people in the Neolithic Burren (Pankratov *et al.* 2020). Estimates of Neolithic population sizes on the islands from other forms of data vary widely, including 120,000 people in Middle Neolithic Britain (Müller 2015) and a boom of perhaps 1 million people in Neolithic Ireland estimated from a summed radiocarbon probability distribution by McLaughlin (2020).

Origins

Archaeologists differ over the areas from which farming became established in Ireland, although the 'Carinated Bowl' strand most probably entered from Britain (Sheridan 2007; 2010; Whittle *et al.* 2011). To investigate further, I estimate shared genetic drift between the Irish Neolithic population and samples from other regions using outgroup F_3-statistics (Fig. 11.4A and B). Unsurprisingly, the majority of top hits come from Britain, with no clear patterning across that island. On the Continent, the highest scoring genomes cluster together in three regions: north-eastern France, the coast of southern France and the Basque region. To confirm these affinities, continental samples were grouped by geography, time period and cultural associations, and F_3-statistics were performed once more. This time, the Neolithic populations of England and north-eastern Scotland were also tested, as well as that of Ireland, with no clear differences found in their continental affinities (Fig. 11.4C).

The highest average value for the English, Scottish and Irish population is seen for a single individual from a causewayed enclosure at Escalles, a coastal site facing out on to the straits of Dover (Praud 2015; Brunel *et al.* 2020). The sample dates to 4230–3879 cal BC, encompassing the period when the first movements into England are thought to have occurred. In his life, he may even have traversed the Channel. However, the proportion of his ancestry derived from European hunter-gatherers is approximately 23% (Fig. 11.2), higher than that seen for any British or Irish Neolithic individual so far tested (14–21%) with the exception of recently admixed outliers. It may be that the Escalles individual is also an outlier in his community or that his population is not the exact progenitor of Britain's and Ireland's Neolithic inhabitants. Notably, the site's pottery shows links with the Spiere Chasséo-Michelsberg group further north in Belgium, while the flint assemblage has affinities to Chasséen flintwork found to the south-west (Praud 2015).

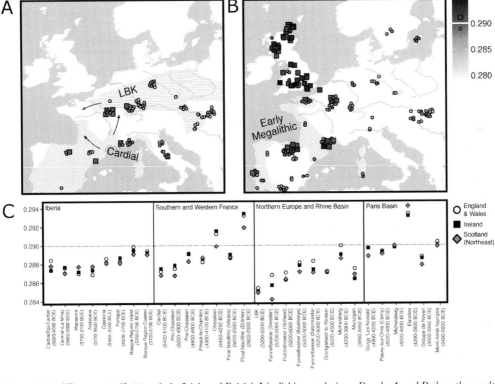

Figure 11.4. The genetic affinities of the Irish and British Neolithic populations. Panels A and B show the results of outgroup F_3-statistics, with darker shades indicating stronger genetic affinity to the Irish Neolithic population. Only samples with over 40,000 sites for pairwise comparison are considered. The top 75 hits (above ~0.29) are shown as squares. Panel C compares the English, Irish and Scottish populations to continental groupings. Samples from Argyll in western Scotland are excluded due to high levels of recent hunter-gatherer admixture.

The Chassey culture emerged *c.* 4350 cal BC with apparent origins in the Cardial cultures of southern France (Gernigon 2016). From there, elements spread north through the Loire, Rhône and Seine river valleys. No genomic data are yet available from northern Chassey sites. However, the next highest values seen in this analysis were for a Chassey site on the south coast, Le Pirou, dating to 4447–4251 cal BC (Erl-13040), and for a megalithic tomb from the same region (Brunel *et al.* 2020). These preliminary results may indicate that the Chassey expansion was accompanied by some level of population movement, which eventually culminated in the colonisation of Britain and Ireland. The Chassey was predated in the Paris Basin by the Cerny culture, whose long mounds represent an early manifestation of monumental burial in the region. Two assemblages from the Paris basin dating to the Cerny horizon, Gurgy and Fleury-sur-Orne (Rivollat *et al.* 2020), do not produce values as high as Escalles or the southern French sites, but they are still higher than most other populations tested. The same is true of samples from Michelsberg sites

(Brunel *et al.* 2020; Rivollat *et al.* 2020), a culture of north-west and west-central Europe, which is believed to have emerged from the Chassey.

When considering the origin of the Irish and British Neolithic, it is also worth noting that Y chromosome diversity on the islands is dominated by a specific lineage, I-M284 (Cassidy *et al.* 2020), that has not yet been identified on the Continent to the author's knowledge. It is possible that this haplogroup was rare in France and rose to higher frequency due to founder effect upon entry to the islands. Y chromosome lineages can also increase rapidly in frequency due to social prestige inferred on perceived male-line ancestry (Zerjal *et al.* 2003). Alternatively, we may find I-M284 at substantial frequencies in a yet unsampled continental progenitor population.

Taken all together, this author's best guess is that the major source of Britain's and Ireland's Neolithic gene pool will be identified in coastal Chasséo-Michelsberg groups south-west of Escalles. She also suspects that populations further north along the coast, who are in closer proximity to the transitional hunter-gatherer-farmers of Swifterbant culture (Dusseldorp and Amkreutz 2020), may have levels of hunter-gatherer ancestry too high for a large contribution, although this is speculative. And what of the Breton strand? While these results do not preclude a migratory stream from Brittany into Ireland and the west of Britain, it is not detectable in current datasets. If a substantial migration from Brittany did occur, it may have derived from sources too similar to those of more easterly streams to distinguish (*e.g.* through a westward expansion of Paris basin populations). Maritime mobility was high at the time of Britain's and Ireland's colonisation, evidenced by the rapid diffusion of megalithic architecture along the Atlantic seaboard from north-west France (according to Schulz Paulsson 2019). In this context, the higher affinity of the British and Irish Neolithic individuals to contemporary populations in the Basque region, relative to other Iberians, is intriguing, as archaeological evidence does not suggest any link. The gaping hole in this emerging and intricate picture is genomes from Brittany itself, although the poor preservation of human remains from this region is discouraging (Scarre 2011).

Society

The Neolithic populations of Britain and Ireland had a very recent shared origin, vibrant exchange networks and minimal ancestral input from local hunter-gatherer groups. This suggests that, at least for the earlier part of the Neolithic, they would have shared closely related languages, customs and beliefs. Recent studies indicate this included a strong emphasis on the patriline among monumental tomb users (Sánchez-Quinto *et al.* 2019; Cassidy *et al.* 2020; Fowler *et al.* 2022; Rivollat *et al.* 2022). By far the clearest example of this comes from Hazleton North, a chambered long cairn of the Cotswold-Severn group, where a five-generation family tree provided evidence of virilocal burial and female exogamy (Fowler *et al.* 2022). The male progenitor of this pedigree reproduced with four women, whose descendants may have been delegated to different sections of the tomb, hinting at possible polygamous practices. Architectural parallels are seen between Cotswold-Severn tombs, the 'Clyde' chambered tombs of south-west Scotland and Irish court tombs, many of which appear to have been built and used over the same short period starting *c.* 3700 BC (Schulting *et al.* 2012). Julian Thomas has suggested that these tombs may have been built for the founding generations of specific communities (Thomas 2015; 2022), who perhaps were growing concerned with territory and lineage in an increasingly crowded environment. Notably, Parknabinnia court tomb also shows evidence of patriliny (Cassidy *et al.* 2020). The majority of males belong to a rare Y chromosome lineage, but no close kinship is seen between them. This could reflect patrilineal affiliations between high-status men that stretched back many generations in time.

Genomes from Irish passage tombs have also shed light on social organisation during the period (Cassidy *et al.* 2020). A network of distant relatives (6th degree or further), spanning a minimum of six centuries, were found interred at three of the major passage tomb complexes – Bru na Bóinne, Carrowkeel and Carrowmore – as well as the related site of Millin Bay. This is best interpreted as an hereditary elite. One of these individuals, a man interred in the right-hand recess of Newgrange, was further found to be the product of first-degree incest. If such unions were socially sanctioned in Neolithic Ireland, then the comparative anthropological data overwhelmingly point to their occurrence within an elite who practised polygyny, patriliny and some degree of political deification (van den Berghe and Mesher 1980; Wolf 2014). The probability of this man's parentage being unknown or frowned upon by his community and unrelated to both his prestigious interment and his kinship with other passage tomb samples is very low. Thus, it may be useful to compare and contrast the developed passage tomb tradition in Ireland to other cultures that engaged in this custom, bearing in mind criticisms of ethnographic analogy (but see Currie 2016).

CONCLUSION

Over the past decade, new technologies and analytical methods have accelerated the pace of archaeological discovery. One key development has been the emergence of ancient genomics, which has shed new light on prehistoric demography and social organisation. In particular, the flood of genomic data has helped cool down heated, lengthy debates over migration, turning population replacement into a testable hypothesis rather than a subjective interpretation. Burgeoning radiocarbon and isotopic datasets are also allowing regional demographics to be examined at a resolution to which ancient genomics can still only aspire (McLaughlin 2020; Snoeck *et al.* 2020). In Britain and Ireland, this has allowed specialists to revisit major transitions in the archaeological record with fresh eyes (Booth *et al.* 2021; Cummings *et al.* 2022; Thomas 2022).

It goes without saying that the truth underlying the archaeological record is far more complex than any model can account for. The Mesolithic to Neolithic transition in Ireland, like any other event in human history, was not a simple affair. However, as archaeology is a field that thrives on interdisciplinarity, it is sometimes necessary to shirk detail and provide 'big picture' narratives to aid in communication, with the implicit understanding that all models are to some extent wrong. My own account of the Neolithisation of Ireland, based on the current genetic data, is then as follows.

The Irish Late Mesolithic population was isolated, with no evidence for frequent and sustained contact with other regions. Early Neolithic communities were large and adept at seafaring, with the overall population eventually probably reaching hundreds of thousands.

To a major extent, the population derived from the same source as that relating to British Neolithic individuals, potentially Chasséo-Michelsberg groups on the French coast between Normandy and Nord-Pas de Calais. Assimilation of Irish hunter-gatherers took place and may even have been quite frequent, but ongoing inward migration and high rates of fertility in farming communities kept their genetic contribution minimal. Neolithic societies were hierarchical and preoccupied with male-line descent. By the peak of the developed passage tomb tradition, an hereditary elite had emerged, some of whose members may have been perceived as having divine attributes.

Further research will surely necessitate small and large adjustments to the above. Going forward, ancient DNA studies must focus on denser sampling of Late Neolithic individuals, not only to place the results from passage tombs into better context, but also to chart the demographic trajectory taken by the Irish population following colonisation, including the ways in which it may have diverged from or dovetailed with that of the neighbouring island. New data from Britain and France are much anticipated. Genomic data from cave sites, including sedimentary DNA, will also be of particular value to our understanding of the lives and legacies of Irish hunter-gatherers. Most importantly, we must continue to grow the vibrant interdisciplinary networks that have made a volume such as this possible.

ACKNOWLEDGEMENTS

I am grateful to Alison Sheridan for her comments, criticisms and many useful nuggets of information that helped improve this paper and my own understanding of the complexities discussed within.

REFERENCES

Antonio, M.L., Gao, Z., Moots, H.M., Lucci, M., Candilio, F., Sawyer, S., Oberreiter, V. *et al.* 2019. Ancient Rome: A genetic crossroads of Europe and the Mediterranean. *Science* 366(6466), 708–14.

Ariano, B., Mattiangeli, V., Breslin, E.M., Parkinson, E.W., McLaughlin, T.R., Thompson, J.E., Power, R.K. *et al.* 2022. Ancient Maltese genomes and the genetic geography of Neolithic Europe. *Current Biology: CB* 32(12), 2668–80.e6.

Booth, T.J., Brück, J., Brace, S. and Barnes, I. 2021. Tales from the Supplementary Information: ancestry change in Chalcolithic–Early Bronze Age Britain was gradual with varied kinship organization. *Cambridge Archaeological Journal* 31, 379–400.

Bortolini, E., Pagani, L., Oxilia, G., Posth, C., Fontana, F., Badino, F., Saupe, T. *et al.* 2021. Early Alpine occupation backdates westward human migration in Late Glacial Europe. *Current Biology: CB* 31(11), 2484–93.e7.

Bownes, J.M. 2018. *Reassessing the Scottish Mesolithic-Neolithic transition: questions of diet and chronology.* PhD thesis, University of Glasgow.

Brace, S., Diekmann, Y., Booth, T.J., van Dorp, L., Faltyskova, Z., Rohland, N., Mallick, S. *et al.* 2019. Ancient genomes indicate population replacement in Early Neolithic Britain. *Nature Ecology & Evolution* 3, 765–71.

Broushaki, F., Thomas, M.G., Link, V., López, S., van Dorp, L., Kirsanow, K., Hofmanová, Z. *et al.* 2016. Early Neolithic genomes from the eastern Fertile Crescent. *Science* 353(6298), 499–503.

Browning, S.R. and Browning, B.L. 2015. Accurate non-parametric estimation of recent effective population size from segments of identity by descent. *American Journal of Human Genetics* 97(3), 404–18.

Brunel, S., Bennett, E.A., Cardin, L., Garraud, D., Barrand Emam, H., Beylier, A., Boulestin, B. *et al.* 2020. Ancient genomes from present-day France unveil 7,000 years of its demographic history. *Proceedings of the National Academy of Sciences of the United States of America* 17(23), 12791–8.

Cassidy, L.M. 2020. Ancient DNA in Ireland: isolation, immigration and elite incest. *British Archaeology* September–October 2020, 32–41.

Cassidy, L.M., Maoldúin, R.Ó., Kador, T., Lynch, A., Jones, C., Woodman, P.C., Murphy, E. *et al.* 2020. A dynastic elite in monumental Neolithic society. *Nature* 582(7812), 384–8.

Cassidy, L.M., Martiniano, R., Murphy, E.M., Teasdale, M.D., Mallory, J., Hartwell, B. and Bradley, D.G. 2016. Neolithic and Bronze Age migration to Ireland and establishment of the insular Atlantic genome. *Proceedings of the National Academy of Sciences of the United States of America* 113(2), 368–73.

Chapple, R.M., McLaughlin, R. and Warren, G. 2022. '… where they pass their unenterprising existence…': change over time in the Mesolithic of Ireland as shown in radiocarbon-dated activity. *Proceedings of the Royal Irish Academy. Section C. Archaeology, Celtic Studies, History, Linguistics and Literature* 122, 1–38.

Conneller, C., Bayliss, A., Milner, N. and Taylor, B. 2016. The resettlement of the British landscape: towards a chronology of Early Mesolithic lithic assemblage types. *Internet Archaeology*, Council for British Archaeology, No. 42.

Cooke, N.P., Mattiangeli, V., Cassidy, L.M., Okazaki, K., Stokes, C.A., Onbe, S., Hatakeyama, S. *et al.* 2021. Ancient genomics reveals tripartite origins of Japanese populations. *Science Advances* 7(38), eabh2419.

Cooney, G., Bayliss, A., Healy, F., Whittle, A., Danaher, E., Cagney, L., Mallory, J. *et al.* 2011. Ireland. In A. Whittle, F. Healy and A. Bayliss, *Gathering time: dating the early Neolithic enclosures of southern Britain and Ireland*, 562–669. Oxford: Oxbow Books.

Crombé, P. and Robinson, E. 2014. European mesolithic: geography and culture. In C. Smith (ed.), *Encyclopedia of global archaeology*, 406–13. New York: Springer.

Cummings, V. and Harris, O. 2011. Animals, people and places: the continuity of hunting and gathering practices across the Mesolithic-Neolithic transition in Britain. *European Journal of Archaeology* 14, 361–93.

Cummings, V., Hofmann, D., Bjørnevad-Ahlqvist, M., and Iversen, R. 2022. Muddying the waters: reconsidering migration in the Neolithic of Britain, Ireland and Denmark. *Danish Journal of Archaeology* 11, 1–25.

Currie, A. 2016. Ethnographic analogy, the comparative method, and archaeological special pleading. *Studies in History and Philosophy of Science* 55, 84–94.

Dowd, M. and Carden, R.F. 2016. First evidence of a Late Upper Palaeolithic human presence in Ireland. *Quaternary Science Reviews* 139, 158–63.

Dulias, K., Foody, M.G.B., Justeau, P., Silva, M., Martiniano, R., Oteo-García, G., Fichera, A. *et al.* 2022. Ancient DNA at the edge of the world: continental immigration and the persistence of Neolithic male lineages in Bronze Age Orkney. *Proceedings of the National Academy of Sciences of the United States of America* 119, e2108001119.

Dusseldorp, G.L. and Amkreutz, L.W.S.W. 2020. A long slow goodbye – re-examining the Mesolithic–Neolithic transition (5500–2500 BCE) in the Dutch delta. In V. Klinkenberg, R. van Oosten and C. van Driel-Murray (eds), *A human environment. Studies in honour of 20 years Analecta editorship by Prof. Dr. Corrie Bakels*, 121–42. Leiden: Sidestone.

Fowler, C., Olalde, I., Cummings, V., Armit, I., Büster, L., Cuthbert, S., Rohland, N. *et al.* 2022. A high-resolution picture of kinship practices in an Early Neolithic tomb. *Nature* 601(7894), 584–7.

Fu, Q., Posth, C., Hajdinjak, M., Petr, M., Mallick, S., Fernandes, D., Furtwängler, A. *et al.* 2016. The genetic history of Ice Age Europe. *Nature* 534(7606), 200–205.

Gamba, C., Jones, E.R., Teasdale, M.D., McLaughlin, R.L., Gonzalez-Fortes, G., Mattiangeli, V., *et al.* 2014. Genome flux and stasis in a five millennium transect of European prehistory. *Nature Communications* 5, 5257.

Garrow, D. and Sturt, F. 2011. Grey waters bright with Neolithic argonauts? Maritime connections and the Mesolithic–Neolithic transition within the 'western seaways' of Britain, c. 5000–3500 BC. *Antiquity* 85, 59–72.

Gernigon, K. 2016. Sphère d'interactions, complexe culturel: clefs de lecture de la variabilité géographique des expressions stylistiques du Chasséen. In T. Perrin, P. Chambon, J.F. Gibaja and G. Goude (eds), *Le Chasséen, des Chasséens… Retour sur une culture nationale et ses parallèles, Sepulcres de fossa, Cortaillod, Lagozza. Actes du colloque international tenu à Paris (France) du 18 au 20 novembre 2014*, 29–45. Toulouse: Archives d'Écologie Préhistorique.

Goggin, J.M. and Sturtevant, W.P. 1964. The Calusa: a stratified, nonagricultural society (with notes on sibling marriage). In W.H. Goodenough (ed.), *Explorations in cultural anthropology. Essays in honour of George Peter Murdock*, 179–219. New York: McGraw-Hill.

Günther, T., Valdiosera, C., Malmström, H., Ureña, I., Rodriguez-Varela, R., Sverrisdóttir, Ó.O., *et al.* 2015. Ancient genomes link early farmers from Atapuerca in Spain to modern-day Basques. *Proceedings of the National Academy of Sciences of the United States of America* 112(38), 11917–22.

Haak, W., Forster, P., Bramanti, B., Matsumura, S., Brandt, G., Tänzer, M. *et al.* 2005. Ancient DNA from the first European farmers in 7500-year-old Neolithic sites. *Science* 310(5750), 1016–18.

Haak, W., Lazaridis, I., Patterson, N., Rohland, N., Mallick, S., Llamas, B. *et al.* 2015. Massive migration from the steppe was a source for Indo-European languages in Europe. *Nature* 522(7555), 207–11.

Jensen, T.Z.T., Niemann, J., Iversen, K.H., Fotakis, A.K., Gopalakrishnan, S., Vågene, Å.J. *et al.* 2019. A 5700 year-old human genome and oral microbiome from chewed birch pitch. *Nature Communications* 10(1), 5520.

Kador, T., Fibiger, L., Cooney, G. and Fullagar, P. 2014. Movement and diet in early Irish prehistory: first evidence from multi-isotope analysis. *Journal of Irish Archaeology* 23, 83–96.

Keller, A., Graefen, A., Ball, M., Matzas, M., Boisguerin, V., Maixner, F. *et al.* 2012. New insights into the Tyrolean Iceman's origin and phenotype as inferred by whole-genome sequencing. *Nature Communications* 3, 698.

Lazaridis, I., Patterson, N., Mittnik, A., Renaud, G., Mallick, S., Kirsanow, K. *et al.* 2014. Ancient human genomes suggest three ancestral populations for present-day Europeans. *Nature* 513(7518), 409–13.

Lipson, M., Szécsényi-Nagy, A., Mallick, S., Pósa, A., Stégmár, B., Keerl, V. *et al.* 2017. Parallel paleogenomic transects reveal complex genetic history of early European farmers. *Nature* 551(7680), 368–72.

Margaryan, A., Lawson, D.J., Sikora, M., Racimo, F., Rasmussen, S., Moltke, I. *et al.* 2020. Population genomics of the Viking world. *Nature* 585(7825), 390–6.

Mathieson, I., Alpaslan-Roodenberg, S., Posth, C., Szécsényi-Nagy, A., Rohland, N., Mallick, S. *et al.* 2018. The genomic history of southeastern Europe. *Nature* 555(7695), 197–203.

Mathieson, I., Lazaridis, I., Rohland, N., Mallick, S., Patterson, N., Roodenberg, S.A. *et al.* 2015. Genome-wide patterns of selection in 230 ancient Eurasians. *Nature* 528(7583), 499–503.

McLaughlin, T.R. 2020. An archaeology of Ireland for the Information Age. *Emania*, 7–29.

McLaughlin, T.R., Whitehouse, N.J., Schulting, R.J., McClatchie, M., Barratt, P. and Bogaard, A. 2016. The changing face of Neolithic and Bronze Age Ireland: a big data approach to the settlement and burial records. *Journal of World Prehistory* 29(2), 117–53.

Meiklejohn, C., Chamberlain, A.T. and Schulting, R. 2011. Radiocarbon dating of Mesolithic human remains in Great Britain. *Mesolithic Miscellany* 21, 20–58.

Meiklejohn, C. and Woodman, P.C. 2012. Radiocarbon dating of Mesolithic human remains in Ireland. *Mesolithic Miscellany* 22, 22–41.

Montgomery, W.I., Provan, J., McCabe, A.M. and Yalden, D.W. 2014. Origin of British and Irish mammals: disparate post-glacial colonisation and species introductions. *Quaternary Science Reviews* 98, 144–65.

Müller, J. 2015. Eight million Neolithic Europeans: social demography and social archaeology on the scope of change—from the Near East to Scandinavia. In K. Kristiansen, L. Smedja and J. Turek, (eds), *Paradigm found. Archaeological theory: present, past and future. Essays in Honour of Evžen Neustupný*, 200–14. Oxford: Oxbow Books.

Olalde, I., Brace, S., Allentoft, M.E., Armit, I., Kristiansen, K., Booth, T. *et al.* 2018. The Beaker phenomenon and the genomic transformation of northwest Europe. *Nature* 555(7695), 190–6.

Pankratov, V., Montinaro, F., Kushniarevich, A., Hudjashov, G., Jay, F., Saag, L. *et al.* 2020. Differences in local population history at the finest level: the case of the Estonian population. *European Journal of Human Genetics* 28(11), 1580–91.

Patterson, N., Isakov, M., Booth, T., Büster, L., Fischer, C.-E., Olalde, I. *et al.* 2022. Large-scale migration into Britain during the Middle to Late Bronze Age. *Nature* 601(7894), 588–94.

Patterson, N., Moorjani, P., Luo, Y., Mallick, S., Rohland, N., Zhan, Y. *et al.* 2012. Ancient admixture in human history. *Genetics* 192(3), 1065–93.

Patton, M. 1993. *Statements in stone: monuments and society in Neolithic Brittany*. London: Routledge.

Praud, I. 2015. Escalles: a Neolithic causewayed enclosure on the Pas-de-Calais coast. *PAST: The Newsletter of the Prehistoric Society* 79, 14–16.

Riede, F. 2009. Climate and demography in early prehistory: using calibrated 14C dates as population proxies. *Human Biology* 81(3), 309–37.

Rivollat, M., Jeong, C., Schiffels, S., Küçükkalıpçı, İ., Pemonge, M., Rohrlach, A.B. *et al.* 2020. Ancient genome-wide DNA from France highlights the complexity of interactions between Mesolithic hunter-gatherers and Neolithic farmers. *Science Advances* 6(22), eaaz5344.

Rivollat, M., Thomas, A., Ghesquière, E., Rohrlach, A.B., Späth, E., Pemonge, M.-H. *et al.* 2022. Ancient DNA gives new insights into a Norman Neolithic monumental cemetery dedicated to male elites. *Proceedings of the National Academy of Sciences of the United States of America* 119(18), e2120786119.

Rowley-Conwy, P. 2011. Westward Ho!: the spread of agriculture from central Europe to the Atlantic. *Current Anthropology* 52, S431–S451.

Sánchez-Quinto, F., Malmström, H., Fraser, M., Girdland-Flink, L., Svensson, E.M., Simões, L.G. *et al.* 2019. Megalithic tombs in western and northern Neolithic Europe were linked to a kindred society. *Proceedings of the National Academy of Sciences of the United States of America* 116(19), 9469–74.

Scarre, C. 2011. *Landscapes of Neolithic Brittany*. Oxford: Oxford University Press.

Scheib, C.L., Hui, R., D'Atanasio, E., Wohns, A.W., Inskip, S.A., Rose, A. *et al.* 2019. East Anglian early Neolithic monument burial linked to contemporary megaliths. *Annals of Human Biology* 46, 145–9.

Schulting, R.J., McClatchie, M., Sheridan, A., McLaughlin, R., Barratt, P., and Whitehouse, N.J. 2017. Radiocarbon dating of a multi-phase passage tomb on Baltinglass Hill, Co. Wicklow, Ireland. *Proceedings of the Prehistoric Society,* 83, 305–23.

Schulting, R.J. 2014. The dating of Poulnabrone, Co. Clare. In A. Lynch (ed.), *Poulnabrone: an early Neolithic portal tomb in Ireland*, 93–113. Dublin: Stationery Office.

Schulting, R.J., Murphy, E., Jones, C. and Warren, G. 2012. New dates from the north and a proposed chronology for Irish court tombs. *Proceedings of the Royal Irish Academy. Section C. Archaeology, Celtic Studies, History, Linguistics and Literature* 112, 1–60.

Schulz Paulsson, B. 2019. Radiocarbon dates and Bayesian modeling support maritime diffusion model for megaliths in Europe. *Proceedings of the National Academy of Sciences of the United States of America* 116(9), 3460–5.

Seguin-Orlando, A., Donat, R., Der Sarkissian, C., Southon, J., Thèves, C., Manen, C. *et al.* 2021. Heterogeneous hunter-gatherer and steppe-related ancestries in Late Neolithic and Bell Beaker genomes from present-day France. *Current Biology: CB* 31 (5), 1072–1083.e10.

Sheridan, J.A. 2007. From Picardie to Pickering and Pencraig Hill? New information on the 'Carinated Bowl Neolithic' in northern Britain. *Proceedings of the British Academy* 144, 441–92.

Sheridan, J.A. 2010. The Neolithisation of Britain and Ireland: the 'big picture'. In B. Finlayson and G.M. Warren (eds), *Landscapes in transition*, 89–105. Oxford and London: Oxbow Books and Council for British Research in the Levant.

Sheridan, J.A. 2016. Scottish Neolithic pottery in 2016: the big picture and some details of the narrative. In F.J. Hunter and J.A. Sheridan (eds) *Ancient lives: object, people and place in early Scotland. Essays for David V Clarke on his 70th birthday*, 189–212. Leiden: Sidestone Press.

Skoglund, P., Malmström, H., Omrak, A., Raghavan, M., Valdiosera, C., Günther, T. *et al.* 2014. Genomic diversity and admixture differs for Stone-Age Scandinavian foragers and farmers. *Science* 344(6185), 747–50.

Snoeck, C., Jones, C., Pouncett, J., Goderis, S., Claeys, P., Mattielli, N. *et al.* 2020. Isotopic evidence for changing mobility and landscape use patterns between the Neolithic and Early Bronze Age in western Ireland. *Journal of Archaeological Science: Reports* 30, 102214.

Soares, P., Achilli, A., Semino, O., Davies, W., Macaulay, V., Bandelt, H.-J. *et al.* 2010. The archaeogenetics of Europe. *Current Biology: CB* 20 (4), R174–83.

Thomas, J. 2015. House societies and founding ancestors in early Neolithic Britain. In C. Renfrew, M.J. Boyd and I. Morley (eds), *Death rituals, social order and the archaeology of immortality in the ancient world*, 138–50. Cambridge: Cambridge University Press.

Thomas, J. 2022. Neolithization and population replacement in Britain: an alternative view. *Cambridge Archaeological Journal* 32, 507–25.

van den Berghe, P.L. and Mesher, G.M. 1980. Royal incest and inclusive fitness. *American Ethnologist* 7(2), 300–17.

Villalba-Mouco, V., van de Loosdrecht, M.S., Posth, C., Mora, R., Martínez-Moreno, J., Rojo-Guerra, M. *et al.* 2019. Survival of Late Pleistocene hunter-gatherer ancestry in the Iberian peninsula. *Current Biology: CB* 29(7), 1169–77.e7.

Waddington, C. 2007. *Mesolithic settlement in the North Sea basin: a case study from Howick, north-east England*. Oxford: Oxbow Books.

Warren, G. 2008. *The adoption of agriculture in Ireland: what are the key research challenges?* Dublin: School of Archaeology, University College Dublin.

Warren, G. 2020. Climate change and hunter gatherers in Ireland: problems, potentials and pressing research questions. *Proceedings of the Royal Irish Academy. Section C. Archaeology, Celtic Studies, History, Linguistics and Literature* 120, 1–22.

Warren, G. 2021. *Hunter-gatherer Ireland: making connections in an island world*. Oxford: Oxbow Books.

Whitehouse, N.J., Schulting, R.J., McClatchie, M., Barratt, P., McLaughlin, T.R., Bogaard, A. *et al.* 2014. Neolithic agriculture on the European western frontier: the boom and bust of early farming in Ireland. *Journal of Archaeological Science* 51, 181–205.

Whittle, A., Healy, F. and Bayliss, A. 2011. *Gathering time: dating the early Neolithic enclosures of southern Britain and Ireland*. Oxford: Oxbow Books.

Wolf, A.P. 2014. *Incest avoidance and the incest taboos: two aspects of human nature*. San Francisco: Stanford University Press.

Woodman, P. 1981. The post-glacial colonization of Ireland: the human factors. In D. O'Corráin (ed.), *Irish antiquity: essays and studies presented to Professor M. J. O'Kelly*, 93–110. Cork: Tower Books.

Woodman, P.C., Anderson, L., Anderson, E. and Finlay, N. 1999. *Excavations at Ferriter's Cove, 1983–95: last foragers, first farmers in the Dingle Peninsula*. Bray: Wordwell.

Woodman, P., Dowd, M., Fibiger, L., Carden, R.F. and O'Shaughnessy, J. 2017. Archaeological excavations at Killuragh Cave, Co. Limerick: a persistent place in the landscape from the Early Mesolithic to the Late Bronze Age. *The Journal of Irish Archaeology* 26, 1–32.

Zerjal, T., Xue, Y., Bertorelle, G., Wells, R.S., Bao, W., Zhu, S. *et al.* 2003. The genetic legacy of the Mongols. *American Journal of Human Genetics* 72(3), 717–21.

Chapter 12

Ancient DNA and modelling the Mesolithic–Neolithic transition in Britain and Ireland

Alison Sheridan and Alasdair Whittle

We examine the impact of the recently-obtained ancient DNA evidence for Mesolithic and Neolithic individuals in Britain and Ireland, and on the Continent, on our own (and others') divergent models of the Mesolithic–Neolithic transition in this archipelago, and draw attention to the outstanding issues which further aDNA analysis may help to resolve.

As many readers will know, we have proposed differing models for the Mesolithic–Neolithic transition in Britain and Ireland and have debated the matter for well over a decade. In a volume devoted to seeking dialogue across and between different disciplines and different approaches, we put our heads together and seek to explore what impact the recently obtained aDNA data for Mesolithic and Neolithic individuals in Britain and Ireland have on our (and others') models. What new issues do the aDNA data and their interpretation throw up? And what questions still need to be addressed through further aDNA work?

In its subject matter, our contribution overlaps with those by Cassidy and by Brace and Booth (this volume); our intention is to complement, rather than repeat, what is presented there. For this reason, we shall not be discussing the latest model proposed by Julian Thomas (2022), as its discussion of genetic data is critiqued in detail by Brace and Booth.

APPROACHES TO THE MESOLITHIC–NEOLITHIC TRANSITION IN BRITAIN AND IRELAND

Past opinions on the nature of the Mesolithic–Neolithic transition in these islands are well known. Suffice it to recap that the dominant older model for the transition was of colonisation from continental Europe (*e.g.* Clark 1966), the main puzzle being the task of deciphering the sources and origin areas for incoming population (*e.g.* Case 1969). Beginning in the processual era of the 1970s and furthered in the post-processual phase of archaeological interpretation from the 1980s onwards, there was in some – but by no means all – quarters a reaction in favour of significant indigenous contribution to (or responsibility for) the processes at work, a position championed by Julian Thomas (*e.g.* 2013; 2022). There was also resistance to that indigenist turn (*e.g.* Rowley-Conwy 2011), and a renewed interest in colonisation models (*e.g.* Sheridan 2010; Whittle *et al.* 2011), albeit not in a revisionist, culture-historical way as has been claimed (Thomas 2013, 157–84; for a response, see Sheridan 2015). The vigorous debate about who were the prime movers in the establishment of a farming way of life continues (*e.g.* Lawrence *et al.* 2022).

As for our own models, one of us has consistently advocated colonisation as the prime mover, with several strands of Neolithisation being identified, from different parts of France to different parts of Britain and Ireland, between *c.* 4300 cal BC and *c.* 3800 cal BC, undertaken for different reasons relating to developments on the near Continent and receiving varied responses from indigenous groups, who were far from passive (*e.g.* Sheridan 2003; 2007; 2010; 2016; Sheridan and Schulting 2020). The earliest proposed strand, around 4300 cal BC, seen in the presence of domesticated cattle bone in a local hunter-gatherer context at Ferriter's Cove, south-west Ireland, is regarded as a 'false start', dying out due to failure to establish a critical mass of farmers and their resources, and to indigenous residents hunting their cattle. A second, Breton, strand, probably *c.* 4000–3900 cal BC, saw small groups of immigrant farmers sailing up the Atlantic façade from the Morbihan region and settling at various points along the west coast of Britain and around the coast of the northern half of Ireland. Those in north-west and south-west Wales failed to flourish, unlike their counterparts in Scotland and Ireland. A third and arguably more populous strand – the 'Carinated Bowl Neolithic' – arrived at various points along the east and south-east coast of Britain from Nord-Pas de Calais from around the 42nd and 41st centuries cal BC, as one of a series of regional groups using Chasséo-Michelsberg pottery. A fourth strand, 'Trans-Manche Ouest', arrived in south-west England from Normandy around 3800 cal BC. Additional immigration from other points along the Channel may also have occurred.

Whittle has travelled on a more zigzag course, initially arguing for colonisation (Whittle 1977; 1985), then experimenting with the notion of significant indigenous contributions (Whittle 1996) and returning again, armed not least with significantly more robust chronology from the *Gathering Time* project, to colonisation being the leading force in a time-transgressive process across Britain and Ireland, starting probably in the south-east of England in the 41st century cal BC (Whittle *et al.* 2011, figs 14.177 and 15.8). He now cautiously proposes a provisional three-stage model for the Neolithisation of Britain and Ireland, subject to anticipated refinements in formally modelled radiocarbon chronology to be achieved through an ongoing revision of *Gathering Time* for England and Wales, undertaken with Alex Bayliss and Frances Healy. (Other upgrades, *e.g.* by Griffiths (2021; 2022) and Whittle *et al.* (2022), have already provided revised date estimates, for the start of Neolithic activity in north-west England and southern Wales, and for the spread and detailed development of causewayed enclosures respectively.) This latest model envisages a first phase featuring increasing, two-way contact (*cf.* Case 1969; Anthony 1990) between the Continent and Britain and Ireland, during the second half of the 5th millennium cal BC, with the various suggested episodes including that at Ferriter's Cove and others at St Martin's Quay, Scilly (Garrow *et al.* 2017) and Bexhill, East Sussex (Lawrence *et al.* 2022). A second phase, from the 41st to the 39th centuries cal BC, constitutes the major period of population movement from the Continent, arriving in south-east England in the 41st century cal BC and progressively expanding outwards from there, arriving in western England and Wales by the 40th and 39th centuries cal BC. The principal ceramic association is with Carinated Bowl pottery. The evidence from Ireland, including the early dates for the enclosure and associated material at Magheraboy, Co. Sligo (discussed extensively in

Whittle *et al.* 2011), still has to be taken into account in this model. Whittle's third phase sees both consolidation and growth of settlement, and a continuation of individual and group migrations, including Sheridan's 'Trans-Manche-Ouest' strand. The 'Pornic-Notgrove' transepted-chamber monuments, for example, found respectively in southern Brittany and around the mouth of the Loire, and in southern Britain, and suspiciously similar to each other (Britnell and Whittle 2022), might signify close kinship or continuing connections (*cf.* Fowler *et al.* 2022).

The main areas of disagreement between our models, and between these and other models, have tended to concern the degree (or indeed existence) of any two-way contact with the Continent during the 5th millennium cal BC; the agency of indigenous Mesolithic communities in the arrival and spread of farming as a way of life; the geographical patterning in the appearance and spread of farming; and the existence of the Breton, Atlantic façade strand of Neolithisation (*e.g.* Whittle *et al.* 2011, chapter 15; Sheridan 2012).

Our, and others', models have been evolving as the evidential base has grown and been reassessed. Many new radiocarbon dates have appeared over the last decade; isotopic data suggest some long-distance movements of individuals (*e.g.* at Penywyrlod, Powys, and Whitwell, Derbyshire: Neil *et al.* 2017; 2020); and Rowley-Conwy *et al.*'s critical review of the evidence relating to the earliest farming in Britain (2020) has shown it to be intensive, complex and skilfully undertaken, reflecting the millennium or so of expertise that its practitioners had built up on the Continent. Moreover, as regards material culture, Hélène Pioffet's technical investigation of Carinated Bowl pottery with regard to its continental *comparanda* (Pioffet 2014) has demonstrated a continuity in tradition, suggesting immigrant potters; and *Projet JADE* has highlighted continental practices in the treatment and deposition of the axeheads made from jadeitite and other Alpine rock that the immigrant farmers brought with them (Sheridan and Pailler 2012). Meanwhile, various claims for post-Channel-formation contact between Mesolithic communities in Britain and Ireland and their contemporaries on the Continent have been made, including that regarding distinctive 'Bexhill point' microliths from East Sussex, as mentioned above (Lawrence *et al.* 2022). The claimed evidence, from submerged sedimentary aDNA from Bouldnor Cliff, for the presence of wheat *c.* 6000 cal BC (Smith *et al.* 2015) has been vigorously – and in our view, justifiably – challenged (*e.g.* Calloway 2015). (See also Sheridan 2018 on claims for continental-style microliths on Scilly, and see below regarding Bexhill.) Arguably the most significant development, however, is the advent of aDNA data from Mesolithic and Neolithic humans in Britain and Ireland, and of relevant individuals on the Continent, particularly France. It is to this, and its impact on the debate, that we now turn.

THE aDNA RESULTS AND THEIR IMPACT ON EXISTING MODELS

As set out by Whittle and Pollard (this volume), aDNA studies across Europe have shown the dominant process in the appearance and spread of farming to be the arrival, and subsequent expansion, of new people with Aegean/Near Eastern genetic ancestry. Two routes of population dispersal have been suggested, one westwards though the Mediterranean and the other through south-east, central and north-west Europe. Along the way and over time, variable degrees of genetic admixture with indigenous hunter-gatherer communities were involved in what was clearly a complex process (as discussed by Richards, this volume).

To date, the aDNA of some six Mesolithic and 111 Neolithic individuals in Britain, plus two Mesolithic and 55 Neolithic individuals in Ireland, has been analysed, with further results from others in the pipeline (Cassidy *et al.* 2016; 2020; Olalde *et al.* 2018; Brace *et al.* 2019; Sánchez-Quinto *et al.* 2019; Dulias *et al.* 2022; Fowler *et al.* 2022; Patterson *et al.* 2022; note that many of the results are to be found in the Supplementary information sections).

As the chapters in this volume by Selina Brace and Tom Booth and by Lara Cassidy make clear, the results obtained so far, along with those for contemporary and earlier individuals on the Continent (*e.g.* Brunel *et al.* 2020; Rivollat *et al.* 2020; *cf.* Beau *et al.* 2017), demonstrate unequivocally the arrival of immigrants from the Continent to our archipelago in the centuries around 4000 cal BC, thereby supporting Sheridan's and Whittle's (and others') overall conclusion, based on non-aDNA data, that the farming way of life was indeed introduced by continental farmers. Brace *et al.* (2019, 768) report that individuals showing Aegean Neolithic Farmers (ANF) ancestry had arrived in Britain from the Continent by *3975–3722 cal BC*. Additional confirmation for this continental ancestry comes from Rohrlach *et al.*'s recent study (2021) of the rare clade H2m – one associated with the Mediterranean route of the Neolithic spread through Europe, and found in individuals in the Paris basin and Normandy. This clade is represented in two individuals from Middle Neolithic Linkardstown-type cists at Jerpoint West and Baunogenasraid in south-east Ireland (Rohrlach *et al.* 2021, fig. 3; note that in their Supplementary information, the placename Jerpoint is wrongly listed as Killuragh). Moreover, the sharing of the commonest lineages between Neolithic individuals in Britain and Ireland indicates a common ancestral genetic pool for those lineages (Richards, this volume); as Cassidy (this volume) points out, previous claims for differing origins for Irish and British Neolithic individuals (*e.g.* Rivollat *et al.* 2020, 9) have not taken into account the differing methods of processing aDNA data that have been used by the laboratories in question. (Most of the British data are reported on the basis of using the cheaper, targeted method of SNP capture, whereas in Ireland, the results of total genome analysis are reported.) The question of the degree of genetic similarity between the Neolithic populations of Ireland and Britain is also discussed by Brace and Booth (this volume) and by Ariano *et al.* (2022).

Both the headline results, and those from finer-grained interrogation of the aDNA data, are revelatory. In Ireland, for example, these incomers (whether they came directly from the Continent or via Britain, or both) were entering a landscape whose genetic pool was restricted, reflecting 'a prolonged period of island isolation' of several millennia (Cassidy *et al.* 2020, 3–4) – an isolation that is also reflected in the distinctly insular Irish Later Mesolithic material culture (Woodman 2015; *cf.* Warren 2021), and which casts doubt on claims for two-way contacts with the Continent during the 5th millennium cal BC (*e.g.* Thomas 2013, but see the Whittle model above for the later 5th millennium). Some idea of the scale of immigration is offered by the results from the early Neolithic portal tomb at Poulnabrone and nearby court tomb at Parknabinnia, both Co. Clare, where the lack of close kin among either tomb's occupants suggests a sizeable community within the monuments' 'catchment' areas, with no inbreeding (Cassidy *et al.* 2020, 1, 3). Other indications that we are dealing with a sizeable influx of people overall, in both Ireland and Britain, include the absence of a 'bottleneck' effect (which would be caused if a small number of incoming families had had large families) and the near-disappearance and subsequent non-resurgence of the indigenous Mesolithic genetic signature following the arrival of continental farmers (Brace *et al.* 2019, 770; Cassidy *et al.* 2020, supplementary data).

The aDNA results also arguably support Sheridan's contention that people were arriving from more than one location on the Continent to more than one location in Britain (and Ireland). The claimed south-west to north-east cline in Britain in the amount of Western Hunter-Gatherer (WHG) admixture in Neolithic individuals – resulting from previous intermixing between farmers and hunter-gatherers on the Continent – reported by Brace *et al.* (2019) reflects 'multiple source populations with variable proportions of WHG admixture having entered different parts of Britain' (Brace *et al.* 2019, 769). Similar conclusions about multiple locations of departure and arrival were reached by Rivollat *et al.* in their study of French and German Neolithic individuals, and their comparison with British and Irish individuals (Rivollat *et al.* 2020, 9). This topic is discussed further by Brace and Booth (this volume).

The finding that Neolithic individuals in eastern Britain (including in areas characterised by 'Carinated Bowl Neolithic' monuments and material culture) tend to have a higher amount of continental-acquired WHG admixture than those in the west might also offer a clue to the directionality of some of this movement. Beau *et al.* (2017) have noted, in their study of early Michelsberg individuals, that a high WHG admixture also characterises Neolithic people in the Paris basin, an area from which groups are known to have emigrated in several directions, from *c.* 4300 cal BC onwards, due to perceived overpopulation. Sheridan has argued (*e.g.* 2010; 2016; 2021) that the 'Carinated Bowl Neolithic' farmers, with their Chasséo-Michelsberg style pottery, came from one of a series of regional groupings of such 'Paris basin emigrés' in northern France and Belgium, more specifically one in Nord-Pas de Calais. Possible confirmation for such a view comes from Lara Cassidy's observation (this volume) that one of the individuals whose remains were found in a causewayed enclosure at Escalles, Nord-Pas de Calais (Brunel *et al.* 2020, SI.1 and 3.3.4, table S1.1: Es97-1) – the closest region of France to Britain – bears a particularly close genetic similarity to British and Irish Neolithic individuals.

As for the other movements proposed by Sheridan, support for the 'Trans-Manche Ouest' strand is offered by Rivollat *et al.*'s study, which acknowledges the possibility that some farmers emigrated from Normandy (Rivollat *et al.* 2020, 7, 9).

As for Sheridan's Breton, Atlantic façade strand, while no aDNA data have yet been obtained for any Neolithic individuals in Brittany (due to the generally poor preservation of bone in the acidic environment there), much has been made in some quarters (*e.g.* Sánchez-Quinto *et al.* 2019) of the apparent genetic similarity, first reported upon by Brace *et al.* (2019, 766), between some British and Irish individuals and Iberian Neolithic farmers. Some have inferred from this that Britain and Ireland were colonised by Iberian Neolithic farmers. The problems with such an inference are dealt with in the next section of this chapter.

Regarding the relationship between the incoming farmers and the indigenous hunter-gatherer groups, while the 'headline' aDNA result is one of a near-total population replacement, with no subsequent resurgence in WHG signatures, in contrast to the Continent (Brace *et al.* 2019), this does not imply a wipeout – and indeed, what geneticists mean by the term 'population replacement' is very different from non-geneticists' understanding of that term (Booth 2019; Booth *et al.* 2021; Brace and Booth, this volume).

That the incomers and indigenes were indeed aware of each other is clear from the small yet growing number of cases demonstrating interbreeding: eight examples from western Scotland (Brace *et al.* 2019; Brace and Booth, this volume) and one from Ireland (Cassidy *et al.* 2020, 4). (Some of these incomers will have looked different from the indigenous Mesolithic inhabitants of Britain and Ireland, being in the main slightly lighter-skinned – but still darker-skinned than typical present-day white inhabitants of north-west Europe – and more likely to have brown rather than light-coloured eyes: Brace *et al.* 2019, 768–9; Cassidy *et al.* 2020, table S12.) As Tom Booth has pointed out (2019), the indigenous genetic signatures could easily have become drowned out if the population size and density of Mesolithic Britain and Ireland were low, yet the number of incoming farmers was high (and rapidly growing). The topics of genetic admixture between indigenes and incomers in Britain, and of the negligible Mesolithic genetic legacy, are discussed further by Brace and Booth (this volume).

Finer-grained examination of the aDNA data has also thrown up some fascinating observations. These include the earliest definitive evidence for an infant with Down's syndrome, at Poulnabrone in south-west Ireland (Cassidy *et al.* 2020, 4); centuries-long familial links between the people buried in passage tombs in different parts of Ireland, and a case of incest attested at the massive passage tomb at Newgrange (Cassidy *et al.* 2020); a relatively high incidence of intra-community breeding among the late 4th/early 3rd millennium cal BC occupants of Isbister chamber tomb in Orkney (Ariano and Bradley, this volume); and detailed 'kith and kin' relationships among the people buried in the Severn-Cotswold tomb at Hazleton North (Fowler 2022; Fowler *et al.* 2022, and note that the family tree diagram presented in Extended Data fig. 4 is considered to be a better fit with the data than that presented in fig. 1 of the main article). No doubt other fascinating insights will emerge from further interrogation of the existing aDNA data, and from the acquisition of new aDNA data.

THE 'IBERIAN' GENETIC SIGNATURE AMONG BRITISH AND IRISH NEOLITHIC INDIVIDUALS: A RED HERRING

The aforementioned genetic similarity, first noted by Cassidy *et al.* (2016) and also observed by Brace *et al.* (2019), between 4th millennium cal BC British and Irish individuals and Iberian Neolithic farmers, has given rise to an argument that the latter were somehow directly involved in the appearance of farming in our archipelago (*e.g.* Sánchez-Quinto *et al.* 2019, 9473). Such a view, however, finds no support whatsoever in the monuments or material culture of Britain and Ireland, and in our view misunderstands both the archaeological and the genetic information; apparent genetic affinity does not automatically signify direct connection. (The same can be said of Sánchez-Quinto *et al.*'s claims (2019, 9470, 9473) for migration of Neolithic monument builders from Britain to Scandinavia; there is no convincing archaeological evidence for interaction between these areas during the Neolithic (*contra* Cummings *et al.* 2022, 5), and any genetic affinity is far more likely to be due to shared ancestry in northern France than to direct contact.)

The 'Iberian' – or, more generally, Mediterranean – genetic 'signature' has been discussed by other geneticists, including Rivollat *et al.* (2020), who have observed that it is by no means restricted to Iberian Neolithic farmers. Associated with the Mediterranean route of the spread of farmers and farming across Europe, the haplotypes in question – which include the aforementioned H2m clade as studied by Rohrlach *et al.* (2021) – are associated with many French Neolithic individuals as well as Iberians, and their incidence in the northern half of France can arguably be accounted for by several possible factors: the spread, along the Atlantic coast, of elements of 'Mediterranean' Neolithic practices and material culture during the 6th millennium; subsequent south–north movements or interactions within France during the 5th millennium; and interactions between Brittany and Iberia at various points during the 5th millennium.

Regarding the first point, Grégor Marchand has described the 6th millennium northerly spread of practices and material culture relating to the Mediterranean 'strand' of Neolithisation up the Atlantic coast of France, and argued for a complex set of interactions between farmers and hunter-gatherer groups at different places along that coast (Marchand 2007) – a picture that seems to be borne out by the aDNA evidence (Rivollat *et al.* 2020). Aspects of this still poorly understood Mediterranean 'strand' are detectable in Brittany in the Augy-Saint-Pallaye ceramic style, which combines Epicardial features (with their Mediterranean 'ancestry') with those of the Villeneuve-Saint-Germain ceramic tradition whose origins lie in the Danubian strand of Neolithisation (Marchand 2007, 235–6).

As regards subsequent movements and/or interactions within France, the processes involved in the adoption, in northern France, of elements of Chassey-style pottery from southern France during the 43rd century cal BC (Gernigon 2016, 40) may have provided another vector for the arrival of a 'Mediterranean' genetic signature in northern France.

Finally, the interactions between Brittany and Iberia at various points during the 5th millennium – as shown, for instance, in the importation of variscite beads and fibrolite axeheads from Spain, and the emulation of Morbihannais-style Alpine axeheads in Iberia (Cassen *et al.* 2020) – could well have enhanced a pre-existing 'Iberian/Mediterranean' genetic signature in the Breton gene pool.

Therefore, Iberia is by no means the only area from which a 'Mediterranean' genetic signature could have arrived in Britain and Ireland. (See also Cassidy, and Brace and Booth, this volume.) Indeed, in their evaluation of the available aDNA data, Rivollat *et al.* (2020, 7) conclude that 'on the basis of the results from our French Neolithic sites, we suggest that English, Welsh, and Scottish groups are connected to the Mediterranean Neolithic sphere not only via the Atlantic coast but more plausibly also via Normandy…, the Paris Basin…, and southern France…'.

OUTSTANDING ISSUES TO BE ADDRESSED THROUGH aDNA ANALYSIS

The aDNA data have clearly made a significant impact on the debate about the Mesolithic–Neolithic transition in Britain and Ireland. Several key issues remain to be addressed, however.

There are significant geographical gaps in the aDNA coverage for western and north-west France (and indeed within Britain), and the absence of any such data for Neolithic Brittany makes it impossible to substantiate or disprove the hypothesised Breton, Atlantic façade 'strand' genetically. It remains to be seen whether the very few extant

Neolithic human bones from Brittany have the potential to yield aDNA, or whether any suitable candidates come to light from future excavations. In addition to this geographical patchiness, the current inconsistency in the way different laboratories process aDNA results – with some examining the total genome data and others targeting particular parts – can affect the comparability of the results, as Cassidy has pointed out (this volume); ideally, wherever possible, non-targeted comparison should be undertaken. Moreover, obtaining larger sample sizes and more haplotype data will be required in order to achieve a clearer genetic picture of different migration streams from geographically and culturally distinct, yet genetically similar, populations in France.

Questions about the absolute number and density of Mesolithic individuals in Britain and Ireland, and of incoming Neolithic farmers from the Continent, remain frustratingly hard to resolve, as pointed out by Cassidy and by Brace and Booth (this volume), and further refinement of methods is necessary to arrive at plausible estimates. The relative size of the various hypothesised 'strands' needs to be clarified, to check whether it accords with that proposed by Sheridan or with that advocated by Whittle in his latest model; while it appears that the arrival of the 'Carinated Bowl Neolithic' involved a substantial influx of incomers, it is less clear whether the other strands involved many fewer migrants. The timing and duration of the population movements also need to be clarified; are we dealing with short-term 'pulses' of immigration, or with a steady (or irregular) flow over several generations, or both?

Other outstanding questions include that of whether any genetic intermixing between individuals in Britain and those on the Continent occurred between the time when the Channel formed (*c.* 6000 cal BC) and the time when Neolithic 'things and practices' were appearing, between the 42nd or 41st and 39th centuries cal BC. Only one of the six analysed British Mesolithic individuals – a female from Cnoc Coig, Oronsay, Scotland – falls within this time period (Brace *et al.* 2019) and the fact that her genome is typical of Western Hunter-Gatherers, rather than of contemporary individuals on the Continent, indicates no continental intermixing in this case. More 5th-millennium individuals in Britain – especially from areas closest to the Continent – need to be analysed to determine whether the Cnoc Coig woman is typical or atypical. Unfortunately, precious few individuals have been dated to this period, and none of these is from southern England (Meiklejohn *et al.* 2011), and so we must await new discoveries before this genetic question can be addressed.

IN CONCLUSION: HAVE THE aDNA RESULTS ENGENDERED CONSENSUS IN MODELLING THE MESOLITHIC–NEOLITHIC TRANSITION IN BRITAIN AND IRELAND?

To judge from the range of views expressed in recent archaeological publications that mention the aDNA data (*e.g.* Cummings *et al.* 2022; Lawrence *et al.* 2022; Thomas 2022), the short answer to this question is 'Not really', and this is also the case regarding the current models favoured by this chapter's two authors. Differences of opinion remain, for instance, about whether any hunter-gatherers in Britain and Ireland ventured over the sea to the Continent. In the opinion of at least one of us, the same objections that have been expressed about past claims for such movement (Sheridan 2015; 2018) can be levelled at the new claims, made by Lawrence *et al.* (2022) in their report on a large Mesolithic assemblage from Bexhill; the widely spaced French and Iberian *comparanda* for the distinctive 'Bexhill point' microliths are not, as the authors admit, precise matches. Moreover, their argument for the association (and, by implication, contemporaneity) between cereal grains and lithics dating to 4400–4300 cal BC (Lawrence *et al.* 2022, 566) remains to be tested by dates on the cereal grains, and the 'association' between some Bexhill points and pottery (of as-yet-unidentified type) is tenuous, given that the contexts are not firmly sealed. Finally, their claim that 5th-millennium T-shaped antler axeheads in Scotland indicate links with Ertebølle and/or Swifterbant groups on the Continent is not substantiated by any other evidence suggesting such continental links (*e.g.* pottery), and the possibility of independent invention of this artefact type in different places is not considered. (Despite these criticisms, the Bexhill publication is to be praised for highlighting variability in Later Mesolithic material culture in England.)

It is likely that the long-running debate on the Mesolithic–Neolithic transition will continue to be characterised by differing interpretations of the same few evidential details – among both archaeologists and geneticists, in their own arenas of research. The need for rigour in evaluating and interpreting evidence, and for being mutually well informed when archaeologists and geneticists debate, is self-evident. Moreover, all models should incorporate the best available formally modelled chronology (or chronologies). Some issues, such as the existence or otherwise of the Breton, Atlantic façade 'strand', can only be resolved through targeted new excavation. Nevertheless, the advent of aDNA results has afforded us a step-change in the debate, and we look forward to the generation of many more aDNA data in the future, with archaeologists and geneticists engaging in informed, two-way discussion.

ACKNOWLEDGEMENTS

The following are thanked for providing information and advice: Tom Booth, Selina Brace, Lara Cassidy, Susan Greaney and Maïté Rivollat.

REFERENCES

Anthony, D.W. 1990. Migration in archaeology: the baby and the bathwater. *American Anthropologist* 92, 895–914.

Ariano, B., Mattiangeli, V., Breslin, E.M., Parkinson, E.W., McLaughlin, T.R., Thompson, J.E. *et al.* 2022. Ancient Maltese genomes and the genetic geography of Neolithic Europe. *Current Biology: CB*, http://dx.doi.org/10.1016/j.cub.2022.04.069.

Bayliss, A., Marshall, P., Richards, C. and Whittle, A. 2017. Islands of history: the Late Neolithic timescape of Orkney. *Antiquity* 91, 1171–88.

Beau, A., Rivollat, M., Réveillas, H., Pemonge, M.-H., Mendisco, F., Thomas, Y. *et al.* 2017. Multi-scale ancient DNA analyses confirm the western origin of Michelsberg farmers and document probable practices of human sacrifice. *PLoS One* 12(7): e0179742. https://doi.org/10.1371/journal.pone.0179742.

Booth, T. 2019. A stranger in a strange land: a perspective on archaeological responses to the palaeogenetic revolution from an archaeologist working amongst palaeogeneticists. *World Archaeology* 51, 586–601.

Booth, T., Brück, J., Brace, S, and Barnes, I. 2021. Tales from the Supplementary Information: ancestry change in Chalcolithic–Early Bronze Age Britain was gradual with varied kinship organization. *Cambridge Archaeological Journal*, doi:10.1017/S0959774321000019.

Brace, S., Diekmann, Y., Booth, T.J., van Dorp, L., Faltyskova, Z., Rohland, N. *et al*. 2019. Ancient genomes indicate population replacement in Early Neolithic Britain. *Nature Ecology and Evolution* 3, 765–71.

Britnell, W. and Whittle, A. (eds) 2022. *The first stones: Penywyrlod, Gwernvale and the Black Mountains Neolithic long cairns of south-east Wales*. Oxford: Oxbow Books.

Brunel, S., Bennett, A., Cardin, L., Garraud, D., Barrand Emam, H., Beylier, A. *et al*. 2020. Ancient genomes from present-day France unveil 7,000 years of its demographic history. *Proceedings of the National Academy of Sciences of the United States of America* 117(23), 12791–8.

Calloway, E. 2015. Ancient DNA dispute raises questions about wheat trade in prehistoric Britain. *Nature* (2015). https://doi.org/10.1038/nature.2015.18702

Case, H. 1969. Neolithic explanations. *Antiquity* 43, 176–86.

Cassen, S., Pétrequin, P., Querré, G., Grimaud, V. and Rodríguez-Rellan, C. 2020. Spaces and signs for the transfer of jade and callaïs in the Neolithic of Western Europe. In C. Rodríguez-Rellan, B.A. Nelson and R. Fábregas Valcarce (eds), *A taste for green: a global perspective on ancient jade, turquoise and variscite exchange*, 121–39. Oxford: Oxbow Books.

Cassidy, L.M., Martiniano, R., Murphy, E.M., Teasdale, M.D., Mallory, J., Hartwell, B. and Bradley, D.G. 2016. Neolithic and Bronze Age migration to Ireland and establishment of the insular Atlantic genome. *Proceedings of the National Academy of Sciences of the United States of America* 113, 368–73.

Cassidy, L.M., Ó Maoldúin, R., Kador, T., Lynch, A., Jones, C., Woodman, P.C. *et al*. 2020. A dynastic elite in monumental Neolithic society. *Nature* 582, 384–8.

Clark, G. 1966. The invasion hypothesis in British archaeology. *Antiquity* 40, 172–89.

Cummings, V., Hofmann, D., Bjørnevad-Ahlqvist, M. and Iversen, R. 2022. Muddying the waters: reconsidering migration in the Neolithic of Britain, Ireland and Denmark. *Danish Journal of Archaeology* 11, 1–25.

Dulias, K., Foody, M.G.B., Justeau, P., Silva, M., Martiniano, R., Oteo-Garcia, G. *et al*. 2022. Ancient DNA at the edge of the world: continental immigration and the persistence of Neolithic male lineages in Bronze Age Orkney. *Proceedings of the National Academy of Sciences of the United States of America* 119(8). https://doi.org/10.1073/pnas.2108001119.

Fowler, C. 2022. Social arrangements. Kinship, descent and affinity in the mortuary architecture of Early Neolithic Britain and Ireland. *Archaeological Dialogues* (2022), 1–22, doi:10.1017/S1380203821000210.

Fowler, C., Olalde, I., Cummings, V., Armit, I., Büster, L., Cuthbert, G.S., Rohland, H., Cheronet, O., Pinhasi, R. and Reich, D. 2022. A high-resolution picture of kinship practices in an Early Neolithic tomb. *Nature*, doi.org/10.1038/s41586-021-04241-4.

Garrow, D., Griffiths, S., Anderson-Whymark, H. and Sturt, F. 2017. Stepping stones to the Neolithic? Radiocarbon dating the early Neolithic on islands within the 'western seaways' of Britain. *Proceedings of the Prehistoric Society* 83, 97–135.

Gernigon, K. 2016. Sphère d'interactions, complexe culturel: clefs de lecture de la variabilité géographique des expressions stylistiques du Chasséen. In T. Perrin, P. Chambon, J.F. Gibaja and G. Goude (eds), *Le Chasséen, des Chasséens… Retour sur une culture nationale et ses parallèles, Sepulcres de fossa, Cortaillod, Lagozza. Actes du colloque international tenu à Paris (France) du 18 au 20 novembre 2014*, 29–45. Toulouse: Archives d'Écologie Préhistorique

Griffiths, S. 2018. A cereal problem? What the current chronology of early cereal domesticates might tell us about changes in late fifth and early fourth millennium cal BC Ireland and Britain. *Environmental Archaeology*, doi: 10.1080/14614103.2018.1529945.

Griffiths, S. 2021. The last hunters of a wise race. In G. Hey and P. Frodsham (eds), *New light on the Neolithic of northern England*, 31–51. Oxford: Oxbow Books.

Griffiths, S. 2022. A chronology of the Black Mountains tombs and their place in the early Neolithic of south Wales and the Marches. In W. Britnell and A. Whittle (eds), *The first stones: Penywyrlod, Gwernvale and the Black Mountains Neolithic long cairns of south-east Wales*, 79–114. Oxford: Oxbow Books.

Lawrence, T., Donnelly, M., Kennard, L., Souday, C. and Grant, R. 2022. Britain in or out of Europe during the late Mesolithic? A new perspective of the Mesolithic–Neolithic transition. *Open Archaeology* 8(1), 2022, 550–77. https://doi.org/10.1515/opar-2022-0249.

Marchand, G. 2007. Neolithic fragrances: Mesolithic-Neolithic interactions in western France. In A. Whittle and V. Cummings (eds), *Going over: the Mesolithic-Neolithic transition in north-west Europe*, 225–42. Oxford: Oxford University Press for The British Academy.

Meiklejohn, C., Chamberlain, A.T. and Schulting, R.J. 2011. Radiocarbon dating of Mesolithic human remains in Great Britain. *Mesolithic Miscellany* 21:2, 20–58.

Neil, S., Evans, J., Montgomery, J. and Scarre, C. 2020. Isotopic evidence for human movement into central England during the Early Neolithic. *European Journal of Archaeology* 2020, 1–18.

Neil, S., Montgomery, J., Evans, J., Cook, G.T. and Scarre, C. 2017. Land use and mobility during the Neolithic in Wales explored using isotope analysis of tooth enamel. *American Journal of Physical Anthropology* 164, 371–93.

Olalde, I., Brace, S., Allentoft, M.E., Armit, I., Kristiansen, K., Rohland, N. *et al.* 2018. The Beaker phenomenon and the genomic transformation of northwest Europe. *Nature* February 21, 2018; doi:10.1038/nature25738.

Patterson, N., Isakov, M., Booth, T., Büster, L., Fischer, C.-E., Olalde, I. *et al.* 2022. Large-scale migration into Britain during the Middle to Late Bronze Age. *Nature* 601, 588–94.

Pioffet, H. 2014. *Sociétés et identités du Premier Néolithique de Grande-Bretagne et d'Irlande dans leur contexte ouest européen: caractérisation et analyses comparatives des productions céramiques entre Manche, Mer d'Irlande et Mer du Nord*. PhD thesis, University of Durham and Rennes 1. http://etheses.dur.ac.uk/11011/.

Rivollat, M., Jeong, C., Schiffels, S., Küçükkalıpçı, İ, Pemonge, M.-H., Rohrlach, A.B. *et al.* 2020. Ancient genome-wide DNA from France highlights the complexity of interactions between Mesolithic hunter-gatherers and Neolithic farmers. *Science Advances* 6, eaaz5344, 29 May 2020.

Rohrlach, A.B., Papac, L., Childebayeva, A., Rivollat, M., Villalba-Mouco, V., Neumann, G.U. *et al.* 2021. Using Y-chromosome capture enrichment to resolve haplogroup H2 shows new evidence for a two-path Neolithic expansion to Western Europe. *Scientific Reports* 11, 15005(2021). https://doi.org/10.1038/s41598-021-94491-z.

Rowley-Conwy, P. 2011. Westward Ho! The spread of agriculture from central Europe to the Atlantic. *Current Anthropology* 52, S431–51.

Rowley-Conwy, P., Gron, K.J., Bishop, R.R., Dunne, J., Evershed, R.P., Longford, C. *et al.* 2020. The earliest farming in Britain: towards a new synthesis. In K.J. Gron, L. Sørensen and P. Rowley-Conwy (eds), *Farmers at the frontier: a pan-European perspective on Neolithisation*, 401–24. Oxford: Oxbow Books.

Sánchez-Quinto, F., Malmström, H, Fraser, M., Girdland-Flink, L., Svensson, E., Simões, L.G. *et al.* 2019. Megalithic tombs in Western and Northern Neolithic Europe were linked to a kindred society. *Proceedings of the National Academy of Sciences of the United States of America* 116(19), 9469–74.

Sheridan, J.A. 2003. French connections I: spreading the marmites thinly. In I. Armit, E. Murphy, E. Nelis and D. Simpson (eds), *Neolithic settlement in Ireland and western Britain*, 3–17. Oxford: Oxbow Books.

Sheridan, J.A. 2004. Neolithic connections along and across the Irish Sea. In V. Cummings and C. Fowler (eds), *The Neolithic of the Irish Sea: materiality and traditions of practice*, 9–21. Oxford: Oxbow Books.

Sheridan, J.A. 2007. From Picardie to Pickering and Pencraig Hill? New information on the 'Carinated Bowl Neolithic' in northern Britain. In A. Whittle and V. Cummings (eds), *Going over: the Mesolithic-Neolithic transition in north-west Europe*, 441–92. Oxford: Oxford University Press for The British Academy.

Sheridan, J.A. 2010. The Neolithisation of Britain and Ireland: the 'big picture'. In B. Finlayson and G.M. Warren (eds), *Landscapes in transition*, 89–105. Oxford and London: Oxbow Books and Council for British Research in the Levant.

Sheridan, J.A. 2011. The Early Neolithic of south-west England: new insights and new questions. In S. Pearce (ed.), *Recent archaeological work in South Western Britain: papers in honour of Henrietta Quinnell*, 21–40. Oxford: Archaeopress.

Sheridan, J.A. 2012. Review of A. Whittle, F. Healy and A. Bayliss, *Gathering Time: Dating the Early Neolithic Enclosures of Southern Britain and Ireland*. *Antiquity* 86(331), 262–4.

Sheridan, J.A. 2015. Review of Julian Thomas, *The Birth of Neolithic Britain: an interpretive account*. *European Journal of Archaeology* 18 (4), 720–7.

Sheridan, J.A. 2016. Scottish Neolithic pottery in 2016: the big picture and some details of the narrative. In F.J. Hunter and J.A. Sheridan (eds) *Ancient lives: object, people and place in early Scotland. Essays for David V Clarke on his 70th birthday*, 189–212. Leiden: Sidestone Press.

Sheridan, J. A. 2018. Review of D. Garrow & F. Sturt, *Neolithic Stepping Stones: excavation and survey within the western seaways of Britain, 2008–2014*, for Prehistoric Society online reviews: http://www.prehistoricsociety.org/files/reviews/Neolithic_Stepping_Stones_Final.pdf.

Sheridan, J.A. 2021. A view from north of the border. In G. Hey and P. Frodsham (eds), *New light on the Neolithic of northern England*, 177–88. Oxford: Oxbow Books.

Sheridan, J.A. and Pailler, Y. 2012. Les haches alpines et leurs imitations en Grande Bretagne, Irlande et dans les Iles anglo-normandes. In P. Pétrequin, S. Cassen, M. Errera, L. Klassen, A. Sheridan and A.-M. Pétrequin (eds), *Jade. Grandes haches alpines du Néolithique européen. Ve et IVe millénaires av. J.-C.*, 1046–87. Besançon: Presses Universitaires de Franche-Comté; Gray: Centre de Recherche Archéologique de la Vallée de l'Ain.

Sheridan, J.A. and Schulting, R. 2020. Making sense of Scottish Neolithic funerary monuments: tracing trajectories and understanding their rationale. In A.B. Gebauer, L. Sørensen, A. Teather and A.C. Valera (eds), *Monumentalising life in the Neolithic: narratives of change and continuity*, 195–215. Oxford: Oxbow Books.

Sheridan, J.A., Schulting, R., Quinnell, H. and Taylor, R. 2008. Revisiting a small passage tomb at Broadsands, Devon. *Proceedings of the Devon Archaeological Society* 66, 1–26.

Smith, O., Momber, G., Bates, R., Garwood, P., Fitch, S., Pallen, M., Gaffney, V. and Allaby, R.G. 2015. Sedimentary DNA from a submerged site reveals wheat in the British Isles 8000 years ago. *Science* 347(6225), 998–1001 https://doi.org/10.1126/science.1261278

Thomas, J. 2013. *The birth of Neolithic Britain: an interpretive account*. Oxford: Oxford University Press.

Thomas, J. 2022. Neolithization and population replacement in Britain: an alternative view. *Cambridge Archaeological Journal*, doi:10.1017/S0959774321000639.

Warren, G. 2021. *Hunter-gatherer Ireland: making connections in an island world*. Oxford: Oxbow.

Whittle, A. 1977. *The earlier Neolithic of southern England and its continental background*. Oxford: British Archaeological Reports.

Whittle, A. 1985. *Neolithic Europe: a survey*. Cambridge: Cambridge University Press.

Whittle, A. 1996. *Europe in the Neolithic: the creation of new worlds*. Cambridge: Cambridge University Press.

Whittle, A. 2018. *The times of their lives: hunting history in the archaeology of Neolithic Europe.* Oxford: Oxbow Books.

Whittle, A., Bayliss, A. and Healy, F. 2022. A decade on: revised timings for causewayed enclosures in southern Britain. In J. Last (ed.), *Marking place: new perspectives on early Neolithic enclosures,* 203–22. Oxford: Oxbow Books.

Whittle, A., Healy, F. and Bayliss, A. 2011. *Gathering time: dating the early Neolithic enclosures of southern Britain and Ireland.* Oxford: Oxbow Books.

Woodman, P.C. 2015. *Ireland's first settlers: time and the Mesolithic.* Oxford: Oxbow Books.

Chapter 13

Looking back, looking forward – humanity beyond biology

Susan Greaney

As the chapters in this volume have shown, the study of ancient DNA is providing a rich new strand of evidence for understanding the Neolithic period in Europe. Large-scale studies of populations and migrations are now being supplemented by much finer-grained research into genetic relations between people. Alongside the many grounds for admiration and optimism, there are nevertheless reasons for measured caution. This chapter will explore the sometimes problematic way in which genetic ancestry has been interpreted using long-discredited notions of social organisation, hierarchy, ethnicity and kinship. It will argue for a 'slow science' approach to collaborative ancient DNA (aDNA) research that makes room for nuanced and reflexive interpretation drawing on the humanities, particularly anthropological and archaeological theory. Genetic change and relatedness need to be considered in the light of the partial nature of the archaeological record and the samples available to researchers, couched using careful terminologies, interpreted alongside other strands of archaeological and anthropological evidence and grounded in critical approaches to social identity and kinship. Some suggestions are made looking forward to a time when aDNA research is fully embedded within archaeological interpretations of the period, and archaeological thinking firmly within interpretations of genetic data.

INTRODUCTION

About 20 years ago, when I was an undergraduate archaeology student, I found myself talking about ancient DNA while sitting in the garden of my aunt's house in Oxford. I was being interrogated by my cousin's father Bryan Sykes (not my uncle – kinship is complex!) on the major questions in archaeology that the study of aDNA could help answer. The immediate and only response that sprang to my mind was biological relatedness: wouldn't it be wonderful to know whether people buried together in Neolithic tombs such as West Kennet long barrow were related to each other? It might help us understand how social groups were organised and who was chosen for burial in such spectacular monuments. At the time I had no concept that genetics could answer questions about mass population movements, major subsistence and technological transitions, or the spread of languages. During the conference in November 2021, I finally saw what had been in my mind that day – a family tree setting out how the burials from Hazleton North long barrow in Gloucestershire were likely to have been biologically related: genealogy from 4700 years ago (Fowler *et al.* 2022).

Since then, my research interests have developed to focus on the landscapes and monuments of the middle and late Neolithic period in Britain and Ireland as well as the Neolithic to Early Bronze Age transition. From this limited archaeological perspective, with no specialist knowledge of genetics, this chapter will explore three subject areas that are central to the interpretation of human aDNA: biological relatedness, social organisation and uneven patterns in funerary practices. It is worth exploring these in some detail, as a deeper and more critical understanding of them may help to influence how aDNA results are interpreted. In the fast-paced world of publication in major science journals and the desire for sensational results, there is an argument to be made for a more considered, slower and more collaborative approach that takes some of these interpretative issues on board; some suggestions towards how we might achieve this are made at the end of the chapter.

LOOKING BACK: DANCE OF THE DISCIPLINES

Since the development of second or next generation short-read sequencing technologies and the recognition of petrous bones as sources of well-preserved DNA, alongside other methodological improvements (see Ariano and Bradley, this volume), the last seven years have seen an increasing deluge of archaeogenetic papers and new data. Initial high-profile research projects focused on mass population movements and the spread of languages (*e.g.* Allentoft *et al.* 2015; Haak *et al.* 2015). These large-scale narrative interpretations were at a scale beyond which most archaeologists felt confident to operate. The return to outdated cultural-historical models and the revival of migration as the only explanation for change were disruptive and unsettling. They exposed unresolved problems within archaeology relating to the definition of material culture groups and how these might relate to identity and social organisation, and highlighted a lack of theorisation relating to migration and acculturation.

There are now well-rehearsed criticisms relating to assumptions within these early papers about archaeological cultures being distinct populations or social groups (Vander Linden 2016; Furholt 2018, 162) and for the way in which interpretations extended well beyond the genetic data (Kristiansen 2022, 11; this volume). It has become clearer to researchers working in both palaeogenetics and archaeology that each discipline uses models to describe and communicate their ideas and findings (Booth 2019, 591). Genetic scientists identify groups of individuals who share more genetic variants with each other than with individuals outside these groups, giving them names such as 'Western hunter-gatherer'. Archaeologists traditionally identify groups of individuals who share more cultural traits with each other than with individuals outside these groups, giving them labels such as 'Corded Ware Culture'. Both types of terminology simply express similarity, but they are imprecise and can be misleading if they are taken to mean bounded population groups or are used interchangeably. This can lead to a blurring of the distinction between genetic variants and cultural traits, even though these are entirely unrelated types of evidence (Frieman and Hofmann 2019). Despite alternative solutions for more neutral nomenclature proposed by Eisenmann *et al.* (2018), it seems that mixed geographical and cultural labels continue to be preferred within archaeogenetics, despite a shift to more neutral variations (Kristiansen, this volume). This seemingly intractable problem means that each paper needs to set out why these labels have been chosen, with an awareness of the potential impact of their use on wider understandings. Similar attentiveness needs to be paid within archaeological publications too; for example, within a British context, the neutral terms 'Beaker-using people' or 'Beaker-associated burials' are far preferable to 'Beaker people'.

One of the reasons that the arrival of aDNA papers enshrining a return to 'culture-historical' models of population change felt so unsettling for archaeologists is because this approach was so far divorced from current interpretative strands within western European and American archaeology. Building on decades of feminist and post-processual thinking that firmly rejects socio-evolutionary labels like 'chiefdom' and the use of archaeological 'cultures' altogether, some archaeologists are actively exploring entirely different ideas relating to materiality, relationality, assemblage theory and non-human actors (Harris and Cipolla 2017). However, by avoiding migration and large-scale movement as a topic, archaeologists have neglected to develop sophisticated theories relating to how different communities segregate, integrate and negotiate their cultural differences to form new identities. This work must now take place as a matter of urgency, enlightened by the wide array of available anthropological evidence.

FAMILY TIES

The 'ontological turn' in archaeology has led to a reframing of ideas relating to kinship, gender practices and more lately, power relations – fields to which aDNA researchers are now contributing fundamental new data and about which they are reaching their own conclusions, albeit from a radically different theoretical perspective (Crellin and Harris 2020). As the papers in this volume show, archaeogenetics is now maturing as a discipline, with a shift to smaller-scale questions and a greater understanding of the complexity of cultural change in the past (Kristiansen 2022, 14). Finer-grained studies are teasing out the detail of how migration and integration took place. Collaborative research projects have begun to combine genetics with other bioarchaeological sciences such as isotope analysis, and sometimes with archaeological analysis of, for example, grave goods (*e.g.* Mittnik *et al.* 2019). A series of recent aDNA papers have been able to reconstruct patterns of biological relatedness, either within single cemeteries or burial monuments (*e.g.* Mittnik *et al.* 2019; Fowler *et al.* 2020; Sjögren *et al.* 2020) or across more dispersed sites (Cassidy *et al.* 2020). Despite some of these aDNA papers having extended discussions incorporating insights from anthropology (*e.g.* Sjögren *et al.* 2020), many of the interpretations apply idealised models of kinship that are somewhat crude and outdated, without sufficient understanding of archaeological context, or of the current debates and nuances surrounding these topics (Frieman *et al.* 2019; Brück and Frieman 2021; Ensor 2021). For example, authors commonly refer to 'marriage' as shorthand for 'had children with', unconsciously applying modern Eurocentric notions of heterosexual monogamous long-term partnerships, which may not have been practised in the past. In response, Brück (2021) has set out a range of ethnographic examples to show how kinship need not be a direct reflection of genetic links, and Booth *et al.* (2021) have set a high standard in their analysis of genetic data, deftly undermining and questioning common assumptions about kinship relations, migration, patrilineality and exogamy, using pertinent anthropological examples. These are needed to help to address the lack of creativity and imagination in interpretations about how people in the past lived, moving beyond 'common-sense' (Eurocentric and modern) assumptions. As Frieman (2021) has highlighted, aDNA results can privilege the biological aspect of kinship relations, which may be far more relevant to us as modern scholars than it was to people in the past.

That said, Fowler and colleagues (2022) offer a counterexample of a collaboration between geneticists and archaeologists with a good understanding of post-modern and relational approaches, helped by strong archaeological peer review and further interpretation (Fowler 2022). Analysis of genetic data from individuals buried within the early Neolithic long barrow at Hazleton North in Gloucestershire has allowed the reconstruction of the biological relations of an extended lineage over five generations (Fowler *et al.* 2022). This lineage was descended from one male and four females with whom he had children, with the social architecture of the tomb, that is the location of the burials within the two chambers, almost entirely based on maternal lines of descent. The people interred were mostly sons and grandsons (adult daughters do not seem to have been placed within this tomb), but these included sons of the female partners by other males. The authors suggest that this indicates adoptive kinship or social fatherhood, using the term stepfather (Fowler *et al.* 2022, 586), although the evidence could equally suggest that descent from the maternal line for these individuals was more important. The evidence suggests that different aspects of both paternal and maternal descent were important markers of identity negotiated through choices made during the construction of the tomb and ongoing funerary practices (Fowler 2022). Interestingly, eight of the sampled individuals buried within the tomb were not biologically related to the main family, but may well have been considered close kin, at least within the context of the funerary sphere. This serves to emphasise how aDNA results can bring useful evidence about non-biological forms of kinship, with adoption, co-residence or other forms of social relationship potentially being of equal importance and expressed through the placement of the dead.

As others (Frieman *et al.* 2019; Brück 2021) have argued, implicit gender bias appears to often influence interpretations in aDNA studies. It is easy to slip from a description of communities as patrilineal and patrilocal, to stating that they were patriarchal. Simply because males and their male descendants stay in the same location does not necessarily mean that these communities were controlled by men. As Brück (2021, 232) has identified, Sjögren *et al.* (2020) describe the people buried in Beaker-using community cemeteries in southern Germany as patriarchal. They write of 'a dominant male line that married in women from other groups and married out their own daughters' (Sjögren *et al.* 2020, 23). Women have become pawns in a game of male alliances, rather than people with agency, who were valued for reasons other than simply reproduction, with extensive knowledge of other places and communities. If these were travelling males, they would have been characterised as explorers or pioneers. The paper's application of a binary model of sex (Frieman *et al.* 2019) leads to conclusions that gloss over two burials where gender-differentiated burial practices were not followed, and isotopic evidence that shows that some males also travelled to other places during their lifetimes.

IDENTIFYING INEQUALITY

It is worth underlining that decisions relating to funerary practices, burial processes and the placement of the dead, as well as possible subsequent removal and disturbance of burials, were ongoing performances, actively creating and negotiating identity and community among the living (Parker Pearson 1999). People may well have been brought together in death who did not live together in life. In some aDNA papers, there is a tendency to assume that grave goods can reflect the status of the deceased in life, but as archaeologists are taught, 'the dead don't bury themselves'. The aDNA evidence from a Bronze Age cemetery in the Lech river valley in southern Germany showed that 'richer' grave goods were buried more often with men who had relatives in that or nearby cemeteries, leading to the suggestion that these men were of higher status (Mittnik *et al.* 2019, 732). Perhaps instead this was because they had more family members in the vicinity to contribute to the funeral, rather than necessarily reflecting their status or position in life.

The identification of distant biological relatedness among individuals buried within geographically dispersed and diverse passage tombs in Neolithic Ireland (such as Carrowmore, Millin Bay, Newgrange and Carrowkeel), as well as distinct genetic clustering of sampled individuals buried in these tombs, has led to the conclusion that these people identified themselves by descent, chose partners from within their circle of relatives, and that, therefore, society at this time had a high degree of social complexity, in short, constituting a 'dynastic elite' (Cassidy *et al.* 2020, 386). However, this genetic information needs to be analysed carefully in combination with modelled radiocarbon dates for these individuals. The distantly related individuals have dates that show that they are unlikely to have lived contemporaneously but instead were spread out over *c.* 1000 years of the Neolithic. The individuals interred at Carrowkeel date from the latest Neolithic and were interred in these tombs well after their main use for the deposition of cremations. Is it possible that one elite extended family controlled these tombs, and retained the exclusive right for burial within them over such a long period, as claimed (Cassidy *et al.* 2020; this volume)? The idea is contradicted by aDNA results from six individuals within Carrowkeel Cairn K who did not show any biological kinship closer than 4th-degree relatives (Kador *et al.* 2018, 23).

Assessing the uniqueness of burials within these passage tombs is difficult due to the fact there are few comparable aDNA samples from non-passage tomb contexts from the middle and later Neolithic period in Ireland, largely because of the archaeologically invisible ways in which most people were treated after death (see below). Could the genetic clustering identified by Cassidy and colleagues simply be an outcome of temporal drift instead, suggesting an increasingly limited island population with little out-breeding in the second half of the Neolithic? The fact that some individuals were distant biological relations of each other may have been a relatively meaningless factor in the creation of their identities. Until more data are available, there is nothing conclusive in the evidence so far to suggest social hierarchy or elite families being buried in these passage tombs. Although the presence of large monuments is often used to assume social hierarchy, this is not a given; there are several societies around the world where communal monuments were built without evidence for strong social inequalities.

The discovery of an individual whose unburnt skull was deposited in the chamber at Newgrange passage tomb, who was the offspring of a first-order incestuous union, has been interpreted as a behaviour indicative of a ruling elite family of a complex chiefdom or early state (Cassidy *et al.* 2020). Abstracting from one individual (whose genetic status may or may not have been known to his contemporaries, or to those who placed his remains in the tomb) to a whole structure of society is problematic, and this is only one of several possible different interpretations for the status of this person. One example cannot determine whether incest was widely practised within a community, nor whether it was deemed socially acceptable or not. Even if this was a practice related to preserving an elite lineage, it may have been very short-lived or even a one-off phenomenon, rather than indicative of the wider trajectory of social evolution. For this reason, terms such as chiefdom or early state need to be avoided, as these form part of long-discredited socio-evolutionary models. Many societies are known that do not fit these categories (*e.g.* Clastres 1977), documented examples of chiefdoms and early states have been shown to often be secondary formations that are reflections of modern world systems (Chapman 2003), and the Pacific Island societies that were the original models for many of these socio-evolutionary models have been shown to have widely varied forms of social organisation and expressions of monumentality (Bedford 2019). Interestingly, a recent aDNA study on Neolithic human remains from the Xagħra Circle on Gozo, Malta, did not reach conclusions relating to inequality or social hierarchy, despite identifying close inbreeding among their ancestry (Ariano *et al.* 2022).

Interpretations of aDNA evidence relating to social hierarchy and status in the absence of other archaeological evidence need to be cautiously applied, and different possibilities considered. There are, of course, widely varying opinions on this topic within the archaeological community (compare Sheridan 2020 with Carlin 2020, for example); aDNA is one strand of evidence to add to these ongoing debates. Unfortunately, there is a tendency for aDNA papers to simply cite the interpretations of previous genetic studies. For example, Dulias *et al.* (2022) cite Cassidy *et al.* (2020) to support their conclusion that strong hierarchies existed among megalithic communities across Britain and Ireland.

THE MISSING DEAD

For much of the Neolithic in Britain and Ireland, people disposed of their dead in archaeologically invisible ways. Where burials have survived, for example within early Neolithic long barrows or middle Neolithic passage tombs, only a small selection of the community appear to have been selected for interment, and aside from this selection, there are very few indicators of status or social hierarchy. Cremation appears to have been the preferred (although by no means exclusive) funerary practice during the middle Neolithic (Willis 2021), with limited numbers of cremations deposited within small and large circular enclosures in the years around 3000 cal BC (*e.g.* at Stonehenge, West Stow and Dorchester-on-Thames). By the late Neolithic, the dead are almost entirely invisible within the archaeological record. It has been suggested that people were depositing cremations in rivers or the sea (Parker Pearson 2020, 497) and this seems likely, but direct evidence remains very sparse. As it is not currently possible to extract aDNA from burnt bones, despite laudable attempts to do so (Cassidy *et al.* 2020, supp. info., 21), a large part of the Neolithic therefore currently lies beyond the reach of genetic analysis. New types of individual burial accompanied with grave goods and in particular Beaker pottery begin in the Chalcolithic period after 2450 cal BC or so, which have been clearly shown through aDNA analysis to reflect new people moving into Britain and Ireland from the Continent (Olalde *et al.* 2018). However, there remains variability in funerary rites, with the practice of cremation likely continuing among both local communities and brought in as an existing practice by incomers, as well as disarticulation and mixed burials (Bloxam and Parker Pearson 2022).

It is against this extremely partial picture of funerary practices that aDNA results must be understood. The paper on Hazleton North neglects to mention the presence of over 200 fragments of cremated human bone within the chambers of this tomb, largely found within the entrance to the northern chamber, where the cremated remains of at least one adult (and likely more) and one child were scattered (Saville 1990, 104, table 50). Similarly, Dulias *et al.* (2022) note their inability to assess cremated remains from the Bronze Age cemetery on Westray, Orkney. Although genetic information from these individuals might not drastically alter the overall picture obtained from the unburnt remains, perhaps particular people from separate lineages or other types of kin were interred in this way. Within Irish passage tombs, considerable quantities of intermingled burnt and unburnt human remains are usually found within the chambers, but aDNA can only be extracted from the smaller amounts of unburnt bone. In addition, selecting the petrous bone from the skull, a part often treated differently from the rest of the skeleton, introduces further bias; these unburnt skulls might represent a particular subset of the community (Charlton *et al.* 2019).

As Booth *et al.* (2021) have demonstrated, the major shift in genetic ancestry at the start of the Chalcolithic identified by Olalde *et al.* (2018) was not a sudden population replacement, but a more gradual transition over 10–16 generations. Certain individuals up to around 2000 cal BC have significant proportions of 'Neolithic' ancestry showing the persistence of unsampled populations who only infrequently had children with the new arrivals and their descendants, and who chose to bury their dead in archaeologically invisible ways (Booth *et al.* 2021, 381). Slightly later, by around 2100 cal BC onwards, there is more integration visible in the genetics, a pattern that must be interpreted alongside changes evident in the archaeological record around this time, including the development of new pottery styles and decoration, increasing use of bronze and changing funerary practices, such as more frequent cremation burials and a marked diversification in grave groups (Needham 2005; Carlin 2020). The existence of such parallel populations, sharing places of residence, landscapes, technologies, fashions and perhaps language for lengthy periods, but not regularly intermixing genetically, can now be seen in various places and times across Europe, as finer-grained aDNA evidence becomes available that more closely matches the complexity visible in the archaeological record (*e.g.* Furtwängler *et al.* 2020; Papac *et al.* 2021; Bánffy, this volume).

More detailed chronologies for late Neolithic monument building, alteration, use and abandonment will help with understanding the impact of new arrivals in Britain, and the social contexts within which interactions took place (*e.g.* Greaney *et al.* 2020). Although major monument construction in southern Britain appears to cease after *c.* 2400 cal BC (the date varies regionally), many of these sites retained their significance, with deposition at these sites continuing, Beaker-associated burials placed nearby, and some, such as Stonehenge, being remodelled. The mapping out of these processes of division and difference, integration and affiliation, and how these contributed to identity building in different regions, is a task that the archaeological community is best placed to undertake. Genetic data form one strand of evidence to be used in these debates, alongside other sources such as isotope and dietary information, radiocarbon dates, material culture and changes in the environment and wider landscapes.

LOOKING FORWARD: TOWARDS THE TRANSDISCIPLINARY

The world of archaeogenetics is exciting and fast-developing. We are learning things about the Neolithic that would astonish archaeologists working in this area only 20 years ago. There is already much to digest, to integrate and to re-assess in the light of these new results (see Bánffy this volume). But what other research questions might we want to address in future? From the perspective of Neolithic Britain and Ireland, we now have data from chambered tombs in Ireland and one from the Cotswolds that show very different patterns of biological relatedness (Fowler 2022, 73). How might these compare with people buried in early Neolithic tombs in Caithness, or Kent? A focus on mass population movements at the beginning and end of the Neolithic means that middle Neolithic burials have been neglected so far in aDNA analyses, but these could provide information about biological relatedness, movement, social relations, disease and demography. Were the four children buried with elaborately carved chalk drums in Yorkshire in the middle Neolithic related to each other? What about the middle Neolithic 'mass grave' at Banbury Lane, Northamptonshire, or the burials at Duggleby Howe, East Yorkshire?

Looking ahead, how can we ensure that these research questions are answered within truly collaborative, transdisciplinary work between archaeogenetists and archaeologists? Frieman and Hofmann (2019) have identified steps that can be taken, for example suggesting that aDNA labs encourage more discursive and lengthy publications in collaboration with archaeologists and arguing for ontological reflection at each stage of research projects. Richardson and Booth (2017) have highlighted the need to develop venues and mechanisms for the two disciplines to come into contact more often: one of the aims of the NSG conference. In this volume, Kristiansen has set out some of the key steps and issues involved in the move towards truly transdisciplinary work.

Meaningful, cross-disciplinary collaboration should create further best-practice models to follow, with research questions formulated, as well as results interpreted, in light of current archaeological and anthropological thinking on gender, kinship, identity, power and social inequality, as well as new thinking on migration and acculturation. Going further, I would argue that there is a need for archaeologists and geneticists to make steps together towards a 'slow science' approach (Stengers 2018; see Caraher 2019 for a discussion of 'slow archaeology'), shifting the value of such work from a focus entirely on research outputs towards research that benefits the general public. It involves giving time and energy to the sharing of information through workshops and discussion groups, where each discipline learns about the methods and theories of the other, rather than simply publishing across each other's bows. It should involve embedding archaeologically trained researchers into aDNA laboratories or projects and the discussion of ethical implications, from sampling decisions to interpretation. One proactive way forward would be to set up a short course on archaeogenetics so that archaeologists can engage more confidently with a basic understanding of the science behind this complex field; conversely, a course on social archaeology may help geneticists working on the archaeological material acquire the same confidence. 'Slow science' is time-consuming and hard work, particularly as it goes against major structural constraints of funding, traditional career progression models, competition for the 'big story' and high-impact publication strategies (Sykes *et al.* 2020). An edited volume such as this falls far short in terms of academic impact models (we therefore extend huge thanks to all the authors for contributing); perhaps we need to re-assess whether all impact is good impact. These are major issues for academia that stretch far beyond the limits of our own disciplines and are common to wider inter-disciplinary research.

Why is it important to build further collaborative projects and move towards a more nuanced 'slow science'? First, it is needed in order to do justice to the complexities and realities of the past, without perpetuating unconscious assumptions or biases. The second reason is preventative – we have seen how initial large-scale aDNA studies over-simplified processes of migration resulting in misleading conclusions. As genetic studies become more fine-grained, interpretations might well contain assumptions about kinship, gender and social hierarchy. It is perhaps possible to predict the areas of disagreement that might come next: further assumptions about gender without reference to queer theory perhaps (Frieman *et al.* 2019; Bickle 2020), or the difficulties of equating population estimates with contradictory archaeological evidence. If we can work together more collaboratively, we may be able to break the cycle of 'big story' followed by critique and counter-narrative. Finally, we know that the great press interest and impact of palaeogenetics papers on the wider public can result in over-simplification and unhelpful public discourse (Richardson and Booth 2017; Frieman and Hofmann 2019; Hakenbeck 2019), often giving the impression that genetic evidence can solve all archaeological questions (Jones and Bösl 2021). Although archaeologists and geneticists have no control over how the media report on their discoveries, we do have considerable influence over the choice of paper titles, university or institution press releases and quotes given to journalists. It is possible to predict the likely press angles and possible controversies, and these should be predicted and mitigated against to prevent interpretative inflation (Barclay and Brophy 2020). It is also important not to perpetuate out-dated approaches to the past that make inequality seem inevitable (Graeber and Wengrow 2021). Relying on long-dismissed evolutionary social models and minimising the complexity of human behaviour limits our interpretation of the past, making extreme social inequality and contemporary stereotypes seem natural and inevitable, both in the past and today. These are fundamental issues for how we reconstruct the lives of people in the past, and how we tell stories about our own future.

ACKNOWLEDGEMENTS

Thanks are extended to Alasdair Whittle, Josh Pollard and Cate Frieman whose comments have vastly improved this chapter.

REFERENCES

Allentoft, M.E., Sikora, M., Sjögern, K-G., Rasmussen, S., Rasmussen, M., Stenderup, J. *et al.* 2015. Population genomics of Bronze Age Eurasia. *Nature* 522, 167–72.

Ariano, B., Mattiangeli, V., Breslin, E.M., Parkinson, E.W., McLaughlin, T.R., Thompson, J.E. *et al.* 2022. Ancient Maltese genomes and the genetic geography of Neolithic Europe. *Current Biology* 32, doi.org/10.1016/j.cub.2022.04.069.

Barclay, G. and Brophy, K. 2021. 'A veritable chauvinism of prehistory': nationalist prehistories and the 'British' late Neolithic mythos. *Archaeological Journal* 178(2), 330–60.

Bedford, S. 2019. The complexity of monumentality in Melanesia: mixed messages from Vanuatu. In M. Leclerc and J. Flexner (eds), *Archaeologies of island Melanesia: current approaches to landscapes, exchange and practice*, 67–79. Canberra: Australian National University Press.

Bickle, P. 2020. Thinking gender differently: new approaches to identity difference in the central European Neolithic. *Cambridge Archaeological Journal* 30(2), 201–18.

Bloxam, A. and Parker Pearson, M. 2022. Funerary diversity and cultural continuity: the British Beaker phenomenon beyond the stereotype. *Proceedings of the Prehistoric Society*, doi:10.1017/ppr.2022.2.

Booth, T. 2019. A stranger in a strange land: a perspective on archaeological responses to the palaeogenetic revolution from an archaeologist working amongst palaeogeneticists. *World Archaeology* 51, 586–601.

Booth, T., Brück, J., Brace, S. and Barnes, I. 2021. Tales from the supplementary information: ancestry change in Chalcolithic–Early Bronze Age Britain was gradual with varied kinship organization. *Cambridge Archaeological Journal* 31(3), 379–400.

Brück, J. 2021. Ancient DNA, kinship and relational identities in Bronze Age Britain. *Antiquity* 95, 228–37.

Brück, J. and Frieman, C. 2021. Making kin: the archaeology and genetics of human relationships. *TATuP* 30(2), 47–52, doi: https://doi.org/10.14512/tatup.30.2.47.

Caraher, W. 2019. Slow archaeology, punk archaeology and the 'archaeology of care'. *European Journal of Archaeology* 22(3), 372–85.

Carlin, N. 2020. *The Beaker phenomenon? Understanding the character and context of social practices in Ireland 2500–2000 BC*. Leiden: Sidestone Press.

Cassidy, L.M., Ó Maoldúin, R., Kador, T., Lynch, A., Jones, C., Woodman, P.C. *et al.* 2020. A dynastic elite in monumental Neolithic society. *Nature* 582, 384–8.

Chapman, R. 2003. *Archaeologies of complexity*. London: Routledge.

Charlton, S., Booth, T. and Barnes, I. 2019. The problem with petrous? A consideration of potential biases in the utilisation of pars petrosa for ancient DNA analysis. *World Archaeology* 51(4), 574–85.

Clastres, P. 1977. *Society against the state*. Oxford: Blackwell.

Crellin, R. and Harris, O.J.T. 2020. Beyond binaries: interrogating ancient DNA. *Archaeological Dialogues* 27, 37–56.

Dulias, K., Foody, M.G.B., Justeau, P., Silva, M., Martiniano, R., Oteo-García, G. *et al.* 2022. Ancient DNA at the edge of the world: continental immigration and the persistence of Neolithic male lineages in Bronze Age Orkney. *PNAS* 119(8), doi.org/10.1073/pnas.2108001119.

Eisenmann, S., Bánffy, E., van Dommelen, P., Hofmann, K.P., Maran, J., Lazaridis, I. *et al.* 2018. Reconciling material cultures in archaeology with genetic data: the nomenclature of clusters emerging from archaeogenomic analysis. *Science Reports* 2018 Aug 29, 8(1):13003, doi: 10.1038/s41598-018-31123-z.

Ensor, B.E. 2021. Making aDNA useful for kinship analysis. *Antiquity* 95, 241–3.

Evershed, R.P., Davey Smith, G., Roffet-Salque, M., Timpson, A., Diekmann, Y., Lyon, M.E. *et al.* 2022. Dairying, diseases and the evolution of lactase persistence in Europe. *Nature* 608, 336–45.

Fowler, C., Olalde, I., Cummings, V., Armit, I., Büster, L., Cuthbert, G.S., Rohland, H., Cheronet, O., Pinhasi, R. and Reich, D. 2022. A high-resolution picture of kinship practices in an Early Neolithic tomb. *Nature* 601(7894), 584–7.

Fowler, C. 2022. Social arrangements: kinship, descent and affinity in the mortuary architecture of Early Neolithic Britain and Ireland. *Archaeological Dialogues* 29, 67–88.

Frieman, C. 2021. Emergent or imposed? *Antiquity* 95, 247–8.

Frieman, C. and Hofmann, D. 2019. Present pasts in the archaeology of genetics, identity, and migration in Europe: a critical essay. *World Archaeology* 51, 528–45.

Frieman, C., Teather, A. and Morgan, C. 2019. Bodies in motion: narratives and counter narratives of gendered mobility in European later prehistory. *Norwegian Archaeological Review* 52(2), 148–69.

Furholt, M. 2018. Massive migrations? The impact of recent aDNA studies on our view of third millennium Europe. *European Journal of Archaeology* 21(2), 159–91.

Furtwängler, A., Rohrlach, A.B., Lamnidis, T.C., Papac, L., Neumann, G.U., Siebke, I. *et al.* 2020. Ancient genomes reveal social and genetic structure of Late Neolithic Switzerland. *Nature Communications* 11(1), 1915, doi: 10.1038/s41467-020-15560-x.

Graeber, D. and Wengrow, D. 2021. *The dawn of everything: a new history of humanity.* London: Allen Lane.

Greaney, S., Hazell, Z., Barclay, A., Bronk Ramsay, C., Dunbar, E., Hajdas, I., Reimer, P., Pollard, J., Sharples, N. and Marshall, P. 2020. Tempo of a mega-henge: a new chronology for Mount Pleasant, Dorchester, Dorset. *Proceedings of the Prehistoric Society* 86, 199–236.

Haak, W., Lazaridis, I., Patterson, N., Rohland, N., Mallick, S., Llamas, B. *et al.* 2015. Massive migration from the steppe was a source for Indo-European languages in Europe. *Nature* 522, 207–11.

Hakenbeck, S.E. 2019. Genetics, archaeology and the far right: an unholy Trinity. *World Archaeology* 51(4), 517–27.

Harris, O. J. T. and Cipolla, C. 2017. *Archaeological theory in the new millennium: introducing current perspectives.* London: Routledge.

Jones, E.D. and Bösl, E. 2021. Ancient human DNA: a history of hype (then and now). *Journal of Social Archaeology* 21(2), 236–55.

Kador, T., Cassidy, L.M., Geber, J., Hensey, R., Meehan, P., and Moore, S. 2018. Rites of passage: mortuary practice, population dynamics, and chronology at the Carrowkeel passage tomb complex, Co. Sligo, Ireland. *Proceedings of the Prehistoric Society* 84, 225–55.

Kristiansen, K. 2022. *Archaeology and the genetic revolution in European prehistory.* Cambridge: Cambridge University Press.

Mittnik, A., Massy, K., Knipper, C., Wittenborn, F., Friedrich, R. Pfrengle, S. *et al.* 2019. Kinship-based social inequality in Bronze Age Europe. *Science* 366(6466), 731–4.

Needham, S. 2005. Transforming Beaker culture in north-west Europe: processes of fusion and fission. *Proceedings of the Prehistoric Society* 71, 171–217.

Olalde, I., Brace, S., Allentoft, M.E., Armit, I., Kristiansen, K., Rohland, N. *et al.* 2018. The Beaker phenomenon and the genomic transformation of northwest Europe. *Nature* 555, 190–6.

Papac, L., Ernée, M., Dobeš, M., Langová, M., Rohrlach, A.B., Aron, F. *et al.* 2021. Dynamic changes in genomic and social structures in third millennium BCE central Europe. *Science Advances* 7(35): eabi6941, doi: 10.1126/sciadv.abi6941.

Parker Pearson, M. 1999. *The archaeology of death and burial.* Stroud: Sutton.

Parker Pearson, M., Pollard, J., Richards, C., Thomas, J., Tilley, C. and Welham, K. 2020. *Stonehenge for the ancestors: Part 1, landscape and monuments.* Leiden: Sidestone Press.

Richardson, L-J. and Booth, T. 2017. Response to 'Brexit, archaeology and heritage: reflections and agendas'. *Papers from the Institute of Archaeology* 27(1), Art. 25, 1–5.

Saville, A. 1990. *Hazleton North: the excavation of a Neolithic long cairn of the Cotswold-Severn group.* London: English Heritage.

Sheridan, A. 2020. Incest uncovered at elite prehistoric Irish burial site. *Nature* 582 (7812), 347–9.

Sjögren, K-G., Olalde, I., Carver, S., Allentoft, M. E., Knowles, T., Kroonen, G. *et al.* 2020. Kinship and social organization in Copper Age Europe. A cross-disciplinary analysis of archaeology, DNA, isotopes, and anthropology from two Bell Beaker cemeteries. *PLoS ONE* 15(11), e0241278.

Stengers, I. 2017. *Another science is possible: a manifesto for slow science.* Cambridge: Polity Press.

Sykes, N., Spriggs, M. and Evin, A. 2019. Beyond curse or blessing: the opportunities and challenges of aDNA analysis. *World Archaeology* 51 (4), 503–16.

Vander Linden, M. 2016. Population history in third-millennium-BC Europe: assessing the contribution of genetics. *World Archaeology* 48(5), 1–15.

Willis, C. 2021. *Stonehenge and middle to late Neolithic cremation rites in mainland Britain (c.3500–2500 BC).* Oxford: British Archaeological Reports.